LIFTING *the* VEIL

Nicholas Moon

Copyright © 2024 Nicholas Moon
All rights reserved
First Edition

PAGE PUBLISHING
Conneaut Lake, PA

First originally published by Page Publishing 2024

ISBN 979-8-88960-974-2 (pbk)
ISBN 979-8-88960-988-9 (digital)

Printed in the United States of America

BRADFORD WAINWRIGHT

While Bradford Wainwright looked at the initial pages of the second manuscript, he paused and said disappointedly, "So the author is Nicholas Moon." He flipped the page. "And like *When the Goddess Returns to Eden*, it also has an Invocation to the Muse and a prologue. I must say I like this approach. Covers all bases. Muses are important. I shouldn't have been so arrogant about my writings without them. But enough with my pity path."

Deciding he needed another cup of coffee, Wainwright placed the manuscript on the table, went to the bathroom, and then returned to the kitchen. While preparing his coffee, Wainwright looked at the donut box. "Ah! Yes! A little sugar while I read." After lifting a couple from their nesting positions between their brothers and sisters and grabbing his coffee mug, Wainwright returned to his reading zone.

Once reseated in his recliner, Wainwright collected the manuscript and began reading a note from Mina Sille.

> Professor:
>
> I trust you have read and reviewed the first two works submitted to you, but I need for you—now—to forget about the initial submission, *Emmaline Singer*. Changes are being made concerning that manuscript, so it in important you focus on the manuscript which has just been delivered to you.
>
> As with the initial manuscript, the characters in this work are not representative of anyone known, but their woven interactions within the

fictionalized plot and setting—both existential and paranormal—are again pertinent for justifiable mention.

This installment continues with the same protagonists and antagonists—both existential and paranormal—but new characters are introduced and play significant roles for the subsequent third, fourth, and maybe—but yet to be determined—fifth manuscripts.

The message to be delivered requires more revelations than was first believed. Recent activity has determined that to be the case. The continued destructive actions in which Homo sapiens sapiens engage is not conducive to the well-being not only for its genus but also other genera.

This manuscript not only tests philosophical beliefs of peoples, but it also continues with the ongoing plague of financial, political, and social criminal activity. The constant fighting both within and outside countries' boundaries concerning political, social, and theological ideologies is securing the downfall of this civilization.

The genres of drama, mystery, science fiction, and horror are utilized to show the constant wars over land, the debate concerning life and death, the schism between the have and have-nots, the inequality of genders worldwide have to stop. What is happening on the planet at present reveals the species has not evolved from its innate egoism. Balance must be secured—period.

I do not know why, but I was instructed to present two messages to you. First, Homo sapiens sapiens need to stop and think about the path they wish to walk: the one of peace and harmony or the one of chaos and annihilation. Second, before the species is permitted to make any significant advancements in space, this planet in this star system has to be healed first.

Again, I remind you, do not—as with the first manuscript—discuss the current manuscript, *Lifting the Veil*, with anyone except your agent, Virgil.

Mina Sille

Wainwright reread the letter again, sighed, and then spoke to the open space of his apartment, "I wonder who's really behind these works. But the real question is, what are the revelations in this manuscript that haven't already been disclosed in one form or another since the origin of writing?"

While he flipped through the pages again, Wainwright answered himself, "Well, I guess I need to read and find out now, don't I, Mina Sille?"

Invocation to the Muse

Calliope—Clio—Melpomene—
I seek thou guidance to continue my script.
But now, I ask Urania and Thalia
For their presence too
When science and comedy be suit.
For if what scribed not clear and true—
Regret be more than due.
I know thou think the script be set,
But walls of doubt be troubling yet.
So list to my prayer *pentaculum*—
Guide my pen to write the cruel effects
Of what be caused by so many in this stream.
For if all not learn from what unveiled—
Destruction becomes the tale.
So I end with plea—
Ensure my pen scribes
Of what *Lifting the Veil* means
For all who live in this stream.

PROLOGUE

The young girl stood in the middle of the door between the kitchen and living room, listening to Iris and her daughter, Carolyn, argue about an insignificant decision neither woman wanted to make concerning that evening's meal. There was to be a picnic for extended family that evening, and the two women, who were relatives of the girl's mother, could not decide which dessert needed to be served. The debate whether to prepare blueberry pies or peach cobblers had continued most of the morning.

Iris turned toward the young girl and asked, "Which one do you want?"

The young girl shrugged. "I don't care." She then suggested, "Why not have both? Then everyone has a choice."

Iris and Carolyn eyed each other, said nothing, and then started gathering utensils and ingredients to prepare the desserts.

But just before the women started measuring the ingredients, the young girl, who always appeared the worst of times, looked directly at Carolyn and asked, "May I see your veil?"

Carolyn had married a wealthy man five years earlier and secured her wedding dress and veil in a trunk at her parents' house. During the ceremony, the veil had covered Carolyn's face quite eloquently, hiding the false visage of her true intentions for her future.

More than once, Carolyn had acknowledged to the young girl, "Money is the name of the game. You can fall in love just as easily with a rich man as you can with a poor one. It's the size of his wallet that determines how much you love someone. Money—and how much—determines everything. You need to remember what I say."

When the women ignored the young girl's request and started to prepare the blueberry pies and peach cobblers, she repeated her request. "May I see your veil? Please?"

Carolyn was shocked by the young girl's persistence. "Why do you want to see my veil? What could you possible want with my veil? You're just being silly."

Without hesitation, the young girl replied, "I just want to see it—that's all."

With her visage revealing uncertainty, Carolyn looked at her mother and asked, "What has gotten into her?"

Iris shook her head as she looked at the young girl. "Can't you see we're busy? It'd be too much trouble to get Carolyn's veil out of the trunk."

"Please," the young girl requested a third time. "I really would like to see your veil." She then pulled on Carolyn's hand, leading her—with Iris following in line—to the trunk where the treasured item lay hidden.

Carolyn looked at her mother then at the young girl. "I don't understand why you want to see my veil." Then, out of curiosity, Carolyn opened the trunk and removed the veil. "Here." Holding the veil in her hands, Carolyn revealed the texture and length. "Look! Now are you satisfied?"

The young girl replied without hesitation, "No. I need to try it on."

"Why do you want to try this veil on?" Carolyn was beside herself with wonderment—even angst about the request. She attempted to thwart further discussion and said, "Besides, your hair might be dirty."

"No, it isn't. I washed it." The young girl eyed both women. "I need to try the veil on—now."

Like an automaton, Carolyn placed the veil over the young girl's face then arranged the layers to hide her visage completely beneath the veil. "Now, are you satisfied?"

The young girl looked into the mirror and observed herself. With the veil completely covering her face, the young girl turned her head to the left then to the right, only to focus again directly into the mirror. She then paused momentarily as if she were thinking what she was to say or do next, but she remained silent, observing herself in the mirror.

Iris and Carolyn looked at each other with neither woman understanding the significance of the young girl's request or actions. Carolyn then asked, "What does this mean?" She looked at the young girl whose face was still hidden beneath the veil.

Still shocked at the scene, Iris replied, "This doesn't make any sense. It's so strange."

Carolyn attempted to resolve the questionable problem the young girl had initiated and laughed. "She's just being a silly, silly girl."

The young girl lifted the veil and cast it over her head ritualistically, looked at Iris and Carolyn who were still shocked from the experience and said, "I needed to lift the veil. That's all I needed to do. It was time. Now, you can return the veil to the trunk. I've done what I needed to do—what I was and am supposed to do. What I am required to do."

Iris and Carolyn looked at each other and then Carolyn eyed the young girl intently as she said, "This made no sense—no sense at all." As Carolyn returned the veil to the trunk, she shook her head. "You really are a silly, silly girl."

The young girl answered, "I'm the one who *lifts the veil*."

1

Rhea stood outside the door of what resembled her classroom with a few changes in the floor plan, observing mayhem. Some people wove and milled around the floor while others sat in chairs alongside the walls. She did not understand why there were so many strangers in her classroom. *Who are these people? Where did they come from?*

While observing their clothes and accoutrements, Rhea analyzed they had arrived from the previous century's forties and fifties and were completely unaware their presence to be an anomaly. *I wonder what they want. Why are they here?*

Two women dressed in floral chiffon dresses—one pink, the other purple—with matching hats squared off in the center of the room. Both pointed their finger knives at each other's solar plexus.

Suddenly, the observers seated around the walls stood and walked liked automatons to the center of the room and began slapping one another's palms.

Unable to stop the battle, Rhea turned away from her classroom, rushed down the main hall of the west wing, jumped over the stairwell, and landed on her feet at its bottom. Geometric symbols appeared over a wide door. Realizing she needed to decipher their meaning, Rhea stopped and, in her mind's eye, translated the symbols to mean *corridor. But where does it go?*

Rhea looked around the open space and saw there were many wide doors with the same symbols. *Which one do I choose to get out of here? I need help.*

Immediately, Rhea noticed a passageway different from the others. When she entered the corridor, a light drew her attention, beckoning her telepathically to change direction toward another corridor's opening where another set of geometric symbols blinked above the opening. Rhea stopped and translated the symbols—*exit*.

Once outside, Rhea did not understand why everything was gray.

Sensing the need to escape, Rhea ran toward an embankment, stopped, and then looked backward. *Ah!* She saw a massive ship. *So that's where I've been.*

Rhea started to run again, but overcome with pain in her side, she stopped, bent over, and gasped for air. *How did I get here? But where is here?*

While observing a man approaching her, Rhea spoke to herself, "I'll ask him." But the longer she watched his fluid movements, she realized he was from the ship.

Traversing the embankment, the man stopped in front of Rhea. With strands of gray mingling within his black hair, the man's vertical yellow eyes focused on Rhea's own with benevolence. Bending toward Rhea's right ear, the man whispered, "You'll be out for three."

Unable to comprehend what the man had just said, Rhea asked, "What? What do you mean?"

The man repeated, "You'll be out for three."

"Three? What do you mean by three?"

"I'm not permitted—"

"What's going to happen to me?"

"I can only tell you—it'll be three."

Rhea looked upward and noticed there were so many stars it was difficult for her to separate one from another. "Oh, just look." Rhea remembered her childhood when she, Charlotte, and their grandparents sat in the backyard and looked and talked about the cosmic light show. She now rubbed her skin as she did then. *I never belonged there. I was in the wrong place—the wrong time.*

Rhea returned her focus to the man beside her as he now waved his arm toward a grassy knoll only to transfer himself kinematically to a fire circle.

Following the male's lead, Rhea too projected herself kinematically to the circle where an ancient waited. With fluid movements around the fire circle, the ancient pulled a scroll from the fire's center.

LIFTING THE VEIL

After unrolling the papyrus, the ancient ordered telepathically, *Read the lines.*

Scanning the cryptic lines, Rhea read the revelation.

> Messenger thou art—messenger be—
> To speak words
> To those who not believe.
>
> So take the reins of the steed
> And ride to destiny's peak.
> For when fire and wind and water and ice
> Become the scene—
> Cries shall rise from depths of sea.
>
> So say what be—
> For if heed not what said by thee,
> Another chance be lost in room,
> And no need will be
> To live on land—feel the wind—swim the sea.
>
> The wars seen
> And bondage accrued
> Need stop
> And disappear in aether soon—
> For all to remain where due.

Rolling the scroll closed, the ancient continued to circle the ring of fire and extracted a dagger only to examine its length, width, and sharpness.

The ancient then tapped the four quadrants of the compass: north, south, east, west. When the ritual ended, the ancient approached Rhea, turned the dagger's blade inward, and extended the mother-of-pearl's hilt to Rhea's right hand then placed the scroll into Rhea's left cupped arm.

Rhea accepted the offerings from the ancient and closed her left arm around the scroll and her right palm securely around the mother-of-pearl hilt. As lightning sliced the air, the dagger's blade transformed into a spear of formidable length, shining brightly in the light of the still blazing fire.

Max Hastings's office appeared in the distance. Sighing with relief and without hesitation, Rhea extended herself kinematically to the street opposite his office. What seemed only moments of her arrival, Superintendent Luther Richmond opened the door of Hastings's office door and rushed to his vehicle. Appearing worried, Richmond opened his car's door and entered quickly.

Rhea remembered her last encounter with Hastings. *Richmond, what did you do to be thrown out of Hastings's office? I wonder, how many people are thrown out of Hastings's office if they say or do something he doesn't want to hear?* When Rhea noticed Richmond's car buck like a wild horse attempting to throw him from the security of his vehicle, Rhea's mind analyzed. *What have you done for me to see your life threatened in such a way?*

Now Rhea stood at Hastings's office door where she saw angry and boisterous men and women argue and complain about property rights and deeds. While some men and women were seated in the reception area's chairs, others stood over Patty Parks's and Bessie Waite's desks, attempting to read the dossiers lying beneath the gazers' eyes. Although both women had disgruntled visages, they remained nonchalant during the mayhem, focusing on their individual computer screens.

After waiting and waiting and waiting, Rhea made another attempt to enter Hastings's office, but this time, the door was locked. After another observation of her surroundings, Rhea realize it was not time to speak to Hastings. He had to make discoveries of his own as she had done.

Rhea left Hastings's scene and continued her journey to a small island. A square building with large windows hugged a small partial of land. Steps connected each level and its rooms to other levels and their rooms. Windows of varying sizes and shapes overlooked a vast turbulent ocean. A storm was imminent. A ten-foot cloaked guide appeared in the doorway to escort Rhea through rooms, pointing to each and every window. Some were large with no glass while others were small with frames and bars to protect the room's contents.

Upon leaving the building, Rhea saw a river of rapids blocking her path to leave the island. Deciding to take a chance, Rhea stepped onto the waves. Instantly, she was in flight across the ocean only to land in a western town just outside a saloon. Rhea placed the palms of her hands on the dirt and pushed herself upward to a standing position. She then brushed the dirt from her gown and walked through the swinging doors of the saloon.

The saloon was filled to capacity. The only available seat was in a booth occupied by a man who had caught Rhea's eyes. Although having a striking physique with long, blond hair and a patch over his left eye, the man's walking cane with a prominent, golden, lion's head captured Rhea's thoughts. *Where have I seen this man before?*

Noticing the man had stood to acknowledge her presence, Rhea inched slowly and cautiously toward his table.

Without speaking, the man offered Rhea a seat at the table. He then looked around the saloon, motioning with his hand at different sections where peoples from different countries were enjoying their drinks, meals, and conversations.

Crackle-ka-boom! Crackle-ka-boom! Crackle-ka-boom!

Lightning sliced the air only for rumbles of thunder to roar and roar and roar on and on and on until Rhea stopped counting the distance of the clouds' reformations.

But when Rhea returned her attention to inside the saloon, everything had changed. She was now standing in an open space. Seeing a building upon a hill, Rhea immediately snaked up the path, stopping at two monolith doors. As if she were expected, the door opened into a grand hall. At its end, a long oak bench sat strategically opposite the entrance. Mint filled the air. *Where am I? What is this place?*

An ancient in a green robe directed Rhea by telepathy. *Move closer.*

Another ancient dressed in a blue robe appeared stern and unforgiving. Eleven other entities appeared instantaneously behind the bench.

One ancient spoke telepathically. *You demanded to meet with us.*

Another ancient asked telepathically. *What do you want?*

The council, Rhea acknowledged telepathically, *I need—*

Suddenly, a form from her right pushed Rhea away, sending her through space-time.

Tumbling and falling, Rhea attempted to regain her balance in flight. But just before she hit terra firma, Rhea was able to control her fall and, with a bounce, landed on her derriere in the middle of Ms. Maggie's and Ms. Pearl's garden.

Smiling, Rhea walked through the garden noticing the roses were in full bloom. The evening was perfect. The sun had just set, but there was still enough light for her to see the vase sitting by the well already filled with water.

With opened mouths and bared teeth, the lions remained in formation, protecting the garden. The cleaned and polished copper caduceus was still coiled in its infinite dance of destruction and creation.

Sighing, Rhea sat on one of the wooden benches to scan the landscape. When a figure in the distance flew toward her, she gasped. *Who?* Fearful, Rhea waited. *What if?* But as the figure moved closer, Rhea recognized the form.

As their bodies touched and they embraced, Rhea placed her head against the male's chest, basking in the warmth of his body, experiencing the security of his plume encircling her own, protecting her, keeping her safe. Lifting her face upward, the male gently kissed her lips, tipped her nose, then returned to her lips, pressing harder against the curves of her mouth only to extend the tip of his tongue onto Rhea's own.

Rhythmically, back and forth, back and forth, back and forth, Rhea and her lover twisted and coiled their tongues around each other. Breathing heavily, Rhea withdrew from her lover's mouth and began her journey across his chest, flicking back and forth, back and forth, back and forth only to pinch each nipple then massage his muscular frame as she continued her tongue's journey upward his breastbone licking and kissing as they stretched and coiled, stretched and coiled, stretched and coiled.

LIFTING THE VEIL

As desire vibrated within the deepest point of her sacrum chakra, Rhea pulled away, ripping the thin white linen gown from her body. Moving forward, she pulled the already naked male to her and acknowledged telepathically. *Please, I need you. I need you—now.*

The male picked Rhea up and carried her to a bed of piled leaves under a monolith tree whose branches dipped down in a canopy of protection. Without hesitation, Rhea mounted her lover, feeling the strength of his manhood swell deep within the moist walls of her vagina. Slowly, Rhea began her ride, losing herself in their rhythmic, sexual dance.

Rhea's lover grabbed her breasts, cupping them inside the palms of his hands as his forefingers and thumbs pinched her hardened nipples.

Please, please don't stop. Harder—please harder, Rhea pleaded, as she continued her rhythmic ride squeezing upward and releasing downward, squeezing upward and releasing downward, squeezing upward and releasing downward. Then, with a final thrust and squeeze, the lovers climaxed simultaneously.

Rhea moaned. *You are wonderful*—eyeing her lover intently—*so very wonderful. I wish we could stay here forever.*

Lightning sliced the atmosphere. Branches on the tree danced and swished back and forth, up and down, around and around, then backward and forward with a large limb breaking free, falling to the ground.

Mesmerized, Rhea watched as the tree's wing splattered leaves and twigs across the garden. The next lightning strike created three giant fireballs, which crashed into Rhea's body. Awakening from the jolt, Rhea attempted to connect with her surroundings. Scanning the attic, Rhea saw Gigi still nestled close to her. "Baby doll."

Gigi meowed.

"What's the matter, baby doll? We must've fallen asleep." Rhea stretched her torso then extended her arms backward and beyond her head while her legs and feet pushed forward. Rhea twisted her toes as she spoke to her cat. "We must've slept a long time, Gigi. I'm hungry. And I bet you are too."

Gigi repeated her meow.

Rhea leaned on her right arm to balance her body, then after rising to a seated position, she almost fainted. "Oh, I really was in a deep sleep, baby doll. Guess I need to be more careful."

Gigi's meow supported Rhea's analysis of her situation.

Pausing momentarily, Rhea scanned the attic again. "Why am I so disoriented? I shouldn't be feeling this way. Something's wrong."

Rhea sighed, paused, then rose from her seated position to descend slowly through the attic's door with Gigi following closely at her heels.

2

Ross Jackson walked into Interview Room A at the Eaton County Sheriff's Office, carrying a cup of coffee and a pack of cigarettes for the interviewee. After shoving the door shut with his right foot, Jackson set the items on the table then seated himself in front of Turner Ashton. "I have donuts if you'd like a couple. Just baked this morning. They're from Ariel's."

Turner Ashton refused Jackson's offerings and waited for the sheriff to begin his interrogation.

> JACKSON. Mr. Turner, I must say, you're a hard man to find.
> ASHTON. I've been out of town. My wife—I's trying to get her to come back to me.
> JACKSON. Any luck?
> ASHTON. I guess it's a wait and see. She doesn't like it here. Says it's too rural. She likes city life better.
> JACKSON. Some people like the city. Others like the country. Me...Well, I like the country air.
> ASHTON, *laughing.* Yeah, me too. I've promised the woman we'd leave once I finish my business here. And where we go will be her choice.
> JACKSON. And why are you here? What business interests do you have in Bell City—Eaton County for that matter?
> ASHTON. Antiques. I heard there's some very old, even rare artifacts in this area. So I'm trying to make connections to discover if anyone knows anything about them or if the tale is a hoax.
> JACKSON. I see. Well, do you know Caleb Norton?
> ASHTON. Yes, Caleb has been helpful with my search.

JACKSON. Terrible about what happened to Calvin and the other two people.

ASHTON. I'm not sure Caleb will ever recover. And what do you mean, other two?

JACKSON. You didn't know? There were two other bodies with Calvin's. Had to use dental records to determine exactly who they were.

ASHTON. Caleb didn't say anything about anyone else being there.

JACKSON. Two drug dealers. And whoever killed them and Calvin must've had a really big beef with all three.

ASHTON. Sad, ain't it? One minute on top of the world, have anything you want, then the next moment lost in a sinkhole of misery.

JACKSON. You's the one who found them, right?

ASHTON, *confused*. No. I wasn't around then. I told ya. I's away.

JACKSON. Oh, yeah, trying to get your wife to come back to you.

ASHTON, *thoughtfully*. Calvin was always taking chances. I tried to warn him. But he'd ignore me and brag about what he could get away with.

JACKSON. Mr. Ashton, you're aware we discovered Maryann Colbert in your garage shed's cellar.

ASHTON. Yeah, Tobias told me. In fact, I had no more than gotten out of my truck when Tobias was at my door.

JACKSON. Just exactly what did Tobias tell you?

ASHTON, *irritated*. Tobias said the cops had been there and found a woman in the cellar.

JACKSON. Is that all?

ASHTON. Yes, I believe so.

JACKSON. The woman was Maryann Colbert. She'd been missing for quite a while.

ASHTON. I don't know how this woman, Maryann Colbert, got into my cellar. I keep it locked at all times. My tools are in there.

JACKSON. What about Rhea Michaels's paintings?
ASHTON. What? Again, I don't know what you're talking about.
JACKSON. Yeah, three paintings. Said she'd placed a curse on the person or persons who stole them.
ASHTON. Is that right? Rhea can be feisty. But a curse? That's new territory.
JACKSON. How do you think somebody was able to get into your cellar, lock a hostage up, steal paintings from your neighbor, and you not know anything about it?
ASHTON, *huffing*. Like I said, I've been away. I told Tobias to keep an eye out, but I guess he slipped up. So somebody knew I had a workshop down there and thought they'd use it to set me up.
JACKSON. Why would anyone want to set you up?
ASHTON. I don't know. Maybe people consider me an outsider and want to get me out of the way.
JACKSON, *hitting the top of the table then rising from his chair*. Well, I appreciate you coming in. But I need for you to hang around for a while whether you find the artifact or not. Just in case.
ASHTON, *rising from his chair*. In case of what?
JACKSON. I have more questions.
ASHTON. Oh, yeah. But now, I think I need to talk to Rhea. Set things straight. Don't want no curse put on me.
JACKSON. Won't hurt. But you might want to prepare yourself for a little fire and fury.
ASHTON. Thanks for the warning. I'll make sure I talk to Rhea soon.
JACKSON. It might be difficult to talk right away.
ASHTON. Why's that?
JACKSON. Nobody can get in touch with her.
ASHTON. Is that so?
JACKSON. You wouldn't know anything about her whereabouts now, would ya?
ASHTON. Not a clue. Remember, I've been gone.

JACKSON. Oh, yes. And you remember—don't leave until things are resolved.

ASHTON. Sorry, I couldn't be more help. But if I hear or see anything, I'll be sure and let you know.

Once Ashton left his office, Jackson immediately called Hastings. "Max, just got finished talking to Ashton. He had all the answers, but something doesn't click. He knows more than he's letting on."

"Ross, did you get any DNA?"

"No. Refused both coffee and cigarettes—even donuts."

"I see." After a thoughtful pause while he inhaled and exhaled the latest draw from his cigarette, Hastings asked, "Have you driven by Michaels's today?"

"No. Haven't had time. Why?"

Hastings's tone revealed irritation. "Wonder where she could be. I've called a couple of times, but it goes to voice mail."

"I'll drive by later. I'm gonna go by and check on Caleb and Edna. There's something Ashton said I want to run by Caleb."

"Good idea. And, Ross, let me know what you find out."

"Yeah. We'll talk then." Ross Jackson smiled as he thought about his excuse to see and talk to Edna Norton.

*****

Once they had descended the steps, Rhea immediately filled Gigi's water and food bowls then engaged her own personal search for anything to sate her hunger pains. Opening the refrigerator's door and eyeing its contents, Rhea saw the milk carton's expiration date. But when she opened the half-gallon container and sniffed the contents, Rhea was shocked. "This milk is sour. Damn it! It was probably ruined when I bought it. I need to pay more attention to expiration dates. I certainly will from now on. I've just wasted money because of my carelessness."

Gigi rubbed her body against Rhea's leg. "What's the matter, baby doll? You still hungry?"

When the cat scampered toward the living room, Rhea focused her attention to a carton of orange juice, but when she opened the container and took a drink, it too was soured. "What's going on!" A soda in the door caught her eye. "Ah, just what I need." Rhea lifted the bottle from its niche and twisted the cap and took a sip.

When Rhea looked at the clock, it digitized 4:00 p.m. "There's something wrong with that clock."

After opening a jar of peanut butter, Rhea then looked inside her stove's oven where she kept her stash of rolls, breads, and cookies. But when she saw everything was molded, Rhea sighed as she said, "I guess it's crackers."

As she swiped the peanut butter over the buttered ovals, her cell phone drew attention away from her snack. After looking at the ID, Rhea answered immediately. "Etta, how are you today?" But Etta's response was not what she expected.

"Thank goodness, Rhea, I've been so worried about you. Where have you been?"

"Etta, what are you talking about?"

"I've been worried sick. I've called and called. Haldan and I have even driven by to check on you. And I must say, I've been a little pissed at you."

"What do you mean?"

"Rhea, the sheriff has even checked on you—and more than once—but there was no response."

"Etta, I's in the attic."

"Since the sixteenth! Hell, Rhea, that's not funny. A lot of people have been worried about you—even Max Hastings."

"Really? That's kinda hard to believe." Rhea realized something was wrong and decided to change her answer. "I've been cleaning and resting."

Etta huffed. "And not answering your phone."

Rhea realized her response needed to be apologetic. "Etta, you know I needed to de-stress. So I kinda shut down."

"Well, I'm glad you're okay. At least, there's been no school with the weather so bad."

Rhea looked out the window. "Yeah, we got our wish, didn't we? No finals before the holidays!"

Etta sighed. "I want to be off, but being off puts me on a roller coaster emotionally. I dread the work when I return."

Rhea's response continued to be guarded as she repeated, "But enjoy the fact—no finals before the holidays."

Etta sighed. "Yes, but we've gotten more than we wish for. It's the first week of January. And it doesn't look like the weather is going to change for the better anytime soon. And February, it's anybody's guess what the weather will be then."

January. Rhea could not believe what she was hearing and attempted to glean more information. "It's been rough." Rhea walked to her kitchen window. "And you're right, it doesn't look like there's any relief in sight. It's snowing right now."

"Yeah." Etta's tone was flat. "Here too."

Rhea laughed. "I guess we'll just have to accept whatever Mother Nature sends us."

"That's obvious." After a pause, Etta said, "Rhea, Haldan has just walked through the door. He has a pizza. So talk to you later."

"Sure, Etta. Talk later."

After her phone conversation ended with Etta Smiley, Rhea looked at the clock again, saw the date, and then in disbelief acknowledged, "It is the first week of January."

Rhea realized now why she and her body had difficulty adjusting when she had awakened in the attic. Rhea walked into the den, seated herself on the sofa, and focused toward the fireplace. *Where have I been?* Stretching her body the length of the sofa, tears cascaded down Rhea's cheeks as she watched the orange flames dance within the synthetic logs. "How can this be?"

The phone rang again, and when Rhea saw the ID, she exclaimed, "Charlotte!"

"Rhea Michaels, I've been worried sick—even called the sheriff for a welfare check."

"Really?"

"Yes, really. And you know what he said?"

"No, Charlotte. What did the sheriff say?"

"He'd been to check on you, and it looked like you had gone on a trip. So where did you go, Rhea?"

Now, wide awake, Rhea attempted another cover-up. "Charlotte, I told you I might go somewhere. It was nowhere in particular. I wanted to get away from the snow."

"So why didn't you come to see us—me and Samuel?"

"I...I didn't want to intrude."

"Intrude! Really?" Charlotte's voice crescendoed. "Rhea, why would you think you'd be intruding?"

"Charlotte," Rhea replied apologetically, "I just needed to get away—that's all."

"Okay, I won't push the subject, but have you contacted the sheriff?"

"Why would I contact Ross Jackson?"

"He found your paintings."

"He what!"

"Yeah, they were in your neighbor's cellar—along with a woman being held hostage."

"What are you talking about?"

Charlotte sighed. "I don't know all the details. I just know when I called to ask for a welfare check, the sheriff said he found your paintings. Max Hastings has them stored in his office. You can pick them up there."

"Really?"

Charlotte was surprised. "What do you mean by really, Rhea? I denote a hint of sarcasm in your voice."

"I'm tired from my trip, Charlotte, that's all. But I also wonder why Hastings would be so generous with his office space."

"Rhea, I do detect sarcasm. So what's happened?"

"Charlotte, as I said, I'm tired. When the snow melts, I'll find out more details, but until then, your guess is as good as mine."

Charlotte continued her verbal pressure to discover where Rhea had been on her trip. "So you're still not going to tell me where you went and if you met anyone special?"

Rhea giggled. "Charlotte, you know I'm always looking for my soulmate. And if he ever shows up, you'll be the first to know."

"Okay, Rhea. I'm glad you're okay. We'll talk soon."

"Tell Samuel, I said be careful."

"I will, Rhea. Take care."

When Rhea and Charlotte's phone conversation ended, Rhea called the supermarket for a delivery. She was hungry, so her list was long and detailed.

After Rhea finished her order, she went to the bathroom and looked into the mirror. As she turned her face to the right then to the left, she said, "Talk about bizarre." She then saw her visage shift and speak. "It time and time be true, thou need accept my view. For it be I who have been with you, and give you what be need to speak the news."

Rhea leaned closer to the glass and acknowledged to herself. "I'm to deliver the message to Hastings then he is to deliver the message to others—to his connections. So Hastings does have a role to play."

Reflecting on the lines written on the scroll, Rhea knew she had to face many obstacles. And the outcome was yet to be determined—whether the final result be a success or a failure.

Rhea sighed. "I may be placed in harm's way, but que será, será—what will be, will be." She then thought about Hastings having her paintings. "But I wonder whose idea it was to suggest Hastings hold my paintings for me. After all, he pushed me from his office's door when I told him about Race Webb murdering his wife and daughters. If he didn't want to listen to me then, he hasn't listened to anything else I've said—even shown him."

I guess you have a problem to solve.

Rhea answered her thought. "It would seem so. But how that's to be accomplished remains to be a mystery because I have no idea what to do—even when to do it."

It was then Rhea heard her doorbell ring. "Ah, food for the weary traveler. It's time I have something to eat." Rhea's visage smiled as she acknowledged, "Then think about my next move in this role—even game—I find myself."

3

Flipping the light switch as he opened the door to his apartment, Maxwell Hastings was glad when Mason and Christopher had offered to go for pizza. Setting his evening meal on the countertop, Hastings removed his gun and shoulder holster and placed them next to his boxed meal.

As he opened the lid to scan the toppings of his pie, church's bells chimed six rings. *Perfect.* After grabbing a beer from the refrigerator, Hastings opened the door and yelled down the hallway toward Mason and Christopher's apartments. "Thanks again, guys. I appreciate the pizza!"

Mason responded, "No problem! Anytime!"

Before he closed the door, Hastings suggested, "If you run out of drinks, I have some extra in the fridge. Just let me know." He then thought about taking a break after a set of papers demanded his attention and asked, "Would you two like to play poker later?" Hastings smiled and said, "It's been a while, so I might be a little rusty."

Christopher replied, "Sounds good to me!"

"Yeah, me too," Mason acknowledged, "just let us know!"

Hastings had to admit he was grateful to William Shepherd and Gabriel Hall for suggesting the two young men work in his office. While they had been assigned to observe Rhea Michaels and protect him, Mason and Christopher had definitely become assets to his office's staff because the paperwork seemed to be doubling every day.

"Okay, sounds great!" Hastings smiled. *And I'll see if I'm still with the game.*

Hastings carried his beer and pizza box to a makeshift table beside his recliner. Once seated, Hastings realized he had left his cigarettes on the counter. "Damn!" He shrugged as he opened the box, pulled a square from the rectangle, and then took a bite from one side.

Suddenly, cacophonous sounds erupted Hastings's dinner. Bodies slammed against the walls in the hallway outside his apartment. Chairs and tables overturned onto the floor while angry unintelligible words filtered through the mayhem. Rushing for his gun, Hastings grabbed the weapon and backed stealthily against the wall and away from the door.

Waiting for what he thought to be the right moment for a surprised intervention, Hastings twisted the door's knob then stepped into the hallway's chaos. As he pointed his gun to a heaping mound of four coiled, twisted, and tangled bodies on the floor, Hastings set himself in a forceful stance and screamed, "Back off! Back off! Back off! Now!"

The woven and webbed mound began to unfold. The two victors, Mason and Christopher, balanced themselves then pushed upward and away from the entangled altercation.

With the two young men standing but continuing to breathe heavily, Hastings asked, "Are you two all right?"

"Yeah." Mason leaned against a wall. "I'm okay."

Hastings continued to point his gun at the two men lying with their backs glued to the floor. "How about you, Christopher?"

"Max! It's me! It's me!" William Shepherd rolled to his side, placed his hands on the floor, and then pushed upward.

Hastings lowered his weapon. "Not a good way to make an entrance, friend."

"I can see we made a mistake." Shepherd looked at the now-standing Gabriel Hall. "But we didn't want anyone to see us enter your office this time. So we decided to come after hours."

"You should've warned us, sir." Mason looked toward Hall and offered, "I apologize for punching you." He turned toward Shepherd. "You too, sir."

Rubbing his jaw, Hall laughed. "Quite all right, Mason. You're doing your job."

Hastings shook his head. "Serves you two right. You should've let me know you were coming. I's beginning to think you had forsaken me. And since you were here, a lot has happened. And I mean a hell of a lot!"

"What's been happening may be the result of who's here," Hall interjected. "We need to talk. It's believed the assassins Rhea Michaels mentioned are here and have connections to the drug cartel."

"So Rhea Michaels was right." Hastings eyed Shepherd and Hall. "And just how do you plan to thwart their attack?"

"We have a plan, Max." Shepherd's answer was defensive. "But we need to clarify some things first."

Hastings extended his arm toward his apartment. "I have a letter from Rhea Michaels. And we—or should I say you—may have a problem."

After following the four men into his apartment, Hastings asked, "Would you like some pizza? I had just started eating my dinner when you two appeared from nowhere."

Shepherd looked at Hall then at Hastings. "If you have enough. We thought about stopping in Will's Store, but everything was closed. When we arrived in Bell City, we decided to check with you first."

Hall looked at the pizza. "We appreciate the offer."

Mason looked at Christopher then at Hall. "We'll get ours. There should be enough for all of us."

While Mason and Christopher went to collect their pizzas, Hastings grabbed paper plates from the cabinet. "Help yourselves. I usually order the largest I can get, so I'll have extra to snack on later." He opened his refrigerator's door. "Do you want a soda or beer?"

Shepherd remembered what Hastings had said about a letter. "What did you mean about a problem with Rhea Michaels? And I want a beer."

Mason and Christopher returned with their meals and eyed Shepherd and Hall intently.

Hastings looked at Hall. "What do you want, beer or soda?"

"I'll have a beer too if you have enough."

Hastings's tone revealed irritation. "I wouldn't have offered if I didn't." He handed the bottle to Hall. "So I'm assuming you checked Rhea Michaels's description."

As he twisted the cap to his bottle of beer, Hall acknowledged, "Yes, and it all checked out."

Shepherd interjected, "But the owner and his wife had disappeared before we arrived." He placed a slice of pizza on the flimsy paper plate.

"So assassins and Rhea Michaels's vision—what can you tell me?'

Hall decided to give the details about the scenario. "According to the locals, the couple posed as lost relatives of Mr. Carver, the owner of the property. He deeded the property to them just before he died. No one suspected anything was wrong."

Hastings analyzed. "But what they really did was take Mr. Carver hostage, stole his property legally, then murdered him."

"Exactly," Hall acknowledged. "They appeared out of nowhere and convinced Carver the man was the only surviving relative. The couple moved into Carver's home and offered to take care of him."

After taking a drink of beer, Shepherd interjected, "And they took him all right. When they exhumed the body, there was evidence Carver had been tortured." He paused then said. "Just like the people in the graves Rhea Michaels saw in her vision."

Hastings took a drink of his beer then stopped to think about what had just been revealed. "Why didn't the mortician discover the reason for Carver's death? It makes no sense the couple wasn't discovered when Carver died."

"It does," Hall answered, "because Carver's will determined no embalming—no services—and to be buried in the family cemetery. So the couple did the honors."

Hastings could not believe the scenario Shepherd and Hall were presenting to him. "Why was Carver's body exhumed?"

"We had it done," Shepherd replied as he collected another slice of pie.

"Why, William, would you have Carver's body exhumed?"

"Because, Max, the scene was exactly the way Rhea Michaels's vision depicted. Her description of the fields, graveyard, and house was exact. So we decided to verify what were in those graves. And it became evidential Carver had tortured and murdered a lot of people, burying them in what he called his family cemetery."

"What!" Hastings exclaimed. "No one suspected Carver was a serial killer!"

Hall confirmed, "Evidently not." He took a bite of pizza.

Hastings shook his head. "Talk about karma."

Nodding in agreement, Hall offered, "But now, we believe the couple who were responsible for Carver's death have been hired by the drug cartel to kill Rhea Michaels and you."

"We also believe," Shepherd interjected, "the couple has established themselves in positions where they think they can be undetected as they were with Carver."

Hastings shook his head. "So how do you know these two people are really imposters?"

"Two educational consultants disappeared on their way to Eaton County," Hall confirmed, "neither family nor friends have heard from them for months—since this past summer to be exact."

Hastings revealed his analysis of the situation. "So this couple stole their identities?"

"Not exactly," Shepherd responded before Hall could answer. "These two have different aliases."

"I don't get it. How would this couple be able to infiltrate a school system? Do you honestly think the couple who killed Carver and the couple who Rhea mentioned being at the high school are the same?" Hastings placed his paper plate in the trash can beside his recliner. "Now, I'll probably need an antacid."

Shepherd and Hall started to laugh at Hastings's comic relief but stayed their act of joviality when they saw the ominous expression on his face then Hall acknowledged, "Yes, we know they're the same." He stood to throw his empty plate away. "Just like we know the descriptive scene by Rhea Michaels—however you want to analyze it—was accurate."

Hastings did not understand why the couple had not already been apprehended. "So why not arrest them and stop their threat against what seems to be a lot of people, not just two."

"It's not a lot of people, Max," Shepherd confirmed. "It's you and Michaels."

"If you're so worried about Rhea Michaels and me, why continue with the charade?"

Shepherd knew Hastings would not like his answer but decided to be blunt. "Because we need to use them to get to the cartel."

Hastings frowned. "So you know this couple is actually in the school system and after Rhea Michaels and me, but you're gonna wait and see what happens. Thank you! That is good to know, William. I really appreciate your thoughtfulness."

Shepherd attempted to placate Hastings's negative response. "Max, from what you've told us about Rhea Michaels—what we've read from her verses—we know Rhea Michaels is quite capable of taking care of herself. I guess you could say she has extra adrenaline."

"I wouldn't call it adrenaline, William."

"So Rhea Michaels will be fine."

Hastings sighed then asked, "So what about me?"

Hall replied without hesitation. "That's why Mason and Christopher are here. Seems to me they're doing exactly what they're here to do." Hall rubbed his jaw. "I can verify from experience."

Hastings paused momentarily then warned, "I have a confession to make. I may no longer be able to be the go-between for whatever you need from Rhea Michaels."

"Why?" Shepherd and Hall asked simultaneously.

Hastings sighed. "When Michaels came to see me the early part of December, she was adamant about her revelations concerning specific information about individuals and their criminal activity. But I've not been able to contact her since then. It seems Rhea Michaels has left the county and, to date, not returned." Hastings pulled an envelope from the drawer of the table beside his recliner. "I received this letter prior to her disappearance."

Shepherd and Hall looked at each other then saw the expressions on Mason's and Christopher's faces and knew something had happened.

Hastings observed the visual exchange among the four men. "When Michaels was here, she gave me verses warning about an attack and a siege at the high school. There's similar verses in the *Book of Ki*. I didn't send them to you because I wanted to wait and show you in person. But a few days later, I received this letter telling me what she thought of me and you."

"I don't understand." Shepherd was visibly distraught.

"You will," Hastings acknowledged. "Rhea Michaels is blunt in her analysis of me—you—whomever she considers to be playing games with her."

"Games!" Hall appeared shocked. "We've not played any games with her."

"She thinks you have. She thinks she's a pawn." Hastings coughed. "And we intend to do nothing to help her." Hastings coughed again. "Excuse me, I need a drink of water."

Hall looked at Shepherd. "We need to hear what she's written."

Hastings handed the letter to Shepherd. "See for yourselves why Rhea Michaels thinks we've betrayed her."

Shepherd eyed Hastings as he accepted the letter, opened it, scanned the lines, then began reading orally.

> Mr. Hastings:
>
> I believe I have wasted your time and mine these past few months. If you remember, I waited a long time to contact you even though Deborah Halsey was quite adamant that I do so promptly. However, it took the theft of my paintings to make me speak to you. But to date, my paintings have not been returned.

Shepherd looked at Hastings. "Max?"

"They're in the library. We found them at a neighbor's house who is a shady character in his own right."

Hall asked, "What's his name?"

"Turner Ashton." Hastings's tone was flat.

Hall and Shepherd eyed each other, then Hall said, "We'd like to see them later."

"Sure. Knock yourselves out."

After a glance at Mason, Christopher, and Hall, Shepherd returned to his oral reading.

> Did you ever contact a cryptographer and submit the verses to him, even the visions, or did you trash the code in your shredder? Whether your answer is an affirmative or a negative, it makes no difference. I know what I am facing with or without yours or anyone else's help.
>
> Maybe you already know to what I am referring. You did say during one of our meetings—the second in fact—"It did not take me long to discover you were on the level, but I cannot tell you why. You have to make that discovery on your own." At the time, I did not understand, but all was revealed to me in a most precarious and provocative way.
>
> I am very much aware of my comforter—formidable to say the least—and whatever shape is formed. All have the capability to ensure the continuation of my well-being regardless of any attack howbeit covert or overt.

Shepherd reread the previous three paragraphs again then looked at Hastings. "She knows she's a shape-shifter."

"Appears so, doesn't it? I didn't think she knew, but now, it's obvious she does." Hastings was irritated. "But you didn't read far enough. There's more—a lot more."

Shepherd continued his oral reading.

> When I met with you, I mentioned an encounter I had with a gentleman at the mall. He was concrete yet abstract—common yet strange—amicable yet formidable. And his introduction to me was quite timely. I assure you I know.

"So is this guy one of yours?" Hastings eyed his visitors intently. "After all, this man appears to be as covert as the two of you when it comes to Rhea Michaels. It's obvious his meeting with her was planned and intentional—to find out something. Just like the two of you are trying to do but using me in the process."

Shepherd scanned the last few sentences then read.

> Before I close, I need to remind you—I trust no one—not even you. But that makes no difference now because I have the edge on my enemies whoever they may be. No one has a clue who I really am. And when they do come after me—and they will—I shall remain standing when they have fallen.
>
> So whatever happens, I assure you I will be able to handle any and all attacks.
>
> Rhea Michaels

Shepherd looked at Hall. "Now, what're we going to do?"

Mason interrupted, "There's always her paintings. Let her paintings be the bait to encourage her return."

Hastings focused his attention toward the counter and eyed the pack of unopened cigarettes. "Excuse me for a moment." Hastings walked toward the pack. "If I'm to plan strategy, I need my supporting cast to help me think."

Shepherd interjected, "Mason is right. You've got to use her paintings."

"If you remember, William, Rhea Michaels doesn't trust me. And quite frankly, I have no desire to talk to a bug."

"A bug?" Gabriel Hall's response was more of a question than a statement. "What do you mean by a bug?"

"The two of you can meet all the shape-shifting creatures from Rhea Michaels you want to encounter. Frankly, I've met all I need to see. It was all I could do to keep my composure when she transformed racially, but when various creatures paid a visit, well, I don't think I have to go into detail about my response."

Hall scanned the apartment for the bathroom. "I need to make a visit."

Hastings nodded toward his bathroom but continued his revelation. "From my observation, I saw a woman transform not only from one humanoid race to at least three others but also from creatures whose extinction occurred thousands of years ago—if my knowledge of history, zoology, even paleontology is correct. And I know it is."

Hall returned from the bathroom. "Did any of those creatures attempt to harm you?"

Hastings huffed. "No."

"Then," Shepherd encouraged, "you don't have anything to worry about. So I don't see why you would care to contact her."

"Oh, so now I'm expendable." Hastings looked toward Shepherd for clarification of his suggestion. "But it doesn't make any difference. I don't know where she is, so contacting Rhea Michaels is impossible."

Shepherd attempted to appease the tension he had created between himself and his old friend. "We'll think of something."

Hastings decided to suggest a different approach to Rhea Michaels. "When she returns from wherever—if she ever does—why don't I arrange a meeting with the three of us in the same room, and the two of you can have a conversation with whatever creature appears."

Shepherd decided to test Hastings's fortitude. "Max, after all your talk, you can't convince me that you're afraid of Rhea Michaels."

"That won't work, William." Hastings eyed Shepherd directly. "I am no longer that ten-year-old boy needing to prove myself to myself. I've more than sufficiently been made aware of my prowess with my ongoing battle with those who are trying to kill me. So don't play with my ego. I repeat—I don't have to prove myself to myself."

4

Rhea Michaels unloaded her just-delivered groceries and began to restock the refrigerator, cupboards, and cabinets. But while she was placing the bread, crackers, and cookies in the stove's oven, Rhea engaged her mnemonic review of where she had been, whom she had encountered, and what she had experienced.

While preparing a bowl of tomato soup and grilled cheese, Rhea talked to herself. "It was a long journey. I was in a lot of different places, met a lot of different peoples, experienced some troubling encounters."

After carrying her prepared dinner to the counter, Rhea seated herself in the barstool then flipped the tab of her soda. As she took a bite of grilled cheese, Rhea continued her verbal analysis of her trek. "I was on a starship. It was a lot larger than the others I've been on before—at least the ones I remember."

Gigi entered the kitchen from the hallway and meowed.

After ensuring the feline was content, Rhea again seated herself in a stool at the counter, continuing her self-conversation. "So there was a firepit, an ancient, a scroll, and a dagger." Rhea visualized. "And I was in a grand hall where the entities communicated with me through telepathy." Rhea stopped to think then asked herself. "Was it twelve, or was it thirteen—even more I didn't see?"

Well, that's not the point now, is it?

Rhea replied to her thought. "No, I suppose it's not." She took a drink of her soda. "It's what they revealed to me, what they made me remember, what they made me watch."

Rhea visualized her initial telepathic acknowledgment to them. *I realize I was warned not to return—*

We did. An ancient in a green robe supported Rhea's introduction of herself then chastised, *But you're a rebel—always doing whatever you are warned not to do.*

Another ancient in a blue robe interjected, *What about entering the ovens during the mass genocide of World War II? And we watched as you experienced the horror of those concentration and gulag camps. What did those experiences teach you?*

Rhea's answer was defensive. *Like this incarnation, I discovered the cruelty of humans and how the species cares nothing for members of its genus—even what happens to other genera inhabiting the planet which is, obvious, on the brink of annihilation. Homo sapiens sapiens don't accept—in this cycle—their greed is responsible for dying of the planet.*

Another ancient in a white robe interjected. *Upon your extended life visits, how many times have you been burned at the stake, buried alive, stoned, decapitated, hanged, boiled, eviscerated, even flayed?*

The ancient in the green robe asked, *How many incarnations will it take for you to listen and remain where you are supposed to be?*

The ancients remained silent momentarily until the ancient in a purple robe warned, *It might be to your advantage to revisit the cruelty of those experiences in order to prepare yourself for your at present situation. That is if you return to the existence in play at the moment.*

Rhea defended her at present incarnation. *Homo sapiens sapiens are destroying the air, the land, the water—the flora which they need to survive. They have hunted and continue to hunt fauna to extinction. They are responsible for the extinction of species, which have as much right to live on the planet as they do—maybe even more so. You do know some are more intelligent.* Rhea spread her wings and hovered as she eyed the ancients. *As you know, Homo sapiens sapiens—as other extraterrestrial species—are not indigenous to the planet.*

The ancient in the purple robe asked, *Since that be the case, what do you plan to do about it?* The ancient paused to give Rhea a chance to respond, but when she did not, the entity continued, *We believe you need to review three of your incarnations—since it has been on your mind and speech—we'll begin with the Romans.*

Rhea decided to reveal her knowledge what it meant to be a Roman. *The Romans—as those who inhabit the planet at present—were* not choosy about whom they exterminated. They killed anybody they considered a threat to their empire. It did not make any difference whether it be a female or male. To be a Roman was to be a part of a machine.

The empire was like a wheel with each spoke ensuring it remained stabilized and in working order. All spokes adhered to its duties and responsibilities. Even though the date 476 CE has been identified as its end, Roman tacticians have been in play for thousands of years and remain at present, just different names, leaders, governments, and religions. But all have been just as deadly and barbaric with their tactics of annihilation.

The ancient in the green robe interjected before Rhea could continue her revelation. *We want you to review three of your executions—just as a reminder of your existential experiences. And we will begin with your crucifixion then show you two additional experiences because your enemy who is with you now was with you then.*

The ancient in the purple robe interrupted and waved for the images to play before Rhea's eyes. *Watch and remember.*

Rhea and the ancients watched together as the screen projected characters being manipulated by the plot in which the Fates—Clotho, Lachesis, and Atropos—had directed them to appear.

The woman walked and talked throughout the countryside, healing and teaching those who followed her. Her lessons stressed the importance of love, humility, truth, and faithfulness. She encouraged her followers to seek peace with one another and to learn the lessons of the present experience to connect with the cosmic realm.

Tears welled in Rhea's eyes as she pleaded telepathically, *Please. I can't watch. It's too painful.*

But the screen continued to flash images as the characters continued their roles.

The ancient in the white robe pointed to the images. *Now watch what happened because of her teachings—what she endured, how she suffered.*

One day, during the woman's mission, there were those in the crowd who saw the woman's shoes and realized she was different and from a foreign place.

A man standing just beneath the rock on which the woman stood accused, "You speak lies. Your teachings cannot be. The Romans won't allow it. They're in control." The man pointed to the woman's shoes. "She's not from here. She's a foreigner. She's here to cause us harm. She's here to get us crucified!"

As the crowd dispersed, the man stopped a Roman soldier and pointed toward the woman. "That woman speaks against Rome."

The scene shifted to the abode where the woman lived. It was noon when the Roman soldiers burst through her door.

One soldier scanned the room and then he eyed a staff next to the hearth. "You plan to destroy us with this?" He lifted the staff into the air. "Strike us dead with this?" The soldier saw the woman's shoes. Pulling her close to him, the soldier ordered, "Where are you from, woman?"

The images froze and the ancient in the green robe revealed, *It was the woman's neighbors who betrayed her. A Roman Centurion bribed them to spy on her, and as she was dragged through the streets, the crowd laughed and followed the soldiers until they entered a courtyard where the woman was to be interrogated.*

The ancient in the purple robe waved for the images to continue their movement.

The men in the courtyard began asking the woman questions.

One man inquired, "Why do you speak against us?"

The woman stood erect as she answered, "I do not speak against you. I am here to teach the importance of peace and to ensure a change occurs. I know and understand the laws, tenets, texts, and prophecies. I am here to help, not harm. I am here to encourage humility and peace."

Another man asked, "Are you a prophet?"

The woman replied, "I am here to encourage a change be made for the future of all species on this planet and the continuation of the planet itself. It is necessary. Again, I am here to help, not harm. Not at present."

As the men talked among themselves, the crowd outside the gate chanted, "See her shoes! See her shoes! See her shoes!"

When the woman's shoes were displayed before the men, the man sitting in the center asked, "Where are you from? How do you know the things you know? You are a woman. You have no right to speak the words you speak."

"I am here to encourage peace and harmony among all peoples."

A man sitting to the woman's right asked, "Do you know what's facing you?"

The woman's answer shocked the men when she revealed her plight. "I know I am to die. It is the only way I can leave this space-time and dimension."

Not understanding the woman's answer, one man inquired, "Do you know what the Romans will do to you prior to your death, the torture you will experience before your execution?"

"I know. I accept what is to be. No one is listening. Lies always win over truth, and what happens to me will be changed into a lie, and those who know the truth will die horrendous deaths."

Rhea responded to the woman's dialogue and prognostication. *And they did. They created a lie to subjugate, enslave, torture, and execute. That prophecy came true. The mother and father must join and become one. One cannot have more power than the other. There must be balance. It is to be.*

The ancient in the purple robe interjected, *We digress. Return to the images and watch.*

The woman was dragged to the Roman Court where she was interrogated a second time. "So you speak against us."

"I am here to initiate a change in thought and action—nothing more."

"Nothing more." The Roman mocked the woman then bragged, "There have been other dissidents who have attempted to destroy our empire." He observed the crowed. "They failed." The Roman then looked at the woman intently. "And you will also fail." He smiled. "Evidently, you do not know what you will endure, so I'm giving you a chance to recant what you've said against Rome."

When the woman refused to answer, the Roman ordered her execution.

The soldiers then dragged the woman away, taking her to an open courtyard.

The woman was stripped and bound to a pole. Remaining quiet, the woman listened to the soldiers' taunts, describing what they intended to do to her.

While they prepared the whip, they mocked, "If you're so powerful, stop us!" One soldier grabbed the staff. "We want to see what you can do with this thing. We want to see if it can stop us. And your shoes—what can they do?"

A soldier threw the woman's shoes across the yard and ordered, "Show us! Tell us where you came from!"

Another soldier taunted, "Maybe they can make her fly."

The first strike from the whip's lash hit the woman's body, and the strike was so forceful, she urinated and defecated.

Her scream after scream after scream did nothing to deter the soldiers from hitting every inch of her form.

After the woman's entire body seeped with blood, the soldiers stopped and inquired, "Had enough, woman? You are almost dead." The soldier laughed as his whip struck again and again and again.

Semiconscious, the woman did not move. Her form was almost indistinguishable. Blood, urine, and feces became her cloak.

Deciding to change their approach, one soldier stuck a sword into hot coals. After ensuring the tip was hot, he walked to the woman and set the hot tip to the woman's back and laughed. "Feel this."

The woman screamed and screamed and screamed.

Sniffing the burning flesh and listening to the woman's screams, the soldier said, "Guess she wasn't dead after all." Now as the soldier looked at his comrades, he continued to place the hot sword at different places on the woman's body with the last burning the flesh between her thighs.

The woman screamed and screamed and screamed until she lost consciousness.

The soldiers whipped and burned throughout the night until they decided to pour water up and down the whip's lash. It was this attack when the Roman soldier sliced her womb with the whip, causing her again to urinate and defecate.

A soldier who watched and directed the torture then ordered, "Take her to the site before she dies. She is almost dead. If she is not alive when we crucify her, we could be next."

Again, the woman was dragged through the streets to the site of her execution. Once there, the crowd watched as the woman was attached to beams formed into an X. She was naked. But her shoes were thrown beneath her feet. The woman was arrested at noon, and she died at noon.

Rhea responded, *I know what I experienced.*

Then, the ancient in the purple robe waved for the scene to continue.

Many who came to observe the crucifixion saw what happened at the time of the woman's death and carried her to the cave where she remained until her regeneration.

Now, to the other scenes, the ancient in the green robe warned. *The burning and decapitation.*

Please, not now. I need your help.

The ancients responded in unison, *We will be watching and observing.*

*****

Scuffling through the pages to be read, Hastings was still angry, and while eyeing Hall intently, he said, "It's time you two meet Rhea Michaels. That's what she wants. So what's the problem anyway?"

William Shepherd returned from his trip to the bathroom. "Max, we need to read the verses you have then we'll discuss our next move."

"Another put off, but you may have a point. I guess you need to be prepared for an encounter with her." Hastings handed Shepherd the pages. "Okay, William, you can start. Then, we all can take turns. Anyone for another drink?"

Shepherd looked at what Rhea had written. "Initially, her prognostication is in sentence form then she shifts to verse."

"Let's hear what she says, William." Hall leaned against the wall.

Shepherd paced back and forth in the middle of Hastings's living room as he read aloud. "When I look and see what see, I hear plan of their scheme. For attack they do from sea of green." Shepherd paused. "I know I've just started, but what is meant by sea of green?"

Hastings answered, "Green River. Sea of green is Green River."

"Oh"—Shepherd thought about the decipherment—"I see." He returned to his reading. "I know they tunnel under beam and make stacks high to set their scheme." Shepherd stopped again. "Now, the writer has returned to verse form."

> Stand against wall—they do,
> And wait till noon
> To start the brew.
> But wait not glee—it seems,
> For around they jump—
> When rats be seen.
> But scream they do
> When they see me at scene.

Shepherd looked at Hastings as he analyzed the verse. "It seems they've built a tunnel."

Hastings shook his head. "The tunnel is already there. It was built by the Underground Railroad."

He was shocked. "How do you know that?" Shepherd repeated himself. "How in the hell do you know that?"

Hastings sighed, remembering the ordeal of discovery. "One afternoon, a couple of friends and I went fishing along the banks behind the school. We hadn't been there very long when I noticed a rock formation that looked like a cave." Hastings paused as he glanced toward a window, thinking about what he had seen that day.

Irritated, Shepherd did not understand why Hastings was not as forthcoming as he should be under the circumstances. "And?"

"Our curiosities got the best of us, so we explored the opening and discovered the mouth of the cave branched off into numerous tunnels whose veins connected areas to the surrounding area. The system of tunnels is like a spiderweb. The assailants could hide a long time in one of those veins until the moment of impact."

"I guess we'd better check it out," Gabriel Hall interjected as he pressed numbers on his cell phone. After waiting momentarily, he ordered, "We're reading more prophecies. And we have work to do. Let the contacts know."

While Shepherd waited for Hall to end his conversation, Hastings offered, "William, I'll read the next few lines. Give you a break."

> And when they come to cut me free—
> Know I be way I need,
> For bad they do
> When fire blast door of room.
> One doth come to shoot me through,
> But shoot not me,
> For he see what be.
> And when he see his due
> Make plan to stab me through,
> But cut not clean,
> So pick me up
> And throw against tree.
> But when he see me dance,
>
> Say he do, "I be free."
> For twist he do
> Where he not need.

"She's giving their attack plans," Shepherd talked quietly to himself. "Tree? Wonder what the poet means by tree?"

Hastings's tone was didactic. "Tree has to be some kind of standing object in the room. Maybe it's a broom or a coatrack."

Shepherd verbalized his thoughts while he shook his head. "Could be a bookcase." He smiled. "The last two lines described what happens to one of the attackers. If it were not so serious, it'd be kinda funny."

"As for the lines you think are comedic, William—especially the twisting of her attacker," Hastings suggested, "I think she wants to make herself known. She's even arrogant about it. Maybe the rest of the lines will give you the answer, but there's other sets describing the scene." Hastings stood as he read. "Listen to this set."

> I hear screams,
> But screams not come from me—the See.
> For it true—
> I be fire when fire doth bloom.
> But when round through,
> Two come to seek duel.

Hastings paused, handing the verses to Shepherd. "I need a bathroom break."

While Mason opened the refrigerator to get a beer for Hall, Christopher, and himself, Shepherd accepted the pages and continued reading orally.

> Yes, when two come to scene—
> Say they do,
> "We kill thee."
> But say I do,
> "Chat all day,
> But dead your due."
> And end be way—
> I rule.

Shepherd shuffled through the remaining pages. "There's more." He looked at Hastings intently. "Are they as ominous as what I've just read?"

Hastings smiled. "William, you've not even touched the waterline of the tip of the iceberg. Rhea Michaels gives a detailed description of the exact day of the siege to the minutest detail. It's as if the attack is in motion, and she describes it as she watches the scene unfold. And what is described is nothing less than war."

"War!" Shepherd was astounded at Hastings's choice of words.

"War," Hastings repeated forthrightly. "War!"

"Do you have those descriptions here in your apartment?" Hall had listened to the back and forth exchange between Shepherd and Hastings. "I think we need them as well—since we're already here."

"Anyone for coffee?" Hastings offered, "Because there's a lot more."

Shepherd sighed. "Yeah, I could use a cup."

Hastings nodded as he walked toward his kitchenette to light a cigarette and to brew their drinks. "And maybe a bottle of bourbon to go with it."

5

Scooting from the barstool, Rhea walked to the den where she plopped down on the sofa. "What am I going to do? I'm surrounded—always surrounded. It's the same always, just different characters in different scenes, but the same plot—an attempt to destroy me."

But that can't happen now, can it?

Gigi scurried into the den, jumped onto the sofa, and curled up at Rhea's feet.

Rhea looked into the fireplace and watched the artificial flames dance. "Well, no more. This time, I'll be their destroyer."

As the doorbell buzzed at the back entrance, Gigi meowed.

"Of all times for somebody to come for a visit." But when Rhea saw who was standing at the door, she hissed. "Now what?"

When she opened the door, Ashton immediately blurted, "Rhea!"

"What is it, Turner?"

"I think I've convinced Megan to come back to me."

Rhea's visage revealed puzzlement. "I didn't know Megan had left you. I've been away."

Ashton was glad an opportunity to talk to Rhea had fallen at his feet. "Yeah, where did you go?"

Rhea eyed Ashton. "Parts unknown to Bell City and its inhabitants."

"Really?" Ashton paused to think about his next statement then smiled. "Well, who did you see?"

Rhea remained silent while she stared at Ashton.

Ashton noticed the tears in Rhea's eyes. "Anything wrong?"

"I'm tired, Turner. I've had one of those days where I've stumbled over furniture, dropped dishes, and lost my keys at least twice. So to cut it short, it's been a shitty day."

"Well, I also wanted let you know I'm completely shocked someone stole your paintings then hid them in my cellar to set me up."

Rhea wanted Ashton to leave. "Charlotte called and told me they also found a woman in your cellar."

"Maryann Colbert. Looks like somebody's got it in for me."

Rhea's response was almost inaudible. "Join the party."

"What?"

"Nothing, Turner. I need to go. As I said, it's been a damn long day."

"I hear ya." Ashton paused to make Rhea think he wanted to continue their conversation.

"What is it, Turner?"

"I just think there's people in this town who'll do anything to cause me problems."

Rhea smiled because she was happy Ashton had given her an opportunity to observe his reaction to her answer. "Turner, in the past, strangers passing through Bell City—even Will's Store and Villa—were waylaid with some attacks resulting in death or dismemberment."

A faint smiled tipped the corners of Ashton's mouth. "So Eaton County was pretty rowdy back in the day."

"Aren't you glad you're one of those who seems to be accepted?"

Ashton shook his head. "I wouldn't say that, Rhea, not at all. I still think someone is trying to set me up. And when I find out who it is, all I'm saying is payback will be worse than what they've done to me."

"Good night, Turner."

After Ashton left, Rhea picked Gigi up and walked to the front door, opened it, and stood momentarily to watch traffic and scan her lawn.

Suddenly, sirens and lights flashed from emergency vehicles, splitting the air. Holding Gigi close to her and while rubbing the feline's chin, Rhea verbalized her thoughts. "I wonder what's happened now."

*****

Hastings had just reseated himself in his recliner when mechanical enunciations from the scanner bellowed instructions to all city and county personnel.

"It's the high school," Hastings said to himself as the scanner identified the origin of the emergency.

"Let's go have a look, Max." Shepherd realized the opportunity to check the high school had just occurred. "Besides, it'll be a good time to check on some other sites in the area."

Hastings shook his head. "It's snowing and heavy." He then remembered the other crime scenes. "But you're right."

When the five men arrived at the high school, the fire had already been contained. But the cafeteria was damaged excessively. What fire had not scorched, water soaked. Sections of the charred ceiling dipped downward with some parts lying strewn across tables. Puddles of water with their draining streams wove within piles of fused trash.

Picking up one of the slips of lined paper, Shepherd read the Latin warning—casas fortuitus. "Look at this." He showed the soaked page to Hastings and Hall.

Hall interpreted, "This is anything but a matter of chance."

"Looks like our visitor intended to be facetious," Hastings analyzed as he scanned the damage.

Hall turned toward Mason and Christopher. "Look around to see if there are any more of these lying around." He returned his focus to Hastings and suggested, "Why don't we walk through the building and check all the exits."

When the men stood at the front entrance, Shepherd pointed to the floor plan and analyzed, "Observe how the two halls join the main corridor. See how the halls connect in the center. Max, haven't you ever noticed this formation? It's obvious it was designed to create the symbol of north, south, east, west. This was not done by happenstance."

"William, all I worried about was getting to class on time and chasing after as many girls as I could."

"Yeah, right," Shepherd agreed humorously. "And I'm sure it was in that order." Then on a more serious note, he asked, "Do you think we could check other points of interests while we're here? This is an opportunity we don't need to let pass."

Hall interjected, "We'd like to see where those tunnels are located," then what appeared to be an afterthought, he asked, "and the gym if that be possible."

Hastings nodded as he reconnoitered the area cautiously. "Let's go this way."

The gym proper was dark with only a faint light projecting from a room behind the stage. "Be careful," Hastings warned, "there's a row of steps, and they're tricky."

The three men inched their way forward when Hastings confessed, "I don't know why, but my nocturnal vision has always been better than my diurnal."

"Yeah, mine too," Hall acknowledged, "even my crepuscular is better than my diurnal."

Shepherd laughed. "Give me a break." But his tone changed when the three men stepped onto the stage. "Is this the area where Anton was found?"

Shepherd and Hall investigated the entire stage then Hall suggested, "Max, we need to check those tunnel entrances. How many did you say you found connecting the grounds to the river?"

"I found at least four, but there could be more."

"We should get started," Hall directed, "and the sooner the better."

The room behind the stage was long and narrow with lines of tables, holding props for plays. Scattered haphazardly, costumes hung from racks with their accoutrements lying on the concrete floor. At the end of the room, a solid door opened to a passage narrowing to where stones replaced concrete. "Here." Hastings pointed to a rock formation. "Here's one. It's six feet down, and then an opening leads to the river."

Shepherd shook his head. "Why hasn't anyone closed this up?"

"I doubt if anyone knows it exists." He looked downward as he verbalized his thoughts. "Or they've forgotten about it being here. With all the construction, you'd think somebody would have found it, but then again—"

"But what happened here?" Hall was stunned.

"From what I know and have been told by genealogists, this property was a holding camp between the north and south. At one time, boats traveled up Green River from the Mississippi to small towns as far as Bell City. I believe Bell City was the last port along the river where the water level was deep enough to sustain the riverboat's cargo."

"Mark Twain," Shepherd said, "identified the necessary depth for a riverboat to travel without endangering the wheel or the mainstay."

"Exactly," Hastings verified. "This property was not only where slaves were brought to be shipped to states of enslavement but also it became a network for those who sought freedom in the northern states."

"The line so to speak," Hall interjected to reveal his understanding of the area.

Hastings sighed. "Yes, the line. And from Rhea Michaels's prophecies, it is the line where horror is to appear again."

Shepherd walked away from the entrance. "We need to see the other three you know about."

Hastings identified two tunnel entrances near the library and the one at the agriculture complex. He then escorted Hall and Shepherd to the second floor where they noted areas described in Rhea Michaels's verses.

After they returned to the first floor and stood in front of Milestone's office talking about what they had observed, Ross Jackson turned the corner. "Max, what're you doing here?"

"Just looking around the old haunt," Hastings volunteered as Mason and Christopher appeared at the scene. "I heard the scanner and decided to come and check things out."

While nodding a greeting to Mason and Christopher, Jackson replied, "I see." He eyed the strangers intently and asked, "So did you find anything worthy of note?" Jackson focused directly toward Hall. "What happened to your eye, buddy?"

With a prominent British accent, Hall answered, "Shrapnel."

Hastings observed Jackson's inquisitive demeanor, "Ross, I'd like for you to meet a couple of friends of mine." He nodded toward William Shepherd. "This is Simon Adams." Then he nodded toward Gabriel Hall. "This is Roderick Rhys."

"Simon and Roderick, this is Ross Jackson, the sheriff."

All nodded their introductions then Jackson looked at Hall and said, "Sorry about your eye."

Hall nodded his acceptance of Jackson's statement of courtesy. "Quite all right. I was one of the lucky ones. Others in the attack weren't."

Jackson shocked Hastings when he replied, "It seems there's always a war somewhere on this planet."

Hall nodded in agreement. "Yes, either for political or religious reason—and greed—a tyrant wants to conquer to subjugate and annihilate which threatens all species on the planet." Hastings wanted to change Jackson's focus and nodded toward Milestone's office. "Does he know what happened?"

Jackson huffed. "Milestone said he saw Rhea Michaels leaving the building just before the explosion." Jackson shook his head. "But I told him it couldn't have been Ms. Michaels because I saw her standing in her front door, holding her cat, and watching it snow, so he must've been mistaken."

*****

On their return trip to Hastings's apartment, Hall suggested, "Why don't we drive by Rhea Michaels's residence?"

Hastings smiled. "William, since Rhea Michaels has returned from wherever she's been, why don't we stop so you two and Michaels can become acquainted—unless you two and Michaels already know one another, and I'm just some kind of minor accoutrement in your game."

Shepherd answered Hastings's insinuation without emotion. "No minor accoutrement, Max."

"Who lives across the street?" Hall inquired nonchalantly.

"Tobias Harding." Hastings smiled. "He is a character with many trades but no talents."

"And the house next to Michaels's, who lives there?"

Hastings paused. "Turner Ashton. Jackson interrogated him and considered him to be anything but on the level. Oh, and Michaels's stolen paintings were discovered in the cellar on the property."

"Really," Hall said to himself more than to the other occupants in the vehicle. "And the house on the other side of Michaels. It looks vacant."

"Traits's." Hastings laughed. "It's supposed to be haunted. People who rent don't stay very long. More than one have said they hear voices." Hastings shrugged. "I really don't know."

As soon as the five men entered the door at the bottom of the steps leading to Hastings's apartment, Hall heard a meow. "What's that?"

Hastings stopped to listen. "Don't tell me a cat has gotten in here!"

"Here." Mason pulled a cage from underneath the steps.

When Hastings saw the carrier with a note attached to the cage's top, he said, "Oh, hell! Damn it!"

"Max." Shepherd laughed. "Who's it from?"

Hastings removed the note from the carrier and read aloud.

> Max, I thought I'd make it convenient for you to take care of Mercy for me. You know she's a special cat. I'm sure the two of you will get along nicely.
>
> If you're hesitant about accepting her, I'm certain, after a few days, she'll win you over.
>
> I apologize for the inconvenience, but I had no other choice. I really didn't. As you can see, I've left what food and litter I had left.
>
> Florinda

Shepherd was curious. "Who's Florinda, Max?"

"Florinda Jones is an elderly lady who is constantly doing things for me. She tries to be helpful but ends up being a nuisance."

"Why would she leave you her cat?" Shepherd tried to avoid laughing because Hastings was so upset—even angry.

Hastings's tone was flat. "Company."

"So she hasn't gone anywhere?"

Looking at the depth of snow, Hastings's answer revealed his irritation. "In this stuff, William, I don't think so."

Shepherd laughed. "I think it's nice an elderly lady wants to take care of you." He thought about the situation. "Are you sure she's elderly?"

"Don't, William. The woman is a little crazy. So I tolerate her, and now, I'm stuck with this cat for a while. Eventually, she'll come for it." He looked at Christopher and Mason. "But until she does, you two have another job."

"Max, give the cat a chance." Shepherd continued to laugh as he tickled the feline under her chin.

"Yeah, Max, give the cat a chance," Hastings repeated disgustedly. "Damn it!"

Christopher volunteered, "I'd be happy to cat sit." As he collected the cage from Mason and carried it up the steps, Christopher looked at the feline. "Come on, Mercy. It looks like I'm your newfound friend."

Mercy purred.

Hall returned his focus to the question at hand. "Why would the principal accuse Rhea Michaels of causing the fire? It's obvious she had not been there." Hall followed Christopher up the steps.

Hastings huffed as he ascended the steps. "You know as well as I do Rhea Michaels could've caused that mayhem."

"Max, the sheriff saw her in her doorway." Shepherd paused to weigh his words and approach to Hastings's accusatory response. "Besides, it could be the way the real culprit wants it. Don't you think members of the drug cartel are capable of setting the school on fire?"

"Yes, but not write Latin. Rhea Michaels translated Latin for me but acted as if she didn't understand how she could."

"Max," Shepherd acknowledged, "I know you're angry with us, and you don't want anything to do with Rhea Michaels, but we need to finish those verses. I know it's late—"

"I'll make another pot coffee, and we can take turns reading. You don't need to leave here until you've heard everything she's written."

Once Hastings, Shepherd, and Hall had settled in their seats, and they had their coffee cups in their hands and a plate of rolls beside their seats, Shepherd began to read.

> Song of war
> Come from Me
> For I say, "All damned who attack me."
>
> But it true—
> Three come
> To start scene,
> But know not what be.
>
> And say they do, "She fake,"
> But when see me due
> Say, "We lose our stool."
>
> ^^^^^^^
> ^^^^^^^
> ^^^^^^^

Hastings looked at Shepherd. "William, I need to confess something."

"What?"

"I'm leery of Michaels, and I have a right to be. But I guess I need to call her."

"Under the circumstances and what we've observed tonight, that's a good idea, Max"—Shepherd was solemn—"for all of us."

"I'll see what I can do tomorrow. I have no choice, do I?"

Shepherd and Hall nodded in agreement simultaneously then sipped their hot black drinks.

Hearing a knock, Hastings rose from his recliner and walked to the door. "What now?"

It was Mason. "Sorry. With all the excitement, I forgot to give you this."

"Vexata quaestio" was written on a small piece of paper.

"A vexing question," Hastings translated, "but I believe it's more of an manus forti and malus animus."

William Shepherd interpreted, "A forceful entry with evil intent." He then looked at Hastings and said, "Now, Max, I hope you realize Rhea Michaels is being set up. She's in the same boat as you." He paused thoughtfully. "Maybe you need to call her, but right now, what about the other verses?"

"Yes." Hastings walked to his bookshelf. "Here they are. They go into more detail."

6

When Max Hastings awakened the next morning, Shepherd and Hall had disappeared. "I guess William and Hall decided to leave—had more important things to do." Hastings walked to his window and opened the blinds. "I need to call Patty and Bessie. There's no way the office can be opened today."

After Hastings finished his conversations with Patty and Bessie, he heard scratching at his door.

"Mercy," Hastings sighed as he opened the door. "Mason and Christopher have forgotten their cat-sitting duties, haven't they? But the major question is how I'm going return you to Ms. Florinda and not hurt her feedings."

Mercy scampered into Hastings's apartment.

After he prepared himself a cup of coffee, Hastings searched through the refrigerator for his breakfast. He eyed a half-empty jar of blackberry jam. "Peanut butter and jam—better than nothing." After taking another scan of the refrigerator's contents, he continued his self-dialogue. "I need some eggs. And bacon. Maybe a little fruit. I need to go to the grocery. Stock up. Even buy some bread."

Mercy purred.

Hastings looked at the cat staring at him. "I'm not pampering you, Mercy, not for one second—and that's final."

Mercy continued to purr.

"I don't care." Hastings walked toward his recliner with the cat following at his heels. After he seated himself, Mercy curled up at his feet. "So you want to be rubbed, do you?"

While flipping the remote to the TV, Hastings tickled Mercy under her chin with his big toe only to jump backward when the cat leaped onto his lap. "Whoa!"

A meow erupted from Mercy when she then leaped onto an unopened envelope.

"Well, I don't have anything else to do—certainly can't go anywhere—not in this frozen mess." Hastings then reflected on the events of the previous evening.

*****

At Shepherd's behest, Hastings called Rhea Michaels, and what the men learned from their conversation was more than what he wanted to accept concerning his actions toward her during their last meeting, but what was even more worrisome was Rhea Michaels's apocalyptic revelations.

Hastings waited for five rings. "It seems Ms. Michaels isn't home." He looked at Shepherd then at Hall. "Oh, but Ross saw her standing in her front door, so she's not answering because she knows it's me."

Shepherd's response was to ensure Hastings made contact. "Wait for a few more rings. Give her time. That's a big house—a lot of rooms."

Hastings huffed in disgust. "Well, there's been at least ten by now." He stopped and dialed another number. "If she wants to talk, she'll answer this number."

The men waited momentarily then Hastings acknowledged, "Nothing. What did I tell you? She has no intention of talking to me regardless of what I do or say. Now, if you can think of something to change her mind, I'm all ears. Otherwise, Rhea Michaels is a lost cause."

Hastings's cell vibrated. Looking at the ID, he motioned to Shepherd and Hall. "It's her." Hastings then answered, "Ms. Michaels!" He pressed the speaker, so Shepherd and Hall could listen to their conversation. "I's beginning to think you'd forsaken me."

"I didn't forsake you. It was you who forsook me. It was obvious at the end of our last meeting you didn't want any further communication."

Hastings shrugged as he eyed Shepherd and Hall. "I don't understand. I thought we had a great discussion during our last meeting."

"I did too, but as I was leaving, you were extremely rude to me."

"Ms. Michaels, I don't know what you're talking about."

"Mr. Hastings, I've really tried to be honest with you. But the afternoon I finally got up enough courage to tell you what I'd seen in my visions, you turned on me."

"Again, I don't know what you're talking about."

The men heard Rhea's sigh before she said, "I know you remember our discussion about Race Webb and his criminal activity—his involvement in all those murders."

"Yes, I remember." Hastings's visage revealed puzzlement.

"When I informed you Race Webb killed your wife and daughters, you pushed me out the door, locked it in my face, then closed the blinds."

Losing all color from his face, Hastings paused then replied, "Ms. Michaels, I was about to lose it. And to be quite honest with you, I don't remember anything about the rest of the night. In fact, I woke up the next morning at my desk. How I got there, I have no idea."

Hall and Shepherd glanced at each other out of the corner of their eyes, but their facial visages remained set, for they had been informed of what had happened by Mason and Christopher.

Rhea continued her dialogue, "And a lot has happened to me since then."

Hastings attempted to placate Rhea's antagonistic verbal assault. "The sheriff has been checking on your property."

"Why?"

"If you haven't heard, your paintings are here in my office." Hastings continued to eye Hall and Shepherd.

"Yes, Charlotte informed me."

"I see." After a thoughtful blanket of silence and Shepherd's encouragement, Hastings continued, "I was wondering when you could come by for us to discuss—"

"Discuss what?" Rhea's tone had not changed. "What is it we need to discuss?"

"Your verses for one thing and some other occurrences—even some people we both know."

"Why? The verses give you what's going to happen. What does the cryptographer think about them?"

"Actually, they're looking at the verses as we speak."

"Mr. Hastings, they're actually sitting in your apartment listening to our conversation as we speak. So to save everyone's time, I suggest reading parts or sections not only of *Warning, The Attack, The Curse,* but also *Two-One Watching Sly,* and *There Are Three.*" Rhea paused then addressed, "Gentleman, the two men who are here to discover just who and what I am about—I have a message to be delivered to specific individuals."

Hastings was shocked, but he saw Shepherd and Hall did not appear to be surprised.

"Ms. Michaels—"

"To whom am I speaking?"

"My name is William Shepherd."

"And the other man, what is your name?"

"Gabriel Hall."

"I see."

Shepherd sighed. "Now that we've been introduced, what can we do for you?"

"First of all, just to be clear, I know you understand you are not speaking to Rhea Michaels."

Hall responded, "We understand."

Hastings was astonished not only by what appeared to be the entity who had revealed herself in his office but also to Shepherd's and Hall's responses to her revelation.

The entity continued to speak. "I need to send a message to those who think they're in control of this planet. There are more members than just nine—but nine is an ending number—so for practical purposes, and my personal satisfaction, I'll identify them as the delta nine."

Hastings motioned to Shepherd and Hall and whispered, "What is she talking about?"

Shepherd and Hall ignored Hastings's question, but it was Hall who asked, "What's the message you want delivered?"

"During the holidays, I met with an individual who is not from around here. I gave him two directives—one was to meet with the universal cosmic council, which I did, and I must say what a visit that was. They made me review the woman's crucifixion."

"And the other?" Hall asked with a concerned expression on his face.

"The other directive was to the delta nine, and so far, they—which I knew they would—have ignored me."

Hall's inhale and exhale was noticeable. "So what do you want from us?"

"I denote irritation and facetiousness, and I assure you…not wise."

"I didn't mean to sound facetious, madam. I just need to know your intentions."

"All right, Mr. Hall and Mr. Shepherd, since they have ignored me, I am sending them this message to change the wrong to what has been happening the past two thousand years. The Jews did not crucify the man whom the at-present civilization calls Jesus—his true name was Yeshua. It was the Romans. The Jews were controlled by the Romans. The Romans were the authoritarians and had complete control over the Jews as they did in every other domain they conquered. But it wasn't a man who was crucified—it was a woman. You know her name. She was the messenger. But she is still being crucified. Now, I want what has been happening for the past two thousand years to stop. The Jews are no longer to be blamed for an execution for which the Romans were responsible. The hateful attacks—verbally, physically, socially, politically—in all forms are to stop. I mean immediately. And while on the subject of hate—all hate groups are to cease their operations and activities. They are harmful to all genera."

Hall eyed Shepherd and Hastings, but the three men remained silent.

"I've been here many times, and my age compared to theirs is incomprehensible. Maybe I need to conduct more demonstrations in order for the delta nine—even the species who thinks it's the apex predator—to realize I'm not bluffing because I don't bluff. I don't have to bluff. They should know that by now."

"I think the delta nine—as you refer to them—are aware of your presence."

"Doesn't appear that way to me, but if they are as you say, then they need to meet with me. If I'm ignored any longer and leave this planet without being able to make the changes necessary for the continuation of this planet's multiple species, including the extraterrestrials, then another cycle shall be initiated—as it has so many times previously in the line—cycle."

Wanting confirmation to what Rhea had said, Hall inquired, "And you want me to use those exact words?"

"You can also tell them I said, 'And there's not a damn thing they can do about it,' then watch their reactions. Please note, I pluralized reactions."

It appeared to Hall the entity had concluded her directive, so he asked, "Is there—"

"Yes, there are a few more items of business or, should I say, messages that need to be delivered. First, more needs to be done concerning worldwide—from all countries—about climate change. If Homo sapiens sapiens think they will be able to contaminate other planets and moons before they find solutions on this planet, they are sadly mistaken." The entity paused then continued, "And yes, I'm aware of technological advancements, but peace must be sustained here before habitation is established on alien surfaces."

Hall was about to speak but the entity interjected, "I'm not finished. I know advanced technological countries are planning to control earth from space. There needs to be a rethinking of that thought."

"Why do you—"

The entity ignored the question and interjected, "Remember, Rhea Michaels is not speaking. I can be anywhere in any form. Second, I am tired of the extinction of species that are vital to this planet. So the raping and razing of ecosystems—*terra firm, marinus, atmossphaira*—necessary for those species' survival is to cease. The hunting and fishing of genera—past and at present—to extinction must stop."

"We understand," Shepherd attempted an interruption.

"I said, I'm not finished. Third, it is time the women, worldwide, stop being treated as slaves—having no say about their well-being, health, and livelihood. The idea life begins at conception is ludicrous—the brain controls anatomical functions. If those who were beheaded could speak, that fact would definitely be understood. But the same politicians who push that agenda not only want to harm the elderly, make them worry and suffer about health care and monetary survival, but also preach and carry the codex of one ideology in one hand while they pack a weapon in another. Wake up!" The entity paused then warned, "By the way, no one—and I mean no one—had better make an attempt on my host's life, whoever it may be. I know you understand the consequences. I will retaliate."

Hall attempted to ask a question.

Hissing, the entity continued with her directive. "Fourth, it is evidential that Homo sapiens sapiens need to follow suggestions and guidelines established by scientists and physicians and not listen to politicians who care nothing for their constituents but their own political agendas. Their lies have effected unnecessary deaths. And to make a prediction, there will be another pandemic. If a person does not learn from the first lesson, and it is repeated for a second time and is not learned, the third repeat will be even more deadly."

"Ms. Michaels—"

"Again, I repeat, Rhea Michaels is not speaking. In fact, her shell is resting comfortably in a chair. So number five, I believe, is in order. My incarnations on this planet and in every country are beyond comprehension. So I am well-aware of the existential mayhem leaders—politically and theologically—need to control the lives of their populations. Autocracies or wannabe autocracies need to relinquish their control of their peoples. Again, if people are not free on this planet, do you honestly think subjugation on other planets and moons will be allowed? The answer is no!"

The entity paused then said, "Since I believe everything needs to be conducted in threes, I shall end with six. It is time illegal drugs are stopped. They are detrimental to the well-being of peoples worldwide. For one country and drug lords—where illegal drugs are prohibited—to funnel drugs to other countries has to stop. It is a high possibility I might be flying around and making appearances at some of these places where they are being manufactured. The individuals who live and work in these compounds will not like my visit—even my appearance—I can assure you of that fact." The entity paused then continued, "Cosmic Mother and Earth Mother are angry. I hope you have recorded my message, which I know you have, in order for the delta nine to understand the brevity to ensure a notable change in conditions. And if I do not witness a change, I will make an appearance when I'm least expected."

The three men looked at one another but remained silent while Hall paced back and forth in front of the window.

Hastings looked at Shepherd and Hall and whispered, "She's still on the phone."

"Yes, Mr. Hastings, I need to repeat a couple of things before I end our conversation."

"We're listening," Gabriel Hall replied cautiously.

"It's time members of worldwide political affiliations, followers of worldwide theological ideologies, and citizens in all countries to stop their wars. I do not care whether the country is democratic, autocratic, or theocratic."

Hastings, Shepherd, and Hall eyed each other, then Hall said, "It will be difficult to—"

The entity interjected, and her response was not what the men wanted to hear.

"If Homo sapiens sapiens like their existence on this planet, then the genus needs to understand its toes are tipping over the abyss. So the political and theological leaders and their inferiority complexes need to understand there's an entity more powerful than they ever thought possible who can just nod her head or flutter her eyelid, and they won't be in control of anything because all they see at present no longer exists. And again, there's not a damn thing they can do about it."

While Hastings and Shepherd looked at each other, Hall responded to the entity's directive. "We understand your frustration—"

"No. None of you understand my frustration. I am tired of what's happening to the flora and fauna. I am tired of how one nationality in a country thinks it has the right to harass, attack, and murder other nationalities. In this country, the debate over immigration needs to be resolved. The peoples who really have the right to the landmass—and everyone else be the invaders—are the Native American tribes. Immigrants charged the shores, invaded the landmass, and took and took and took. There are sacred lands, which need to be returned to Native Americans."

Hall made another attempt to speak but was unsuccessful.

"I am tired of racism among all races. I am tired of attacks and murders because of hate. I am tired of slavery in all forms. I am tired of poverty and hunger in all countries. I am tired of religious and political wars. I am tired of politicians playing to the fears of their constituents for self-aggrandizement. I am tired of dictatorships. I am tired of bullies. I am tired of what I see, hear, and experience every day in this form I now exist. How Homo sapiens sapiens are conducting themselves at all levels of society is detrimental to the planet."

Hall's response was cautionary. "William and I will deliver your message."

"Homo sapiens sapiens have not changed since they arrived on this planet. They destroyed their planet of origin—they won't be permitted to destroy this one. That will be done for them, and they will go with the tide. So, you see, a lot is at stake even for the extraterrestrials who enjoy their habitation here. And I'm certain the extraterrestrials who like to visit and live on this planet want it to remain existent." The entity entered Rhea Michaels's form. "Gentlemen, good night!"

As soon as their conversation ended, Hastings turned toward Shepherd and Hall and exclaimed, "What the hell! I repeat—what the hell, you two!"

Shepherd and Hall remained silent and noncommittal.

"Start leveling with me."

William Shepherd interjected, "What we need to do now is read the verses."

Hastings realized any attempt to glean information from Shepherd and Hall was futile. "Okay, but before we start, I need a drink—and a stiff one. Either one of you want to join me? I'm having a glass of bourbon. And after I drink one, I just might have another."

Shepherd acknowledged, "Yeah, I'd like a shot."

"Me too," Hall verified as he removed the verses from the envelope. "I'll read while you two drink. I'll start with *Warning*."

> What happens to thee
> That day
> Will be the month of May.

Hall affirmed, "We need to check incidents which have occurred in May."

> So prepare you must
> And be hurrying thus,
> For the test
> Be the best.
> And it be time
> Of sad relief
> When all complete—
> You know not what you do,
> But coming door walk through.

"The last four lines have appeared in other verses, so she's being told she'll survive." Handing the verses to Shepherd, Hall asked, "Will you read a few lines? After our conversation with Michaels, or should I say entity, I need to visit the bathroom."

Shepherd accepted the pages and began to read. He, Hastings, Christopher, and Mason then heard Hall's violent, oral response to the entity's revelation. The regurgitation of his last meal gave all of them a moment to pause and think.

> *The Attack*
> I can describe for you
> A round or two.
> "A witch, a witch," they call thee,
> But a witch they not see.
>
> I know you want a description such,
> So I say they begin
> By beating your skin.
> Cut wrists—they try,
> But by and by,
> You take away
> Their knives of crime.
> Make no difference
> What they attempt against thee,
> For pick them up—you do—
>
> Throw one then two.
> Two falls on floor,
> Then pick him up for a while—
> Dance him around with a smile.

Shepherd scanned the lines silently. "Listen to this. There's another description of her physically. It would seem she's shifted."

> If I ever depart this play,
> I hope I remember the day,
> For all to know
> You will kill the foe,
> And never lose eye one.
> For eye be big and green,
> And never face so clear

Even when baby dear.
I know you keep writing this piece,
But piece will be your teeth—
So sharp and wide
When man falls on his side.

Shepherd stopped to warn Hastings and Hall. "Now she goes into another description and what the foe attempts to do when Michaels thwarts his attack."

Adding more to what's been said—
The man is playing dead,
But I hope you see once more—
He wants to cut
To settle score.
So he jumps around,
But you grab his knees.
To pick him up,
And throw against wall—

For the fall.
Soon he tries to crawl away,
But you stop his way.
Pick him up by his feet—
He screams for defeat.
And defeat be his alone
When you slit his throat.

Blood…blood…blood everywhere—blood for the fair.

"So we have the month, time, and description of scene, even what happens. But I guess we need to see what else is here before we jump to any conclusions." Shepherd looked at Hastings and asked, "Do you want to read a few lines?"

Hastings accepted the pages and began his turn at reading the verses.

> You seem
> To return to thee,
> But not meant to be—
> For there's another
> To sing unhappy song.
> Keeping up—1, 2, 3
> And he'll attempt to stab thee,
> But stab not me will he
> For I stab him
> In knee.
> Now, he's lying on the floor,
> And cries are flowing
> To stop the roar.
> But roar not stop,
> For others are coming
> To the spot.
> The man—two—on floor
> Moans and groans
> For he's lost his store.

Hastings paused. "It seems the battle will continue into the night because the next few lines verify it will. But there's also more description of the fight."

"She seems to need the assurance we understand every detail—when the attack occurs, her reaction, and what will happen to the aggressors." Shepherd smiled. "Again, like the initial verses we read—however horrific—still comedic at times."

Hastings returned to his oral reading.

> While all who come this way
> Think day will be day,
> But nighttime too
> Cause much panic and dismay.

> Noise be far and wide,
> But a few will escape to tide.

"Max, it sounds like she's talking about the river," Shepherd interrupted. "What do you think?"

Hastings nodded. "Possibly." He then continued to read.

> You'll fight two
> With broom in room,
> And broom be
> Answer for thee,
> When the man grabs his knife
> To counteract his death in sight.
> He swings—he swings foursquare
> Just to trip on blood there.
> You talk with plans and laugh away—
> As you dance his way.
> He does not see his doom,
> But addled he is
>
> When his body be
> Twisted from his head.

Hastings placed the papers on the table.

Hall sighed. "I guess we need to be finding rooms."

"You can stay here. One of you can sleep in the recliner. The other one can have the sofa. It's just been delivered."

*****

Hastings heard a knock at his door. After ensuring Mercy landed on the floor safely, he yelled, "Just a minute!"

"It's us, Max. We've got breakfast and a lot to discuss."

Hastings opened the door. "I thought you'd left." He looked at the boxes in Shepherd's and Hall's hands. "You do have food."

Entering Hastings's apartment, both men placed the containers on the kitchenette's countertop. "Yeah," Shepherd replied, "we decided to splurge. You hadn't planned to go in today, had you?"

"No. I called Patty and Bessie and told them not even to try to come in."

"Okay." Shepherd opened the boxes. "Your friend, Ariel, sent you a message—'tell Max to make sure he comes by later for lunch or dinner.'" Shepherd smiled. "You know, Max, you've got a lot of people who watch out for you."

Hastings looked at the containers. "Are those mine? Because I'm hungry."

Shepherd and Hall eyed each other then walked toward a makeshift table. As Shepherd lowered himself into a chair, he said, "We need to tell you what we've discovered."

"I'm listening." Hastings took a bite of bacon, paused, then said. "But first, I want to say I've been thinking about our—or should I say—your conversation with the entity last night."

Shepherd looked at Hall then replied, "If you're going to ask—"

"I'm not asking you anything." Hastings grabbed a napkin then continued. "I'm telling you that it would be wise to do as the entity directed. It's obvious she wasn't mincing her words. In fact, I believe the correct analysis of her directive was blunt and definitely uncompromising. At least, that's my interpretation. But if you have another, please feel free to express yours."

Shepherd and Hall remained silent.

Hastings eyed both men directly and said pointedly, "I see." Hastings took a sip of coffee. "The fire beneath the cauldron is firing up, and I believe the flame is blue."

7

Rhea had just walked into her kitchen when she heard the bell at her back door. "Who could that be so early in the morning?" When she opened the door, Rhea exclaimed, "Etta! Come in. You must be a glutton for punishment." Rhea looked at the snow. "What tempted you to venture out on this, I must say, beautiful morning?"

"Just thought I'd stop by—see if you wanted to check things out at the high school."

"Why?"

Etta was shocked. "Rhea, don't you know? Haven't you heard?"

"Heard what?" Rhea realized she was not completely awake. "I've just gotten up. I haven't even had my cup of coffee yet. What's going on?"

Etta shook her head. "Don't you listen to the news?"

Rhea laughed. "This early in the morning. The news is too newsy."

"What about last night?"

"I just walked around the house and talked to myself, making plans."

Etta's curiosity heightened. "Making plans for what?"

"Nothing special—just trying to decide what additional chores I could do while we're off during these wonderful snow days we've been blessed with."

Etta smiled as she plopped down on a barstool. "We'll probably be off longer."

"What's happened?"

"Rhea, you have been out of it. Didn't you hear the sirens last night?"

"Yes, but I didn't pay any attention. Sirens are blaring all the time."

"Somebody set the high school's cafeteria on fire." Etta paused as she eyed the just brewed coffee. "But I think the somebody was somebodies, and those somebodies were Herman and Burke." Etta smiled sinisterly. "Of course, I blame them for everything." Then thoughtfully added, "I could start blaming Shirley Bass." Etta giggled. "Wouldn't that stir things up? Pay her back for all the diarrhea, which spurts from that mouth of hers to me and about me."

"This conflict between the two of you needs to stop, Etta. It's not any good for either of you."

"Yeah, you're probably right, but she's always starting something with me. Now, it's my turn. Besides, I think she's on somebody's payroll. She likes to hint and brag to see what we'll say. I'm not stupid, and neither are you."

Rhea nodded in support of Etta's analysis of their experiences with Bass. "Shirley does like to brag about things, and I agree, it's how she brags. It's as if she's plotting her boasts to get our reactions."

Etta continued to eye the coffeepot. "I'm to the point I don't even want to be around her."

Rhea saw Etta's focus toward the just-brewed coffee. "You want a cup?"

Etta laughed. "I've already had two, but yes, I'll drink a third."

After pouring their coffees and setting the cups on the countertop, Rhea asked, "So you really want to go to the high school? Do you really think it's a good idea?"

"Yes and yes. Besides, you need to get out of this house. If you haven't since December 16, I don't know how you're not bonkers."

"Who says I'm not?"

Etta smiled. "All right. After we drink our coffee, we'll go and see what's up."

Rhea frowned. "Maybe I'm the one who is a glutton for punishment. Go to the high school when I don't have to. Yeah, I need my mind checked. And, Etta, you do too."

"Oh, shit, Rhea. Stop it. You know you're curious. Do you want to bet Herman and Burke are snooping around?"

"No, Etta, I don't because I know they'll be there with rings on their fingers and food on their clothes."

*****

Max Hastings observed Shepherd and Hall while they ate their breakfasts. "So you went to Ariel's."

Shepherd looked at Hall then at Hastings. "Max, I guess we need to tell you—"

"Tell me what?"

> SHEPHERD. We met with Ross Jackson.
> HASTINGS. Really? What for?
> SHEPHERD. We thought it might be better if we were a little more transparent.
> HASTINGS. I see. So what do I need to know? I hope you didn't betray me—Simon Adam and Roderick Rhys.
> SHEPHERD. We didn't give you way, but I did show him my credentials.
> HASTINGS. And what about your British friend here?
> SHEPHERD. Roderick Rhys is here to observe.
> HASTINGS. I see.
> SHEPHERD. He asked us to go back to the high school with him. Take another look.
> HASTINGS. Really?
> SHEPHERD. He wanted to know our perspective of the scene.
> HASTINGS. And what did you tell him?
> SHEPHERD. We told him it was probably one person.
> HASTINGS. So when you returned, did you see anything different?
> SHEPHERD. Jackson stopped two people.
> HASTINGS. Who were they?
> SHEPHERD. Maybe or maybe not the couple we're looking for.
> HASTINGS. Anything else?
> SHEPHERD. The principal appeared to be nervous.

HASTINGS. Do you think Milestone had anything to do with the fire?
SHEPHERD. He knows more than what he's saying. Maybe somebody is threatening him?
HASTINGS. I guess time will reveal his role in the scenario.

"I guess so." Shepherd looked at the papers lying on the table, "I believe we lack *The Curse, Two-One Watching Sly, There Are Three.*"

Hastings offered, "I'll read for a while, let you finish your breakfasts. If you want anything to drink—more coffee, sodas, or fire water—help yourselves," then Hastings began reading *The Curse.*

Time is here for you to know—

There be a show—a show
For thee to kill,
And kill you will
On day falls to nineteen still.

Many think you are dead
But survive you do,
And all will see
Change in thee.

No more the same
As always been—
You be ever
So different then.

Curse you talk,
For bait you walk.
And you will see
The curse by me
Change your taunt.

Hastings analyzed the fifth line. "Nineteen is mentioned again. We really need to figure out the significance of that number—even the date."

Shepherd agreed, "I guess we need to look at the repetitions then compare what is before and after those lines."

Hall reseated himself after refilling their coffee cups. "Probably a good idea."

*****

When Rhea and Etta entered the front doors of the Eaton County High School, the first people they saw were Zachary Milestone, Jules Herman, and Dee Burke.

"Ladies, what brings you out here in all this mess—out there and in here." Milestone avoided Rhea's and Etta's eyes.

Etta stiffened as she looked at Milestone then directly at the educational consultants. "We could ask the two of you the same thing. No school, so why be here?"

Herman's response was anything but cordial. "Paperwork!"

Etta smirked and countered, "Paperwork! You drove here to do paperwork! Why not stay home where it's all warm and cozy, where you can snuggle up, and do paperwork?"

Milestone entered the conversation. "Ms. Smiley, I could ask you the same question. Sheriff Jackson and some other investigators don't want the scene contaminated."

Etta Smiley retaliated, "It's already contaminated!"

Milestone turned toward Rhea. "Ms. Michaels, I see you've returned."

With a puzzled expression, Rhea asked, "What do you mean?"

"I saw you leaving the building around the time I arrived to check on the cafeteria."

Rhea quickly countered Milestone's accusation. "I've not been on these premises since school was called off before the holidays. In fact, my car has not left my driveway."

"Yeah, the sheriff said there was no way. But the likeness of you was spot-on. You must have a twin and don't know it."

Rhea looked at Etta then at Milestone. "I suggest you need a new prescription for your glasses." She turned toward the consultants. "And we really are here to do paperwork."

As Rhea and Etta walked away, they both noticed Milestone, Herman, and Burke enter Milestone's office. Etta then said, "Rhea, they're up to something."

"They're always up to something, and that something is to cause us problems."

"And I wonder what's next." Etta verbalized her thoughts as they ascended the steps to the second floor. "If it's worse than what's been done to us before now, we're really in trouble."

Rhea nodded in agreement. "And I'm sure it will be." She laughed. "Now do you see why I had no intention of accepting your bet?"

Etta smiled. "I had to try."

*****

Shepherd offered to read. "I'll read *Two-One Watching Sly*. Give you a break, Max."

> Two-one watching sly
> Two-one thinking survive—
> "Not true," I say to thee,
> "For they see me."
>
> Acting the way they do
> Be a front
> To survive you.
>
> And knowing they have nothing to say
> Makes them feel
> Out of touch and away.
>
> For time be here
> When something moves
> With their stools.

LIFTING THE VEIL

Shepherd paused. "Do you think these verses are revealing three different incidents, just mixed together? One incident could be an attack by one person. Another incident could have two attackers. The third incident could have three or more attackers."

"Could be," Hall agreed, "but let's see what *There Are Three* says, and I'll read."

> You see
> There be three,
> And there's more
> By the door.
>
> But climb—climb
> You do—forsooth.
>
> Then they jump—jump
> Away from sin—
> Just happy to flee you then.
>
> I wish I could tell true,
> But not for me to do.
> For it's only the bell—the bell that rings
> The day—the day
> The month of May.

"Another mention of May." Shepherd shook his head, speaking more to himself than to Hastings and Hall. "We've just been told the month of the attack when multiple people will appear. As for the other two incidents, it's anybody's guess unless something else is revealed later." He focused his attention to both Hastings and Hall. "Now we need to check significant dates in May, which could be a clue for this incident."

Hastings grabbed his phone. "Let me look." He then scrolled and said, "May 4, 1886, Haymarket Square Riot; May 8, 1942, Battle of the Coral Sea; May 10, 1882, riot outside Astor Opera House."

Hall interrupted, "It's the number 19 which stands out."

Ignoring Hall, Hastings continued his identifications. "May 11, 1969, Battle of Hamburger Hill; May 20, 325, Council of Nicaea set the formulated date for Easter; May 26, 1940, Dunkirk evacuation; May 29, 1453, Constantinople captured by the Turks."

Again, Hall interrupted, "What about other dates in history? There has to be something on May 19."

Hastings response was spontaneous. "It did! On May 19, 1536, Anne Boleyn was executed."

Hall's deduction of the date shocked Shepherd and Hastings. "Maybe, nineteen fall means the days instead of people. Nineteen fall could actually mean the days leading to the incident. So 19 is the date the attack occurs."

There was a long pause and total silence while the three men pondered the possibility of Hall's analysis then Shepherd said, "Let's finish these last few lines to see if there's anything else we need to discuss."

Hastings volunteered, "I'll read."

> I wish you could see
> All to be,
> For the monster
> Does not want to go.
>
> How we survive
> Is turmoil and strife,
> But all who cause this pain
> Will end up with life of stain.
>
> Say I must
> To all who be due—
> Never—never a bad thing do.
>
> For it is the bad that hurts so much—
> It be the bad that teaches such.
> Those who attack you
> Can never be
> After the incident—against Me.

Hall analyzed what Hastings had just read. "It seems whoever is planning these attacks or skirmishes or sprees or whatever you want to call them has no idea what the outcome will be. And their failure starts a wave or a roller-coaster ride of events."

"Hall," Hastings supported, "I think your analysis has hit the center of the board." Hastings then turned toward Shepherd. "And, William, you need to acknowledge my calls when I attempt to contact you."

Putting their coats, scarves, and beanies on, Shepherd acknowledged, "I will, but now, we have other places to go and people to see."

As Shepherd and Hall left the apartment, Mercy whined.

Hastings looked at the cat. "You want to go with them, Mercy?"

The feline's answer was a rub against Hastings's ankle and shoe.

*****

Rhea and Etta had made a few stops on their return trip to Rhea's home. "Thanks, Etta, I've been cooped up so long I'd forgotten how nice it is to get out of the house."

"I know you don't like to drive in the snow, so if you need anything or go anywhere, just call. Either Haldan or I can take you where you need to go."

Looking at her car, Rhea laughed. "I guess I need to do some snow removal and start my car. The battery is probably dead."

"You want to check it now?"

Rhea smiled at Etta's offer. "Thanks, but I have one of those chargers I can attach. Besides, I think I need to remove the snow first."

"Okay. Talk to you later, Rhea."

Rhea was removing her coat when she heard her back door bell ring. "Be there in a second." But when Rhea saw who was waiting to enter, she was more than shocked. "Megan, so you decided to come back to Turner after all."

Megan nodded as she looked around Rhea's kitchen and den. "I almost didn't, but when Turner promised we'd leave when he finds what he's looking for, I'm here—for a while at least."

"You've really had a change of attitude since this past summer."

"What? What do you mean?"

"Megan, this past summer, you were willing to follow Turner to hell—remember."

Megan Ashton appeared not to understand then she acknowledged, "Oh, yeah. I did say that, didn't I?"

"You did." Rhea paused. "What kind of artifact is Turner trying to find anyway?"

"I'm not sure, but I think a dagger."

"A dagger, you say. That's interesting." Rhea looked at the clock over the refrigerator. "I'm sorry, Megan. Please, have a seat. I've been gone most of the day, and I need something to eat."

"Rhea, I probably need to go."

"Don't be silly. You just got here. Besides, I need for you to read something I've written. See what you think. It won't take long." Rhea smiled as she offered, "I have chocolate cake."

Megan nodded her acceptance of Rhea's tempting invitation. "I won't refuse a slice of chocolate cake."

"Good. What do you want to drink?'

"Coffee is fine."

"I believe I'll have another cup too."

8

While Megan sliced her chocolate cake and took a bite, Rhea printed the short story she wanted Megan to read. Rhea had been curious about how Turner Ashton treated Megan and decided her spontaneous visit this morning was an opportunity to discover what she had suspected—even knew—for some time.

Megan appeared to be hesitant. "I don't have long."

"It's just a short story. I'm curious about what you think about it. There's just a few pages."

Megan nodded. "This cake is really good. What have you done that's different? My chocolate cakes never taste like this."

"Almond extract is the key. It does something to the chocolate. I also add almond extract to the frosting."

"Well, all I can say is it's delicious."

"Thanks." Rhea saw Megan's coffee cup was almost empty. "Would you like another cup?"

"Yes, please." Megan eyed the pages Rhea had placed atop the counter. "So you really have been writing."

"Yes. Writer's block has left the house, and I hope never returns. But I need to acknowledge Calliope, epic poetry; Clio, history; Melpomene, tragedy."

Megan's facial expression revealed puzzlement. "Who are they?"

"They are three of the nine Muses." Rhea paused thoughtfully then said, "I probably also need to acknowledge Urania, astronomy, and Thalia, comedy. Usually, tragedy has a hint of comic relief somewhere in the lines."

Now Megan appeared to be curious about what Rhea had written. "So is your story comedy, science fiction, mystery, romance, or horror?"

"I'll let you decide. Why don't you read it orally to me? That way I can hear my mistakes. But I'd also like to see if you think it has an audience—one that can relate to the theme—even the setting, character, and plot."

Megan shook her head. "Why don't you read the story to me? That way you can see and hear your mistakes at the same time. And while I listen, I can eat chocolate cake and drink coffee."

"Okay, Megan, if you insist." Rhea smiled as she began to read.

*FREE*DOM

Although there had been evidence—even sightings and cries—of panthers in the area for years, many people refused to acknowledge the possibility of their presence.

Now while the woman sat at her kitchen table and held a shotgun across her thighs and listened—from a distance—to the signature churning and roaring of her husband's dated truck's engine, she wished for the sightings to be true, especially this night.

The woman's body stiffened as she thought about the steps she had taken, directing her to this existential predicament. Rebellion, she knew, had been the source of her entrapment; and like so many rebellions, the woman was paying and suffering for her actions.

As she focused on the gun, the woman spoke to the open space of her kitchen. "Abuse has many faces, takes many forms, causes irrefutable damage to those who suffer from its forceful attack. Abuse has many names—all waiting for that moment to reveal themselves. Sometimes, abuse is a word. Sometimes, abuse is an action. Sometimes, abuse becomes a character unto itself—never faltering in its mission—always waiting for the opportunity to reveal itself behind the mask."

The woman sighed as she thought about her actions leading her to this predicament she now endured. Again, looking around the room and listening to the truck's engine scream its tortured viscera into the nights air, she confessed to herself. "And like abuse, rebellion takes many forms, has many characters, causes woe for some while liberation from tyranny for others. Some rebellions occur to seek retribution toward family."

That had been the woman's journey. Rebellion to seek retribution, but her retribution had failed, and now, she was paying for her defiance. And that defiance fed and played the causal chain of events. For this woman refused to admit she was wrong—never admitting remorse.

As the woman sat, waited, and hoped not to falter, she thought about the steps and choices that had ushered her to this moment.

She had lost count of the times she had asked, "Is there such a thing as Providence, divine intervention, miracles?" If there were, they had evaded her.

Maybe I'm not worthy?

But tonight, the woman had determined, worthy or unworthy, her release was imminent. One way or another, tonight Death would arrive at her door, and the plot to unfold would determine whether Death captured hers or her husband's existence.

Often, the woman played the scenario in her mind's eye from the beginning to the ending with the same result—nothing changed. She had never followed through with her plot—to kill.

The plot had always been the same. An altercation erupted over something she had said or had done. It could be significant or insignificant. Once, it had been a broken glass, resulting in a twisted knee and broken cartilage. She had limped for months.

Another attack erupted when her husband traded what she considered a piece of junk for a crossbow. To test it, he pointed the weapon toward a door and fired. Laughing hysterically, he bragged, "Just think what could happen if that door had been you." With a sneer plastered across his face, he then demanded, "What's your name? I say, what's your name?"

The woman always remained silent.

Sometimes, the woman envisioned knocking him out and setting him on fire. The most recent plot included poison. That plan occurred when he had walked into the house with a new shotgun—the one lying across her thighs—and shot above her head. If she had moved from where she had been sitting, the woman's head would have split from her body as those who experienced the guillotine during the French Revolution.

After the kill, the woman planned her escape. Feigning insanity had been her first choice, but she did not want to experience bondage in an asylum.

"*What will happen to me there*" was the thought that deterred that particular kill. "*Imprisoned for life*" was another thought that deterred any action of retribution.

Over and over and over, the woman played the scene, but over and over and over, she stopped the attack just as she was about to stab, slice, or bludgeon her prey.

Tonight, his attack had been different. It crossed and cut through a barrier she had never experienced during previous assaults. Death was in his eyes, and now, she had no choice. The woman placed her hand on the trigger. "I can shoot him and make it look like an accident. He's drunk. He's always drunk. I can say he tripped while he's loading the shotgun. Or I can say he was just showing off. No one will question what happened. Everyone knows what he is—how he is. I just have to remain cool—even cold. Show no emotion. Not give him a chance to overpower me. Attack without hesitation—that's the key to my survival," she affirmed.

What had appeared to be a normal afternoon had transformed into a nightmare. He had pulled her hair then grabbed her shoulders, shoving her against the wall. She had become his punching bag with his fists hitting her back and head until she thought she would lose consciousness. After the beating, the man stood backward, walked outside, entered his truck, and drove away.

Now, while listening to the roar of the truck's engine, the woman rubbed her bruised cheek, flicked her tongue across her blooded lips as she brushed her hair away from her swollen eye only to feel the knot on her forehead to be bigger than what it had been earlier that afternoon. She sat upright in her chair, but when she attempted to inhale then exhale, her entire body shuddered from pain, causing her to double over to her right side. "I have to kill him. I have no choice."

The truck's tires screeched as the man attempted to make a turn.

"If only he would flip. Please flip over." *If he flips, the truck might catch on fire, and he'll burn.* "Please burn."

But the woman's wish did not come to fruition. The truck's roar revealed her plea had been ignored. He had survived the turn. "No one's listening. I am alone." She remembered her childhood. "I've always been alone."

The truck's engine roared louder and louder. Suddenly, a burst from the horn shot through the air like arrows with a systematic rotation on then off, on then off, on then off.

Grimacing, the woman worried. *What are the neighbors thinking? Will they call the police?*

The woman's thoughts then shifted to one particular incident when she was in the seventh grade. Her fellow female classmates constantly played psychological games with her at the behest of the girls' mothers who did not realize their daughters were quite adapt at creating their own menacing attacks.

Another blast from the truck's horn sliced the air as the woman's husband swerved into the driveway.

It won't be long. She tightened the grip on the shotgun. "He won't suspect a thing."

The truck's engine stopped. Momentarily, there was weighted silence. The door then squeaked open only to be slammed shut.

As he staggered up the steps, the woman's husband yelled, "You know what's coming, so open the damn, fucking door!"

The woman lifted the shotgun from her lap and rose from her chair. She walked cautiously toward the door, but just before she opened it, the woman dimmed the lights.

There's another way.

Opening the door slowly, the woman's husband started to lunge toward her, but just as he was about to grab her arm and gun, a loud screech erupted from his inebriated cavern. "Ugh!"

Just as he was about to step inside the door, the woman's canines splayed as she leaped for her prey.

Later when the police asked what happened, the woman answered, "I guess panthers are in this area after all. From the evidence at his throat, it's the only logical explanation. What do you think?"

"Mam, what's your name?"

"Freedom. My name is Freedom."

"So what do you think, Megan?"

"It's dark. It's horrific."

"I know I need to work on it some more but—"

Megan appeared to be deep in thought then tears welled in her eyes.

Rhea waited momentarily then said, "As in the story, abuse takes many forms, has different faces, speaks different words. And the abuser knows exactly what he or she is doing—even saying. And it appears you can relate to the character in the story."

"No, no, not at all." Megan sighed. "I'd better be going. I've got a lot to do." Megan rose from her seat at the counter. "Rhea, your story reveals how a lot of people live. And it's sad. As to whether it's a mystery, science fiction, or horror, I believe it has elements of all three." Megan shook her head. "But it's definitely not a romance or a comedy."

"Megan," Rhea smiled as she replied, "I appreciate your listening to the story. I know I need to make changes."

"Then again," Megan responded, "maybe not. The story captured what a lot of people endure on a daily basis—both women and men." She looked at the chocolate cake.

Rhea observed Megan eyeing the dessert and asked, "Would you like to take a couple of pieces with you—maybe even three or four? It'll ruin before I can finish it."

"You could freeze it," Megan offered only to realize she had talked herself out of additional slices, "but I would be more than happy to relieve your burden of having too much cake. I'm going to try adding almond extract to the next one I bake."

Rhea prepared the cake. "I'm glad you like it."

"If you want me to listen to any more stories, just let me know." Megan laughed. "That is…as long as there's dessert."

Rhea nodded. "I will. And thanks again. And, Megan, have a good evening."

"You too, Rhea."

After Megan Ashton closed the back door, and Rhea saw her cross over into her own lawn, Rhea said to herself, "It looks like I've been correct about Turner Ashton all along. He's a man with many faces, and most are devious and dark. The way he threw those planks and mocked Megan when I was returning from falling into that pit is his true persona. He may be even worse than I expected. So I definitely need to be more careful."

That would be wise.

"Yes, so I'm going to play the game with Turner like I always have with everybody else." Rhea shook her head. "But I have other attacks to survive first because the verses have warned there's more than one."

Rhea smiled as she placed her short story on the desk. "Maybe a panther will show up for me. Wouldn't that be a shock for my enemies?" She then answered herself. "Of course, it would definitely be effective."

Bradford Wainwright's Review 1

Bradford Wainwright placed the manuscript on the table beside his recliner, paused, and then said, "What a roller-coaster ride. I need a break, and like Rhea Michaels and Max Hastings, I need to order groceries and carryout. But what I want to order is another question. Maybe, like them, I need a little of everything. Stock up." He looked at the remaining chapters lying on the coffee table still to be read. "Because it looks like I have sixteen left."

Wainwright walked into his bathroom, looked at himself in the mirror, then mechanically unzipped his pants. Once his urination and ablution were complete, Wainwright returned to his kitchen. "I hope I still have some of those lemon cookies. Tea and lemon cookies would hit the spot right about now."

After finding the cookies and tea bags, Wainwright smiled while he pressed numbers on his phone to restock his refrigerator and cupboards.

Returning to his recliner with his tea and cookies, Wainwright reseated himself; and after taking a sip of tea and a bite of cookie, he said, "So Mina Sille or Nicholas Moon, you certainly have revealed a lot of information about Rhea Michaels's being the host to an entity who appears to be a formidable character. But now, I need to analyze what I've just read. Like the first manuscript, there's a lot of shifts. And like the first, they are necessary for the time line, character interactions, and plot development. But I have to say, there's a lot of controversial issues revealed. So the manuscript is definitely true to its title.

"Chapter 1 begins with Rhea Michaels leaving a starship. She then transports to a knoll where she is given a scroll to read and a sword to carry. Rhea's trek continues through numerous scenes only to land finally in the garden where she encounters a lover. After Rhea and her lover engage in coitus, lightning slices the air and causes Rhea to awaken in the attic. At first, she's disoriented and doesn't understand why her body feels the way it does. When she hears Gigi's meow, Rhea realizes she and her cat are hungry. So they leave the attic and return to her kitchen for something to eat.

"At the beginning of chapter 2, Ross Jackson is interrogating Turner Ashton about Maryann Colbert and Rhea Michaels's paintings being discovered in his cellar. The chapter then shifts to Rhea's kitchen where she can't understand why the food in her refrigerator is ruined. Etta Smiley, her colleague, calls and Rhea realizes she has been gone since December 16. When Charlotte Meadows calls, Rhea has to acknowledge to herself she has had a paranormal experience.

"The entire setting in chapter 3 is in Max Hastings's apartment. William Shepherd and Gabriel Hall appear to inform Hastings Rhea Michaels's visions about the serial killer have been verified. While eating Hastings's just-delivered pizza, the men read a letter from Rhea Michaels chastising Hastings and them. The chapter ends with William Shepherd teasing Hastings about being afraid of Rhea Michaels, but Hastings doesn't accept the bait. He informs Shepherd he no longer has to prove himself to himself.

"Chapter 4 opens with Rhea unloading her groceries and restocking her refrigerator, cupboard, and cabinets. While eating her dinner, Rhea attempts a mnemonic review of her journey—where she had been, whom she had encountered, and what she had experienced. Rhea soon realizes she was made to review an inquisition, torture, crucifixion, and regeneration of the female. The chapter then shifts to Hastings's apartment where he, Shepherd, and Hall are reading Rhea Michaels's verses about future attacks against her.

"At the beginning of chapter 5, Rhea cries while she is thinks about what she has seen concerning the woman's torture and death. Turner Ashton appears to tell Rhea he was set up concerning the stealing of her paintings. The chapter shifts to Hastings apartment where the three men hear about a fire at the high school, so they go and investigate the scene. While there, Hastings escorts Shepherd and Hall to specific points where the school could be attacked. The chapter ends with the three men reading additional verses.

"Chapter 6 continues from chapter 5. Hastings awakens to discover Shepherd and Hall have left. His thoughts then shift to the previous evening's events, especially Shepherd's, Hall's, and his conversation with Rhea Michaels and her directives concerning numerous controversial subjects and issues. The chapter ends with Shepherd and Hall returning to the apartment with breakfast for Hastings from Ariel's. Shepherd comments about how many people care about him, but Hastings ignores the comment. While the three eat their breakfasts, Shepherd and Hall inform Hastings they need to discuss what they've discovered while they were gone.

"At the beginning of chapter 7, Rhea Michaels has just entered her kitchen to prepare coffee when her doorbell rings. It's Etta Smiley who has come to encourage Rhea to go to the high school with her. A shift occurs to Hastings apartment where he, Hall, and Shepherd are reading verses Rhea had suggested they read the previous evening. Another shift occurs when the women arrive at school, and they encounter Milestone, Herman, and Burke. But as they ascend the steps to check their classrooms, the women's dialogue reveals they are worried about what Herman and Burke have planned for them in the future. The chapter then returns to Hastings's apartment where the three men are attempting to discover the date in May, which could be the day of the major attack on Michaels. The chapter ends with Rhea returning home, but as soon as Etta leaves, Megan Ashton rings Rhea's doorbell.

"In chapter 8, Rhea attempts to verify Turner Ashton abuses Megan. Rhea offers Megan chocolate cake then asks Megan if she would read a short story entitled *Freedom*, but Megan suggests Rhea read to her. The story is about a woman who transforms into a panther and murders her abusive husband. The chapter ends with Megan crying and Rhea realizing the different personas Turner projects and acknowledges to herself she and Ashton will engage in battle. I wonder if the next set of chapters will be another roller coaster ride."

Only one way to find out.

Collecting the unread pages, Wainwright responded to his thought, "Yeah, only one way to find out, and that's to read." After taking a bite of cookie and a sip of tea, he confirmed, "So I might as well get started." He looked at the chapter and asked, "So, chapter 9, what revelations and controversial issues do you have for me?"

9

Rhea walked into Ariel's to order her dinner. She was hungry for someone else's cooking, and since Ariel and Stanley had remodeled and expanded their business, it was difficult to find a seat in the popular establishment. Tonight, Rhea was happy to see she had her choice of tables, counter stools, or booths.

"Rhea Michaels, where have you been? I's just telling Albert I hadn't seen you—well, I guess before Christmas."

"Ariel, I guess the best word would be hibernating. But tonight, I decided I wasn't rummaging through cupboards or the refrigerator and still not be able to decide what I wanted to eat. So here I am for one of your specialties—even one or two carryouts."

"Since no one seems to be out and about, I've just prepared soups and corn bread." But just as Ariel was about to take Rhea's order, Max Hastings walked through the door. "Max, so you've decided to come in for a meal and after how many messages I've sent you."

Hastings laughed. "I did, and I want you to know your deliveries to the office, especially the breakfasts, were perfect. But tonight, I's running low on choices." He looked at Rhea. "Ms. Michaels, what brings you out on this cold evening?"

Rhea replied, "Like you, what I had in the refrigerator wasn't too enticing this evening."

Hastings nodded toward Ariel and acknowledged, "Most of my meals come from here—even carryout."

Ariel smiled. She had been worried about Hastings. "Okay, tonight it's chili, beef stew, or vegetable soup."

Hastings ordered, "I think I'll have the beef stew, corn bread, and coffee."

Rhea agreed, "Sounds good to me, Ariel, but I want a soda."

"Ms. Michaels, I'm sorry. Did I jump in front of you?"

"That's quite all right, Mr. Hastings. I hadn't decided yet, so you're good."

Hastings glanced around the restaurant. "Looks like we're the only ones brave enough to test the elements."

Rhea nodded in agreement. "The house was closing in on me. Besides, I needed a little exercise."

Hastings was shocked. "You're walking?"

"Yes." Rhea was surprised Hastings would question whether she walked or drove to town. "It's not that far."

"Yeah, but it's cold."

"I'll be all right."

Hastings motioned toward a table. "Would you like to sit over there? It might be more comfortable."

Rhea thought this was an opportunity to give Hastings another chance. "If I can sit where I can watch the door."

Hastings nodded then suggested, "How about we both sit where we can watch the door?"

"That sounds reasonable, Mr. Hastings."

Hastings pulled a chair from the table for Rhea. "Why don't we stop the formalities? I'm Max."

"All right, Max. I'm Rhea."

When Ariel returned with their meals, she was surprised to see Rhea and Hastings had moved to a table. "If you two need anything else, just let me know. Remember dessert. You have the choice of chocolate pie or coconut cake."

Rhea nodded affirmatively. "I definitely want dessert, and I believe I'll have a slice of your chocolate pie. I don't need the calories, but I'm sure I'll walk them off on my way home."

Hastings nodded in agreement. "Chocolate sounds good to me. And if you have an extra, I'd like to take it with me."

Ariel smiled. "You got it. If you need anything else, just let me know."

"Thanks, Ariel, we will." Hastings turned toward Michaels. "Rhea, if it's okay, I'd like to discuss some things with you."

"I think that's a good idea, Mr. Hastings. After all, you appeared in a timely manner." Rhea then remembered their agreement. "I mean, Max."

Hastings did not understand to what Rhea was referring with her statement about appearing in a timely manner but decided to let it pass. "I really don't know where to begin."

> RHEA. Wherever you think is best.
> MAX. All right. I guess the first person we need to discuss is your neighbor.
> RHEA. Tobias?
> MAX. No. Turner Ashton.
> RHEA. What do you want to know?
> MAX. What's he like?
> RHEA. He and his wife or live-in—I haven't decided which it is—are constantly at my back door for one reason or another. But I have to weigh my words if I want to glean information from them.
> MAX. What does he do? Why is he here? Where did he come from?
> RHEA. I really don't know. He comes and goes. During the day, he's gone, but I don't know where. Megan has told me he's after an artifact. I think he's responsible for digging a hole in the garden, but she blamed Tobias.
> MAX. What's his association with Caleb Norton?
> RHEA. He's never mentioned Caleb to me, but he wouldn't if he knew how Caleb and Calvin feel about me. I've heard Caleb hasn't accepted Calvin's death.
> MAX. Do you think Ashton stole your paintings?
> RHEA. Not a doubt in my mind. Before I discovered their being gone, he was snooping around, saw the paintings, and went into a lengthy discussion about them.
> MAX. What about Maryann Colbert? Do you think he kidnaped her?

Rhea. If he did, then he must've needed her for some plot he's developing. But since she's been found, he'll go after somebody else.

Max and Rhea stopped momentarily to continue their meal with each thinking about what needed to be discussed before they left the restaurant.

"This stew is delicious." Rhea looked at the new decor of the restaurant. "Like you, I intend to order carryout for tomorrow."

"I do a lot. I have a small kitchen in the apartment, but I just usually depend on Ariel to keep the calories landing on body parts where they're not needed."

"I thought you had a house on the other side of town—even a farm."

"I do, but since"—not wanting to mention the deaths of his wife and daughters but realizing it was time to accept they were gone—"things have changed, I live above my office. Besides, it's handy for me."

Rhea nodded. "I understand. There's only a few rooms where I spend most of my time. The remainder of the house is closed both winter and summer. I believe the spirits in the house are happy with the arrangement."

Hastings laughed.

"I assure you, Mr. Hastings—I mean Max—I'm not trying to be comedic. My home is very much alive and has multiple personalities."

Ariel walked to the table. "I'm assuming you're ready for dessert?"

Simultaneously, Rhea and Hastings answered, "Yes."

All three laughed.

Rhea acknowledged, "And I want carryout of chili, this stew, and the vegetable soup. I won't have to cook anything for a couple—maybe even three—days."

"I want the same and remember a pie if you have extra."

Rhea nodded. "Why not? Me too. Only, I'd like a couple slices of your coconut cake."

"Okay. I'll fix you right up."

"And I'll drive you home," Hastings suggested. "There's no way you can carry these items by yourself."

"Why, thank you, Max. I appreciate, and definitely accept, your offer."

*****

The cartel's monthly review of business was held in its latest state-of-the-art facility. The bunker housed marijuana and cocaine stacked on wooden pallets, and if one package were removed from within the base frame, the entire cache would collapse. An entrance incline serviced the in and out traffic of tractor trailers.

After the tour, members with forlorn expressions on their faces entered the office just off the main entrance, and while some seated themselves in metal chairs in front of a temporary makeshift desk, other members positioned themselves along the walls.

Oscar Wheels sat behind the metal blockade and prepared for the night's agenda by tapping his glass of bourbon with a ballpoint pen. "Meeting come to order." Wheels appeared tired. "Since Race is dead, Otis, you take the minutes."

Otis Borden acknowledged his new role.

Just as Wheels opened his mouth to begin the proceedings, Arlo Willard interrupted, "Before we discuss monetary problems, I want to say things have gotten out of hand."

"Arlo!" Wheels bellowed. "We need to talk about—"

But Arlo ignored Wheels's outburst. "Race and Eldon are dead. There's nobody to run against Hastings. It appears their deaths was or, should I say, is a warning for the rest of us."

"And what makes you think their murders is a warning for us?" Daniel Rafter smirked. "You know how headstrong Race was. He wouldn't listen to a damn thing anybody said."

Arlo Willard responded to Daniel Rafter's chastisement. "That may be true, but I doubt Race wrote those messages with Nolan's blood—even set him on fire. I also doubt Eldon hog-tied Race to those beams and used him as target practice with a crossbow." Willard trembled. "I just want the whole thing ended. So whatever you decide, I agree. But I don't want to have anything to do with strategy. Nothing has worked so far, and as far as I'm concerned, nothing will. Hastings and Michaels have many lives—more than nine evidently."

Wheels bellowed, "Well, whether you want to or not, you're part of this group. If you don't want to interject, don't. But you're as much a part of this operation as the rest of us. I know I'm clear."

"Yes." Willard's acknowledgment was almost inaudible. "You're clear."

"Excuse me." Daniel Rafter looked toward Norton. "Where's Caleb's buddy, Turner Ashton?"

Caleb Norton slumped in his chair. "Don't know. Ain't seen him for a while—ain't heard from him neither."

Oscar Wheels volunteered, "He couldn't make—" He stopped in midsentence observing Caleb Norton's astonishment. "It. He had business to take care of."

Tim Barns held two crutches vertically, leaning forward on both. "I think we need to plan something when they return to school." Taking risks was second nature to Barns. Today, he had been careless when checking on his cattle, spending the biggest part of the afternoon in the emergency room at Eaton County Memorial.

Daniel Rafter turned his body sideways in his chair, projecting his right arm and shoulder over the back's frame. He then clasped the curved, metal back next to his torso and crossed his left leg over his right knee. "We're gonna have to hire somebody who can't be traced back to us."

Otis Borden raised his head from note-taking. "Do you realize how much money we've already spent on those two? And you're talking about more?"

Daniel Rafter responded to Borden's concern about money. "I must admit we've extended our purse, but it looks like we're going to have to extend it further whether we like it or not."

Rudd Dewey rose from his chair and paced back and forth in the artificial aisle created by the chairs and bodies of his confederates. "It's more money to ensure we keep and add to what we have or no money and lose everything we've built. We could take our chances and involve students."

Daniel Rafter shook his head. "That's already been tried but didn't work. The students we used in the last attempt are either locked up or dead from swallowing or injecting our blends."

There was a moment of silence with each member trying to think of a solution to their problem.

Rafter stood, stretched, and then said, "If worse comes to worse, we could call out our extremists' and dissidents' connections, but if that's not feasible, I have my secret weapon to use if nothing else works."

Caleb Norton nodded. "Calvin and I'll do what's necessary. We've had people killed and said nothing to the rest of you about it. Didn't ask a penny from any of you neither."

The other members looked at one another then Wheels turned toward Norton. "Caleb."

"What is it, Oscar?"

"Calvin is dead. You've got to accept the fact Calvin is dead. He's gone, and he won't be coming back."

A cacophonous scream erupted from Norton. "I don't know why people keep saying Calvin's dead—he ain't, I tell ya! He's on a trip. I just don't know when he'll be coming back. But I know he'll be coming home soon. I just know it. And as for getting Hastings and Michaels, we'll do it. I promise."

Booth Strand interjected, "And we appreciate your complete and total dedication to the cartel, Caleb, but it's obvious your hires have missed their mark so far. You've wasted your money. Looks to me like you've even been taken for a ride—been a sucker for—"

Norton thundered, "Don't you mock me and my boy, Booth! I don't see you ever putting yourself out on a limb. Come to think of it, maybe you're the one betraying the rest of us."

Booth sneered, "Damn it, Caleb, you know better than that."

"No. Can't say I do, Booth."

Oscar Wheels screamed, "Enough out of both of you! This bickering has to stop! It's getting us nowhere!"

Arlo Willard started to speak only to realize he had made a mistake.

Daniel Rafter smiled slyly as he said, "Thought you weren't gonna say anything, Arlo."

"I'll say whatever I damn well please when I damn well please, Daniel." Willard was adamant. "I have as much right to talk as anybody. I just said at the beginning of the meeting I don't want to plan strategy. I'll go along with whatever is decided, but I want no part of planning."

Rafter accused, "Whether you sit, stand, talk, or keep your mouth shut, you're still as guilty as the rest of us, so you're plotting and planning regardless. And there's no way out—period. Besides, you're always around when the money is being divided, now ain't ya."

Wheels huffed. "I want to thank all of you for making a point not to accomplish anything this evening."

"Oscar—" Tim Barns attempted to make a statement but was cut off by Wheels pounding the desk in front of him.

"Not now, Tim." Wheels eyed each member. "Nothing is going to be resolved if we're fighting among ourselves all the time. And I mean nothing. What kind of reaction do you think Rhea Michaels or Max Hastings would have if they knew the problems we're having to plan their send-off from the planet. But from all the bickering that's going on, they'd know we're losing our edge. And they'd be right."

Oswald Flynn nodded toward Wheels. "Oscar is right. We're not accomplishing anything. Some of us are worried Michaels is with a covert agency. Others think she has paranormal powers. Others believe something else entirely. But whatever anyone thinks, it makes no difference. She has us backed into a corner—a corner where I don't want to be."

Oscar Wheels coughed, releasing phlegm from his mucous membranes. After spitting into the trash can by the desk, he said, "We're to the point we have to assume Michaels knows somebody. And we have to find out who that somebody is."

Oswald Flynn rubbed his inflamed, swollen knee. He was suffering from a bout with gout. "Whatever we do, it had better be quick."

LIFTING THE VEIL

The group of disgruntled men nodded their heads and mumbled indistinguishable affirmations as they passed through the entrance to the cafeteria.

10

Ariel set slices of her chocolate pie in front of Rhea and Hastings. "Would you like another round of drinks?"

"Yes." Hastings's reply was swift.

"I would too, Ariel, but I'd like a cup of coffee to go with my pie."

"Coming right up." As Ariel poured their drinks, she said, "Take your time. It'll take me a few minutes to prepare your carryouts."

After Ariel returned to the kitchen, Rhea and Hastings continued with their conversation.

> MAX. Now, I need to shift to the educational consultants. Your vision panned out.
>
> RHEA. I see.
>
> MAX. Do you really think the couple is the same as the one in your vision?
>
> RHEA. Are you really testing me again? I didn't see a couple. I saw a man who was a serial killer. But when I saw Herman and Burke during the in-service training, I knew they were connected in some way to the serial killer.
>
> MAX. What can you tell me about this couple?
>
> RHEA. I've seen them in other visions—ones which I haven't shown you yet.
>
> MAX. Do you think they're represented in your verses? It seems your verses are giving details about three separate attacks. But the information is jumbled.
>
> RHEA. That hasn't crossed my mind. But I think at least one incident has multiple attackers.

Max. So what do these consultants do?

Rhea. They set people up for altercations. Do you know Etta Smiley and Shirley Bass?

Max. Etta, yes—Bass, no.

Rhea. If there has been any good come from Herman and Burke being at the high school, it's helped to release a character in Etta I never thought existed. But on the down side, Etta and Shirley could end up in a physical altercation.

Max. Why?

Rhea. Shirley likes to push Etta's buttons to the boiling point. And Etta thinks Shirley is in cahoots with Herman and Burke.

Max. What do you think?

Rhea. I think Shirley Bass has been purchased by somebody. So if Herman and Burke have been purchased also, the three could be in cahoots.

Max. I see.

Rhea. When I come to get my paintings, I'll bring those visions.

At that moment, Ross Jackson walked into the restaurant. "Well, wouldn't you know. The very people I want to see."

Hastings's response was amiable. "Pull up a chair, Ross. We're having Ariel's stew—even taking some with us."

When Ariel heard she had another customer and saw who it was, she asked, "Ross, what can I get for you?"

"What do you have?"

"Chili, beef stew, and vegetable soup with corn bread."

"Vegetable soup."

"What do you want to drink?"

"I'll have a soda—and regular, no diet."

"Be just a minute."

As Ariel walked toward the kitchen, Jackson eyed Rhea and Hastings. "So what brings the two of you out this evening? The streets are deserted."

Hastings replied, "I think we both wanted to get out of the house and apartment regardless of the weather."

Rhea remained silent as she observed Jackson and Hastings talk.

"Don't we all," Jackson supported, "and probably more when we finish this meal."

All three laughed then Jackson looked toward Hastings. "Max, I need to update you on what I've found out. Will you be in your office tomorrow?"

"Yes, court's been canceled. But I have cases to review."

"Oh," Jackson remembered. "Esmeralda Blake has moved to town." He focused toward Rhea and said, "She's your neighbor now."

Rhea nodded. "I'll need to welcome her to the neighborhood."

"I did Esme's closing." Hastings frowned. "She didn't want to leave her farm but said, 'It's time I give it up. I need to let somebody else worry about the land.'"

As Jackson rearranged the salt and pepper shakers on the table, he nodded toward Rhea. "Ms. Michaels, I believe you may be able to return to school by the end of the week. I was at the high school earlier, and they're getting things in order."

"I see."

Jackson was blunt. "Do you have any idea who'd vandalize the cafeteria, other than students, because I don't think students started the fire. Other people I've talked to, who should know, and I'm not talking about the Fire Marshall—don't think so either."

Rhea eyed Jackson intently. "I suspect a couple, but I'll have to wait and see when school is back in session. I'm sure the culprits will give themselves away—either by what they say or how they act."

"If you hear anything, I'd like to know." Jackson paused then said, "I'm sure Max would too."

Hastings nodded. "Ross, Rhea—"

Jackson was shocked. "Rhea? You two on first-name basis now?"

"I don't see why not, Ross. We're having a meal. So Rhea and I decided to drop the formalities."

Jackson's reply was unemotional. "I see."

Rhea did not understand the sheriff's tone or reaction and confessed, "It's automatic for me. I guess it's more of a shield than anything else. Our grandmothers taught my sister and me to address people formally until we were given permission to do otherwise."

Hastings and Jackson eyed each other, then Jackson shifted his gaze to Rhea. "So you're walking?"

"Yes, I needed the exercise."

"I see. Well, it's late, and from what's been happening the past few months, I'm offering to drive you home."

"I appreciate your offer, Sheriff, but Max has already said he'd take me home. I hadn't really thought about what could happen walking home after dark. I'm usually more cautious, but I guess I wanted to get out so badly, I let my guard down."

Jackson sighed. "We all need to be more careful."

*****

The men had just lined up to prepare their bowls of potato soup or pinto beans and corn bread when harsh discordant sounds erupted from the loading dock. Rushing to the blast of screaming voices, chaos boiled before the men's eyes.

A forklift had jumped out of control, ramming into wooden pallets supporting the marijuana and cocaine already prepared for shipment. The lift's impact on the stacks had forced it backward causing the major part of the body to burrow into the contraband.

"What in the fucking hell is going on out here!" Wheels eyed the piles of white and green salad covering the concrete floor in front of his feet.

The man who had been driving the forklift lay beneath its frame with his torso pinned under the weight of the machinery. "Who's this man!" Wheels screamed. "Get that damn thing off him!"

An anxious worker stood helplessly next to the victim and exclaimed, "We can't!"

Wheels glared into the worker's face. "And why in the fucking hell not!"

"If we raise the lift off his body, he'll die."

Booth Strand attempted to calm Wheels's agitated state. "It looks like he could die anyway."

"Well, he's going to die anyway!" Wheels stomped. "And I may kill him myself!"

While the man pinned beneath the weighted metal monster remained conscious and pleaded for help, the other workers scurried in all directions with no one being able to obtain the necessary equipment to remove the overturned machinery.

Wheels shouted over the ceaseless mayhem with his beady eyes reduced to slits. "I want this damn fucking lift off him! And now!" Wheels looked down to the man pinned under the machinery. "We're gonna help you, son." He observed the cannabis and cocaine blend on the floor. "I want all of this mess cleaned up and what can be repackaged—do just that! Now!"

The workers looked at one another but said nothing.

Booth Strand shook his head. "They can't do that, Oscar. It's a loss."

"Oh, no, it's not! Some of it can be salvaged. And I want what can be saved just that—saved!"

Booth Strand shook his head again then volunteered, "All right, Oscar, I'll see what can be done."

Wheels turned toward a worker standing behind him and asked sarcastically, "What do you want?"

"Clint is dead, sir."

"Clint." Wheels shoved his face into the worker's own. "Who in the hell is Clint!"

The worker's shoulders slumped as he looked at Wheels anxiously. "Clint was under the lift."

"Get rid of the body! And now!" Wheels turned toward the cleanup.

The worker was aghast. "But what do you want me to do with it?"

"I don't give a fucking damn what you do with it. Just get rid of the damn thing!"

The worker was horrified. "What about his wife? What do we tell her?"

Wheels paced the floor. "You tell her nothing. That's what you tell her. You don't tell her a damn, fucking thing."

The worker pleaded, "But he has a two-year-old."

"I don't give a damn if he has two-year-old triplets." Wheels looked scornfully at the worker. "Get rid of the body! Tell no one." Wheels scanned the blending of the cannabis and cocaine again. "Or you'll be next." With his gait being more of a stomp, he ordered, "I repeat. Get rid of the damn body! Do you understand what I'm saying to you!"

The worker nodded and acknowledged Wheels's commands and threats.

"And you pass the word along to everyone else. Nothing—and I mean nothing—is to be said about this incident." Wheels continued to stomp. "As far as the dead man's wife is concerned, he's gone missing. And I mean what I say!"

With his shoulders slumped, the worker complied with Wheels's demand. "I understand."

The other cartel members listened to Wheels's threats but remained silent until they returned to their dinner in the cafeteria.

Wheels filled his bowl with beans then grabbed a square of corn bread only to pause and, without a verbal warning, threw its contents as far as he could. The beans and corn bread splattered against a wall, creating nothing that resembled a work of art.

Rudd Dewey looked at the other members then at Wheels. "Oscar, let's go back to the office."

Wheels, as did the other members, nodded in agreement.

Once the men had reseated themselves in the bunker's office, Rudd Dewey shook his head and said, "Don't you think it's kind of risky getting rid of the body like that, Oscar?"

While some members nodded in agreement, others froze.

After observing his colleagues' disapproval, Wheels shrugged and answered, "Risky, you say, Rudd. And the rest of you agreeing with him." Wheels lowered his head, paused to think about his response, and then said, "Well, let me tell all of you what risky is—risky is being involved not only in drugs, prostitution, slavery, but also terrorism."

The members erupted simultaneously. "Terrorism!"

"Yes, terrorism!" Wheels had returned to his agitated state. "All of you know as well as I do some of our dealings are with terrorists. So we're traitors in every sense of the word. Everyone who's accepted our money on Max Hastings's and Rhea Michaels's lives are accessories to any and all activities—even terrorism. And if we're caught, we could meet Death in a most precarious way."

Wheels thought about Webb and Nolan. "And our end could be the same way Race and Eldon received their sentences—maybe something even more horrendous. And I don't want what happened to them to happen to me." Wheels paused and scanned his confederates. "And I doubt very much if any of you do either."

Daniel Rafter huffed. "None of us are going to die because of treason. People get away with everything now, especially if they have money or if people think they have money."

Glances were exchanged cautiously then Nicholas Patrick, who had just arrived, interjected, "I bet Rhea Michaels had something to do with it."

"Oh, hell! Here we go again," Oswald Flynn moaned. "How could Rhea Michaels be responsible for the chaos out there tonight?"

"It's time we realized what we're up against with that bitch still walking the planet." Nicholas Patrick removed his gloves, revealing the rash that had consumed both hands from the tips of his fingers to his wrists. "This rash isn't going away. Nothing works. And I'm in constant pain." When Patrick heard the men's groans, he said, "The doctor still says it could be contact dermatitis. And it may be contact all right, but the contact was with Rhea Michaels. She's the dermatitis. I still think she put a curse on me. And to tell you the truth, I've thought about going to her and begging her to take it away. I'm that desperate."

While the other members remained quiet as they eyed the serpentine strips shooting up his arm, Daniel Rafter tried to cover the impact the unveiling had on him. "Oh, come on, Nicholas."

Nicholas Patrick moaned. "I can't take this itching much longer. It's driving me crazy."

Elmo Thornton attempted to lighten the severity of what he was witnessing and suggested, "This isn't the twelfth or thirteenth centuries, Nicholas."

Nicholas Patrick screamed at Elmo Thornton, "Rhea Michaels put a curse on me!" He then focused toward the other members. "And I'll agree to do whatever is necessary to get rid of her and Max Hastings. It's time they're stopped once and for all. Maybe if we kill her this rash will go away?"

"We're all in agreement with you, Nicholas," Daniel Rafter encouraged, "but the problem is how we're going to do it." He appeared to have thought of a solution. "Has anyone considered Samuel Meadows? He's with us now. Meadows could kill his sister-in-law and make it look like an accident."

Directing his gaze toward Rafter, Wheels admonished, "Samuel Meadows is too important to this organization to risk getting caught killing his sister-in-law. His import-export business gives him connections we need now and will need later on. We also need Meadows's monetary expertise. I've already discussed the details with him." Wheels paused then said, "There's something else I want to say while I'm talking. We need to think about letting the cannabis go."

Suddenly, the men heard a knock at the door.

Wheels opened the door. "What now!"

The worker standing just outside the office's door jumped backward then, after balancing himself, said, "Most of the powder and marijuana have been collected, separated, and repackaged." He stopped as if to plan the wording of his next sentence then said, "Clint's body has been taken care of."

A broad smile plastered Oscar Wheels's face. "Gentlemen, there is always a way. Our commodities are repackaged. And the body has been taken care of." He turned toward the worker and replied, "That'll be all for now."

Booth Strand ensured Oscar Wheels never discovered the contraband was a total loss.

Once the worker had left, Daniel Rafter interjected, "Now, back to our discussion about Michaels and Hastings."

Caleb Norton interjected, "I've told you and told you—I have the people. They just need time. Time is everything in a situation like this. So give them a chance. They know what they're doing."

Tyler Burrows's voice thundered. "We argue about Hastings and Michaels every fucking meeting. And I'm tired of all the shit!" Burrows huffed then suggested, "I say we stay with Caleb's hires for now." He shrugged. "Then if they fail, we'll take a look at another approach."

Oscar Wheels nodded. "I agree with Tyler. Let's stay with Caleb's hires. See what happens."

Elmo Thornton had listened to the back and forth arguments until he was tired. "I need to say something before we leave."

"What, Elmo?" Otis Borden was curious because Elmo usually remained quiet.

When Thornton realized he had everyone's attention, he warned, "Michaels has something with her."

There was a fog of silence permeating the office when Wheels motioned to Otis Borden and ordered, "Turn the air conditioner on. It's getting hot in here." Wheels's shirt collar was soiled from perspiration. "We don't need anything to go wrong with the air in this place. I hadn't realized how hot it's gotten in here."

Otis Borden turned to the wall behind him and adjusted the thermostat to sixty-eight degrees. "That should take care of it."

As the unit hummed into action, the other members sighed in relief, for they too had not noticed the rise in temperature until Wheels had bellowed his order.

Elmo Thornton smirked. "Now, I need to finish what I's telling you before I was, as usual, interrupted."

Wheels waved his arms. "The floor is yours, Elmo."

"Rhea Michaels knows things there's no way she should know, and I'm not talking about her curses or her knowledge of the cameras. She's got something with her. I saw it."

"Thanks, Elmo," Nicholas Patrick acknowledged with gratitude. "I'm glad at least one person thinks the way I do around here."

"Here we go again." Caleb Norton laughed. "Elmo, you're crazy. Who told you that junk anyway?" Norton then answered himself. "Well, I'll tell ya. It had to be one of your tea-leaf drinkers, card-dealing spreaders, palm readers, or crystal seers. Or maybe this time, you asked a cloud observer. Which one, Elmo? Huh? Which one told you that bullshit?"

Thornton lunged toward Norton but was held at bay by Booth Strand and Daniel Rafter holding each arm.

"Calm down, Elmo." Wheels rose from his seat behind the table.

Still refusing to retreat, Thornton hissed at Norton. "You asshole, shithead, mouth fart. How dare you mock me!"

Norton blasted, "Everyone knows about your visits to the card readers, Elmo, so shut the fuck up!"

Elmo Thornton was not deterred. "No card readers, Caleb. It's what I saw with her. It was big and tall—a shadow of sorts."

"Now, you're seeing things, Elmo." Norton laughed. "How long has it been since you had your eyes checked?"

"Enough is enough—out of both of you. Let's calm down." Spittle projected from Wheels's mouth. "I'm ready to go home. I've had enough of this shit tonight! Meeting's adjourned!"

11

As Rhea opened the door of the vehicle and collected her cartons of food, Hastings decided he and Rhea needed to continue their conversation. "I believe I need to help you with those containers." He remembered Rhea's dialogue with Hall and his physical response to her directives, so Hastings warned, "You certainly don't want to slip and fall and lose any of their contents."

Rhea smiled. "Yes, I would appreciate your help. I'll even offer you a drink."

As Michaels and Hastings ascended the steps of her deck, Turner Ashton appeared from what seemed the aether. "Need any help?"

Rhea's reply was anything but cordial. "No, Turner, I think we've got it."

But Rhea's tone did not deter Ashton from his inquiry. "Who is that with you? Got a new friend or something?"

Irritated, Rhea stopped where she stood and replied, "Turner, I really don't think it's any of your business who's with me, but I'll introduce you anyway." She turned toward Hastings. "Max, this is Turner Ashton." Then she nodded toward Ashton. "Turner, this is Max Hastings. Mr. Hastings is Eaton County's district attorney."

"You don't say. I've heard a lot about you—just haven't had a chance to make your acquaintance, Mr. Hastings."

Hastings laughed. "I guess it depended on who you were talking to at the time whether the comment was favorable or otherwise."

Ashton's answer suggested he had heard negative comments. "Can't please everybody now, can ya?"

"No, you certainly can't."

Ashton smiled at Rhea. "Guess I'd better be going."

"Good night, Turner."

Once Hastings and Michaels entered her kitchen, Rhea verified, "See what I was talking about. Somehow—someway, I've got to get Charlotte to buy that house, so I can get rid of him. It's something all the time."

"I needed to make his acquaintance. This was a good happenstance. It might come in handy later on—never know." Hastings smiled. "Sometimes, people appear exactly at the moment I need to see or encounter them." Hastings laughed. "I'm glad he intruded."

Rhea nodded in agreement. "You might be right because I think he's plotting something. And I believe he's capable of anything and everything."

"I'm sure you—maybe even I—will find out soon enough. But now, I need to ask you about something else that's been bothering me."

Rhea set the containers in the refrigerator. "So is it bourbon, whiskey, coffee, tea, or soda?"

"I'd like bourbon or whiskey, but I guess I'd better have coffee instead."

"Coffee it is." Rhea motioned for Hastings to have a seat in her den. "I'll be just a minute."

While Rhea prepared their coffee, she noticed Hastings was scanning the den and dining room. "I see you're curious about my guests."

Hastings laughed. "You weren't joking when—"

"I don't joke." Rhea walked toward the den. "Come with me. I'll show you around."

Hastings shook his head. "That's not necessary."

"It's all right." Rhea laughed. "Actually, I'd like to observe their response to you."

"What?"

"Things happen when certain people show up."

Hastings's visage revealed disbelief.

After Hastings and Rhea entered the hallway, she presented an anecdote. "When Charlotte and I were young, we stood at the dining room's door and listened as a man ascended the steps to the second floor. We even counted his steps. When his foot touched the landing at the top, he paused to our count of fifteen then entered the bedroom to the right. We even heard the door open and close. Of course, the door was already closed."

"You're kidding." Hastings was amazed.

"Finally, after we wore our grandparents out talking about our encounter, they finally added carpet to the steps."

Hastings eyed the steps. "And that stopped the man's appearance?"

"Oh no!" Rhea laughed. "We still heard him open and close the bedroom's door." After sighing, she continued, "But now, when I tell Charlotte about paranormal activity, she brushes me off."

Hastings eyed the living room. "And are there any visitors in here?"

"Always. They come and go. I know you've heard about portals. This house and property are portals."

"Really?"

"I'll show you sometime. The garden also has a personality. It reacts to visitors."

"How so?"

Sometimes, it's just a garden. Other times, it reveals its true self. It's another dimension."

"I see."

Rhea laughed. "I don't think you do. That's why I'll take you on a tour of the vineyard and garden someday."

Rhea and Hastings heard a huff.

"What was that?" Hastings asked, but when he saw the shadow, he uttered, "Oh!"

"What's wrong?"

"There's someone behind you."

Rhea smiled. "Yes, the shadow—my guardian. He appears periodically when he wants to make himself known for whatever reason. His introduction to me was quite frightening. I thought he was trying to kill me. But now, I understand why he is here."

"He's tall."

"Yes, and very protective, but he approves of you."

"How do you know?"

"I just know." Rhea sighed and repeated herself. "I just know."

The shadow disappeared.

When they returned to the den, Rhea suggested, "Let's sit at the counter in the kitchen." She motioned to a stool. "Please have a seat." As Rhea poured their coffee, she asked, "Cream or sugar?"

"Black is fine."

Rhea smiled as she seated herself at the counter. "So there was something else you wanted to ask me."

"Yes." Hastings nodded affirmatively. "And I'm not sure how I want to begin."

"Just begin. Ask what you want, or should I say what you think you need to ask."

Hastings saw a marked shift in Rhea's visage. "But I need for you to remain in the persona of Rhea."

The entity returned to Rhea's form. "All right. I just needed to let you know the answers to the questions you have are true. They're not fantastical. I'm not lying or fabricating anything I tell you. If you haven't accepted what's been revealed in the verses yet, then you need to understand when I leave Rhea's body, she is nothing but a hollow shell."

Hastings nodded as he remembered the entity casting Rhea's shell against the back of his chair.

"Now ask your questions."

Hastings took a sip of coffee. "When you were talking to William and Gabriel—"

Rhea nodded. "The cryptographer and his associate?"

"Yes. You mentioned the delta nine, age, and extraterrestrials."

Rhea paused, eyeing Hastings intently. "All right, Max. First, I want to let you know I know you think I'm the culprit responsible for all the murders, or at least that's what you tell William Shepherd and Gabriel Hall. And their reaction is a put off always, and regardless of how you attempt to trip them up, they manage to avoid your inquiries."

"Yes." Hastings's mind's eye reviewed the encounters and discussions he had with Shepherd and Hall."

Rhea smiled. "I want you to continue your accusations and inquiries."

Hastings appeared to be shocked. "Really? Why?"

Rhea's response was not what Hastings expected. "Let's just say it's important that you do so for now."

Hastings took another sip of coffee. "I need a cigarette right about now."

"Be my guest."

"You don't care."

"Not at all. I'll protect you."

"Protect me from what?"

"Illness."

Hastings could not believe what he was hearing, but he pulled a pack from his coat pocket, pulled a stem from the pack, tapped it on the counter then flicked his lighter to its tip, inhaled, and then exhaled.

After Rhea watched the ritual, she suggested, "But you might want to slow your activity slightly. It might help."

Hastings nodded in agreement. "I know I should, but cigarettes help with stress."

"And your angst is working overtime at the moment—I suppose."

"You could say something like that."

Rhea rose from her stool and walked to her kitchen's window and peeped toward the Wynn house. "Maybe we need to end our conversation here and continue at a later date—when you're ready to listen and accept my answers to your questions."

Shaking his head, Hastings's reply was swift. "I'm ready to listen, but if my reaction appears to be negative, that doesn't mean I don't believe you. I'm sensing what I'm about to hear from you is unbelievable—even incomprehensible. But I still want to hear what you have to say." Hastings was silent momentarily then said, "It might help me to understand things that have appeared and happened to me since my childhood. Your conversation with Shepherd and Hall the other night made me think about some of my experiences. So please begin with the delta nine."

*****

Turner Ashton stood at the Wynn's bay windows, holding a beef-lettuce-tomato sandwich in his hand, attempting to observe any activity in Rhea's den, kitchen, or dining room. "Damn it! That's all I need—Hastings inching his way into Rhea's life. That just means more worries and a lot of fucking unnecessary plotting." He took a bite of his sandwich. "I'm just gonna have to be more careful."

Ashton saw Rhea glance toward his window. "Fuck!" He stepped backward. "What if she saw me peeping? What am I gonna say if she says something?"

Ashton answered himself and confirmed, "Well, I'm gonna deny it. Tell Rhea she's seeing things." He smiled as his chest swelled. "Then I'll throw it back at her and ask, 'Why would you care if I's looking out my window? What were you doing you didn't want me to see?'"

Thinking how that would sound, Ashton stomped. "Hell, fucking fire! Can't go there." He threw the remainder of his sandwich onto his plate. "I'll just have to play the game and act innocent. That is if Rhea says anything." He shook his head. "Maybe she won't. But Rhea is full of surprises—just never know what she's gonna do or say next."

*****

Rhea reseated herself at the counter. "Members of the so-called delta nine allow leaders of governments to do as they choose to their peoples and the planet. As you have observed, there's no stoppage of leaders committing genocide of ethnic groups just because they don't like the ethnic group's religion or creed. They are letting things go. The members think they can't be touched. They tell one another, 'Wait and see.' But they've waited and seen long enough. Their actions or lack thereof have placed this planet—whether that be flora, fauna, land, oceans, and air—in jeopardy."

Hastings took a draw from his cigarette then upon exhale asked, "In jeopardy of whom?"

"Who do you think?"

"Are the members of the delta nine—as you label them—really aware of you?"

Rhea smiled. "What do you think?"

"How do you know all this?"

"I observe."

"You observe?"

"Yes, Max, I observe."

"Then, if you observe, why not show up? Crash their parties so to speak."

Rhea's visage revealed a smirk. "I require an invitation."

"Why?"

"I expect that courtesy."

Hastings was confused. "Why are they ignoring you?"

"They don't want to face me, but they know eventually they will have to." Rhea laughed. "They don't want to experience my revelation—maybe a demonstration—so close and personal."

Looking around to extinguish the last remnants of his cigarette, Hastings said, "I don't understand."

Rhea smiled as she handed Hastings a makeshift ashtray. "Eventually, you will, but you need to ask the last two questions about which you are more curious."

Hastings paused, lit another cigarette, took a draw, inhaled, and then exhaled. "Yes, extraterrestrials and your age."

Rhea's visage shifted slightly. She was humanoid but no longer Rhea Michaels. "What do you want to know?"

"Are extraterrestrials really here?"

The woman nodded as she answered forthrightly. "Of course, they're really here. And there's a lot of different species from other planetary systems. The ancestors of Homo sapiens sapiens are from another star system in another galaxy." The woman paused to ensure her next statement was understood. "And yes, there were other hominid species already existent. But the species from the other star system in that distant galaxy did not change its actions toward other species on this planet."

Hastings eyed intently the woman sitting in front of him and started to speak then changed his mind.

The woman read Hastings's thought and answered, "The genus, Homo sapiens sapiens, did to that planet what it has done to this planet—conquer, torture, subjugate, and destroy. Isn't it obvious? The evidence of extinctions, genocides, wars, famine flash across the television screen every day—24-7. Talk is cheap. It takes action, and there are those who are doing nothing to save earth and its multiple species whether they be terrestrial or extraterrestrial. So to be blunt—brevity is in play. There must be peace. So it would not be wise for both terrestrials and extraterrestrials to stop their avoidance of my presence. What is occurring on this planet every day in every country should verify that statement."

Hastings took another sip of coffee but remained silent.

The woman continued her dialogue. "How many entities do you think have arrived to aid, to guide, to teach only to be greeted with torture and execution in horrendous ways by political and religious leaders—even by their sycophants who worship them. And I am accusing all in the past and at present. When those who held, and hold, positions of authority did, and do, not like or fear what was, and is, said by the messengers, those messengers were, and are, labeled as witches and heretics."

Hastings took a draw from his cigarette, inhaled deeply then exhaled, but he remained quiet and continued to listen to the entity's observations and her warning. He then extinguished it next to its brother in the makeshift ashtray.

"I know you are aware and have studied what happened to scientists, physicians, teachers, and artists. If they did not agree to subjugation by those in power, then they were chastised, mocked, and murdered. But the sad truth was—and is—those who committed the tortures and executions knew whom and what they were destroying. At present, it's the same scenario just different characters—although it seems some of those barbarians have returned to this cycle."

Hastings withdrew another cigarette, showed it to the woman, and said, "Stress release."

The woman looked at Hastings as he lit the third cigarette then continued her dialogue. "There have been species from other planetary systems visiting this planet—which they call Eden—for millions of years."

"Are these different species aware of one another?"

"Yes."

"So certain humans know about all the other extraterrestrial species and really aren't letting the rest of us know."

"There are extraterrestrial species about whom so-called humans do not know."

"Really?"

"Some fall into the mythological category so to speak."

"So what about you? Are you an extraterrestrial?"

"I'm an interdimensional traveler. And my dimension is an umbrella for all others."

"So the dimension you're from—"

"Communication is by telepathy. There is no form there. There is awareness, but no transparency. There's a void." Rhea smiled. "And even though I'm considered a rebel because I don't listen to advice, I am still the leader. I'm the one in front—the one who is sacrificed. The council likes to chastise me, but not one of them would play the role I play—not one."

"And the shadow who follows you around sometimes?"

"He appears when it is considered to be necessary to do so."

"So," Hastings sighed, "why are you here?"

"I can have form. Besides, I like this planetary or star system, whichever you prefer to call it. It's beautiful. In fact, whether any species likes it or not, I consider this planet to be my planet—even my star system."

"There has to be another reason."

"This planet is about to be destroyed, so it's time the members of the delta nine invite me to a conference. It's that simple. It's time Homo sapiens sapiens understand the error of their ways and change their course toward total annihilation. That's why William Shepherd and Gabriel Hall need to convince those who are ignoring me to be more respectful of my presence. If they don't—"

"Then what?"

"I might throw a tantrum. I've thrown enough tantrums over millions of years. It is evidential what I can do."

"One last question—"

"Yes, my age."

Hastings nodded. "So you read my mind."

"Of course."

"Okay then, if you're from another dimension, how old are you?"

"If I answer you mathematically, I would say I am older than what the members of this dimension identify as a googol. If I answer you using a term or word, I would say infinite. Therefore, I am older than any extraterrestrial who walks, flies, swims this planet. It would be advantageous for the delta nine to seek my presence and be done with it."

"So they don't know what to expect."

"They wonder—even worry."

Hastings started to rise from his stool.

The woman returned to Rhea Michaels's visage. "Max, before you go, I need to tell you a couple more things."

Hastings nodded. "Forewarned is forearmed is the way I see it."

"I know you consider Ross Jackson a friend, and he is to a point—"

"But..." Hastings paused then asked, "What do I need to know?"

"I've observed him and seen things."

Hastings sighed, eyed Rhea, and then asked, "And?"

"It depends on the scenarios that occur. If one happens, Jackson might be tempted to betray you. But if the incident is resolved before he is bribed, then he won't."

"It depends on how the plot unfolds."

"Yes, it depends on what the actors do or choose to do in a particular setting."

"And it has nothing to do with the director."

"No, it's the actors being manipulated by the weaving of the plot."

Hastings braced himself. "And the other revelation?"

"There are some incidents that are about to occur—"

"So there's no deviation of plot concerning these incidents?"

"No, and I just need for you to play your role."

Hastings eyed Rhea intently. "And follow your lead—is that correct?"

"Yes. That's what I need for you to do. Also, I want you to continue to doubt my innocence to Shepherd and Hall."

Hastings was shocked. "Why? They want us to become friendly."

"I know, but I want you to continue to remind them of things I've said and done when they return to check on you."

"I don't understand."

"I just need for you to play your role. All will be revealed eventually. Everything will make sense to you. I promise."

Hastings nodded. "If you say so. So for now, I guess it's good night." He crushed his cigarette in the makeshift ashtray.

"Good night, Max, and be careful." Rhea then warned, "Don't let your guard down."

"Never. It's always active."

After Hastings left, Rhea immediately showered and went to bed, but when she fell asleep, a recurring warning inundated her journey through the night world.

A gray mist floated through the forest, making the path almost invisible. Copper snakes with geometric shapes covering their skins lay along the dirt road and watched like diligent sentinels. A house with darkened windows stood on a hill overlooking a steep bank filled with green trees and layers of golden, brown leaves. It appeared as if someone had thrown them—like a giant blanket—across the hillside. A wooden and wire fence around the lawn served as a boundary against intruders with one of the serpents coiled around a post supporting the entrance gate.

Rhea opened the gate to walk up the stone steps. *You're expected at the river*, the serpent warned.

Immediately, Rhea turned away and began her trek to the river.

Sharp, jagged boulders blocked the already narrow path, cutting her feet, making them bleed.

A clear stream of water cascaded down a hillside, overflowing onto the road, forming a deep puddle where Rhea waded freely, washing the blood away, soothing her skin.

Realizing she was close to the river, Rhea walked faster. Just beyond, a group of sycamores stood with the moon's beams permeating them and the countryside.

It was peaceful here, and Rhea wanted to stay—be safe, be happy, remain forever. But just as she was cloaking herself in the serenity of the moment, a chill surged through her body, making her feel weak and defenseless. *I must protect myself.*

Instantaneously, the scene changed. The moon disappeared. Rhea heard a roar in the distance. A wall of water churned, twisted, and rolled toward Rhea, sweeping her into a deep cavern. Landing on the edge of a stone cliff, Rhea grabbed a jagged buttress, fearing she would fall into the abyss below.

"Please...Please help me...Please."

But her pleads were to no avail. Rhea lost her grip and fell freely through space-time, awakening to Gigi's meows and the coldness of her bedroom.

12

Rhea stood outside her classroom's door when Etta Smiley stopped for a chat. "Can you believe we're back today? It's Friday. Of all days, what do they think we're going to accomplish? It'll be nothing but babysitting."

Walking to where Rhea and Etta were standing, Shirley Bass huffed. "And it'll be sack lunches in our classrooms until God knows when."

"It doesn't look like much has been done to the seating area. I guess they focused on the kitchen first." Rhea looked up and down the hall. "The population is sparse this morning."

"Can you blame them?" Etta inhaled deeply then exhaled slowly. "Since I've been off, I'm spoiled. I've been watching late-night shows, sleeping until ten or eleven, then wearing my robe the rest of the day."

"I hear ya," Shirley Bass agreed then changed her tone. "I'd leave now if I could find a sugar daddy." Bass looked directly at Etta. "How are you and your new sugar daddy getting along?"

"You're nothing but a troublemaking hussy, Shirley Bass," Etta hissed. "Just wait until I tell Haldan what you've said."

Shirley Bass smiled. "Everyone knew it was Peter Anton for years, but it sure didn't take you long to find yourself another lover after Anton no longer could bed you."

"You bitch!" Etta leaned her head close to Bass's face. "I have no idea what you're talking about. I don't have a sugar daddy. Haldan and I are happily married. As for Peter Anton, I felt sorry for him. And that's all."

Shirley Bass focused her eyes toward the hallway's ceiling. "Maybe it was his alcohol keeping you two as so-called friends." She smiled. "But your latest, Etta, I must say I'm impressed."

"For the last time, Shirley, I'm not having an affair."

The three women heard the intercom click then Milestone ordered, "Teachers, check your email."

The three women walked to Rhea's computer where they read the message.

"Use today to organize. Next week, we'll spend a couple of days on those missed finals. Then you'll have another couple of days to post grades."

Shirley Bass moaned. "Oh, hell—that's just great! I's hoping Milestone would forget about those damn finals since we've been off for so long."

Rhea frowned. "Do what you had planned before the break." She thought about how disgruntled she was at the moment. "If I knew when I was younger what I know now—all the hell I'd experience being a teacher—I certainly would've chosen another career. In my next life, I plan to be a dramatist—maybe even an actress. I've had enough practice in this one."

Etta was shocked at Rhea's response to Milestone's directive. "You're right—no point in stressing about today. For all we know, there'll be another five or six inches of snow before Monday."

As the bell rang for first period to begin, Rhea verbalized her thoughts. "I wonder if the consultants are here today?"

"Yeah," Shirley Bass verified. "I saw them downstairs with Milestone. He didn't look happy by the expression on his face."

"Great! That's just great," Rhea sneered. "Wonder what they'll do today?"

Etta replied, "Whatever it is, it'll be something to cause us problems."

"You can say that again." Rhea spoke to herself more than to Etta and Shirley as students entered her classroom.

*****

This morning, Hastings had awakened with one of his molars throbbing on the right side of his mouth. For a few days, he had felt a sensitivity and hoped it was just a filling that needed replacement, but from experience, he knew the arrows shooting through his gum were revealing a different story entirely.

After another horizontal strike, Hastings pressed numbers on his phone. "Patty."

"Yes, Max, what's wrong?"

"I need for you to call Bart. I think—no, I know—I have an abscess. Will you call and see if he can see me today?"

"Yes."

According to the annual survey in the *Messenger Budget*, citizens of Eaton County had chosen Dr. Bartholomew Mills as the best dentist—even social media posts supported the accolade.

When Hastings entered his office, Patty's first comment was "You're swollen." Her visage revealed concern. "Dr. Mills's line has been busy, but I'll keep trying."

"I'm going upstairs until you get in touch with Mills's office. Please tell them I need something done and soon."

Upon his return to his apartment, Hastings pressed his fist against his jaw as he paced back and forth from his kitchenette to the windows overlooking the street below. "Maybe, some whiskey might help?"

While he was holding the liquor in his mouth, drumbeats resounded on his cell phone. After spitting the whiskey into a trash basket, Hastings asked, "What did they say, Patty?"

"They'll have to work you in."

"I'm gone."

"Ad Haslett called about the fiscal court meeting Wednesday night."

"What about Wednesday night?"

"He needs to cancel. There's a family situation, but he didn't say what the situation was."

Hastings sighed. "Whatever. I need to get this tooth taken care of. I can't think about anything else right now."

*****

When Hastings entered Mill's office, it had not been too crowded; but as the morning progressed, the number of patients increased, creating an overflow in the reception area. *I wonder how long I'm going to have to wait.* He looked at the door, leading to the individual procedural rooms and continued to think. *How can he see all these people this morning?*

A little boy sat in his mother's lap, pushing his chubby hands against her arm as tears rolled down his cheeks. "Mommy, I don't want to go." He grabbed his mother's neck.

Trying to calm her son, the boy's mother used a tissue to pat the tears away from his brown cheeks. "Don't worry. It'll be okay."

"Promise?"

The little boy's mother smiled. "I promise."

Just as Hastings noticed the office was cooler than usual, he heard the drone of the heating unit rumble into action. He then sent a telepathic message to the dentist. *Bart, shuffle through your patients a little faster.*

A song from the office's sound system interrupted Hastings's thoughts and telepathic communication. As he sat and listened to the soothing lyrics, Hastings forgot momentarily where he was, shifting himself to a place far away where he was completely alone. When the song ended, he was immediately attacked by an arrow penetrating his tooth and gum. Now, the entire right side of his face throbbed.

Hastings noticed a farmer observing the child. From the expression on his face, the farmer also was hoping the child would stop crying. But the deeper message revealed a story of excruciating pain. Shifting his body back and forth in the chair, the man could not seem to position himself to relieve the torture in his jaw.

Hastings pressed harder against his jaw. *Another abscess. Must be abscess attack day.*

The door opened leading to the procedural rooms, and Hastings saw Mill's assistant standing in the doorway and sent another telepathic message. *Please call me back, Bart. Please.*

But the dental assistant announced, "Jamal Adams."

The toddler whined, "Mommy, she'll give me a shot."

Smiling, the dental assistant nodded toward the little boy. "Shot! I'm not going to give you a shot." She pulled a miniature tractor from her white coat's pocket. "Look what I have." As she handed the toy to the child, the dental assistant attempted to calm the child's angst. "Now, that's much better than any old shot, isn't it?"

The toddler smiled, accepting the offered toy as a security token to help him survive his visit to the padded chair.

As the pain in Hastings's jaw continued its pulsating mode, he scanned the reception room. An off-white, shaded floor lamp stood in one corner while a wooden coat tree guarded the entrance. Two prints hugged the walls. One scene depicted a road disappearing beyond the horizon with a row of trees on each side of the line. A pond was positioned in the foreground with ducks enjoying the afternoon sun. The second print presented a group of houses on a busy street during winter. Streetlights with yellow and orange hues glowed in the distance.

The bell on the office's door jingled to notify everyone another patient had entered the office. It was Caleb Norton who immediately seated himself in a chair against the wall.

An elderly man already seated offered his condolences. "I was sure sorry to hear about your troubles, Mr. Norton. Did they ever find out what happened?" The man pulled a handkerchief from his hip pocket and blew his bulbous, reddened nose. After examining the phlegm collected on the cotton cloth, the elderly man returned it and its latest addition to his hip pocket. "You know, every day, there seems to be more and more crimes being committed—robberies, shootings, burnings—just one thing right after the other."

Becoming noticeably irritated, Norton stared straight ahead, attempting to avoid any social interaction with the speaker.

While the elderly man shifted his eyes to other patients in the reception room, he said, "I just want you to know I understand. Somebody set my barn and house afire. I found out later a so-called friend paid to have them burned because he wanted my property. He thought he'd get the land cheaper if all the buildings were gone."

The dental assistant reappeared at the door. "Mr. Seward. Mr. Amos Seward."

Caleb Norton shuddered as Seward rose from his chair. It had been John Seward, Amos Seward's son, who had lost his life as a result of bullying by Calvin Norton and three of his buddies.

John Seward had been hanged in a tree just off Branch Creek. Although the case had gone to trial, there was no sufficient evidence to convict the four who had been charged.

The defense the four presented: "All of us tried hanging ourselves for fun, but something went wrong with John."

Amos Seward limped toward the dental assistant, but just before walking through the door, his tone changed to contempt. "Mr. Norton, justice will be served—if not in this life, then the next. What keeps me going is knowing the people who murdered my boy will pay. John never bothered nobody. And for him to be killed for kicks. Hell is firing up."

Caleb Norton dropped his lower lip. "I don't know, Mr. Seward. I really don't."

"Well, I do. Could be one or two are already there. Ya think." Seward turned toward other patients still waiting in the reception room. "Ain't that right!"

The other patients remained silent, but it was obvious from Hastings's observation of their visages the activity in their cranial cavities was charging actively.

After Amos Seward disappeared behind the door, Norton shrugged and blocked any mental attachment to his most recent verbal attack. It was only when Norton noticed a man standing at the receptionist's window he gasped involuntarily.

The receptionist inquired, "May I help you?"

Dressed in a white hooded sweatshirt and blue jeans, the man laughed. "Yeah, I guess you can, little lady. I need a checkup."

The receptionist looked at the appointment book. "It'll be two weeks. Friday, the fifteenth, one o'clock."

"Sounds good to me. Just need to get acquainted with a local dentist."

"What's your name?" The receptionist appeared uncomfortable.

"Turner Ashton."

Hastings noticed Norton was staring at Ashton. *Caleb is afraid of this man.*

"So Friday, the fifteenth, at one o'clock, I'll be here." Ashton then turned and walked out the door but left it ajar.

Jamal Adams and his mother approached checkout. "That wasn't too bad now, was it?" The receptionist smiled. "No shots."

The toddler smiled and nodded affirmatively.

"Mr. Norton. Mr. Caleb Norton," the dental assistant repeated.

Norton rose from his seat, grabbed his back, and limped toward the procedural rooms, but just before he walked through the door, he said, "Been busy today, haven't ya?"

The dental assistant nodded and smiled. "We're busy every day."

After Norton entered the procedural area, and the door closed, Hastings approached the receptionist. "How long do you think it'll be before Bart can see me?"

The receptionist looked at Hastings and shook her head. "Mr. Hastings, I'm sorry. I didn't see you. We were supposed to work you in, weren't we?"

Hastings grimaced. "I'm having a lot of pain."

"Let me check." The receptionist looked at the appointment book again. "Could you be here at one o'clock?"

Hastings turned away from the counter. "I'd appreciate it. I don't think I can endure this pain much longer."

*****

It was fourth period, and Rhea's students had just settled in their seats returning from the cafeteria with their sack lunches.

Rhea had brought her lunch. She resented the increase in the teachers' fees for both breakfast and lunch. But what she resented more than the increase cost of meals was some members never paid a cent for anything they ate as long as they had been employed by the system while others were chastised or charged double if they grabbed an extra cookie. At present, Milestone and now Herman and Burke were in the elite group.

Norma Preston broke Rhea's concentration when she hit her lunch sack. "I can't eat this—this hog shit!"

Pulling her cell phone from her jean's pocket, Norma punched numbers, looked at Rhea, and nodded for permission to leave the classroom.

Rhea nodded her permission then returned to her lunch and thoughts of what she needed to do after school dismissed.

Suddenly, Norma's conversation was anything but private. "I can't eat this shit! You bring me something to eat. I don't care what, but anything is better than this fucking hog shit!"

Rhea realized Norma was listening to the other party because she was silent momentarily.

Norma then screamed, "I don't give a fucking damn about your fucking job! You tell that son of a bitching boss of yours I said he can go to fucking hell! I need my lunch brought to me!"

Rhea had listened to all she intended to hear and walked to the classroom's door. "Who're you talking to, Norma? The entire second floor and maybe the first can hear you."

"I don't give a fucking damn, you bitch!"

Rhea froze. "Go get your things, and come with me."

"I ain't going nowhere!"

"Oh, yes, you are. We're going downstairs."

Norma screamed, "I hate this fucking place! I hate you! I hate everybody!"

As they walked down the hallway, Norma kicked lockers then turned and stopped, faced Rhea, then hit the locker with her fist. "This is you, bitch!"

"I know the locker is me, Norma, in more ways than one. And every time I look at this locker, I'll remember this locker is me. But for now, you need to leave and go get your lunch. And I really hope you enjoy your lunch, but you need to be careful."

"Be careful?" Norma was curious, for she had calmed herself somewhat since Rhea had not reacted the way she had expected or wanted Rhea to respond. "Be careful—I don't understand."

When Rhea and Norma entered Milestone's office, he was reading a letter. "What can I do for you, Ms. Michaels?"

"Norma says she can't eat the damn hog shit in the sack lunches. So I've brought Norma to the office in order for someone to take her to town." Rhea eyed Milestone intently. "But Norma needs to find another class during fourth period. That would be wise for everyone."

Milestone's chest swelled then he huffed. "Is that a threat, Ms. Michaels?"

"A fact—nothing more." Rhea turned toward Norma. "I'll remember I'm that locker. And now, you have a good lunch. Enjoy every bite, especially all the added ingredients."

*****

It was after one o'clock when Hastings returned to his office. The dentist had worked Hastings into his lunch schedule, taking x-rays then writing a prescription for an antibiotic. "Patty, I'm going upstairs. Maybe I'll feel better by tomorrow morning, and this swelling will be gone. But I want to be left alone the rest of the day."

13

The reception area at the Eaton County Board of Education was empty, so Rhea seated herself in front of the secretary's desk then scanned the decor as she waited.

A healthy fig tree and a colossal elephant plant sat adjacent to the stone fireplace with fluorescent bulbs supplying the necessary light for their survival. Another three-tiered display of historical documents decorated the west wall guarding a row of stained, ladder-back chairs stationed as sentinels beneath the documents. The identification of the documents as being historical was a ruse to support an affiliation with one religious ideology and a rejection of others both past and at present.

Voices and laughter rang in adjoining rooms, but the door to the superintendent's office remained closed. Rhea yawned as she looked at the clock sitting atop the secretary's desk. It digitized 3:45.

The door to Luther Richmond's office opened slowly.

Milestone appeared in the entrance, but his visage and demeanor depicted angst. "Ms. Michaels?"

Rhea's greeting was cordial. "Mr. Milestone."

"Did you hear?"

"Hear what?" Rhea did not understand Milestone's response to her. "What are you talking about?"

"Norma Preston is ill—very ill."

Rhea feigned concern. "What's wrong with Norma?"

Milestone eyed Rhea intently. "Norma's lunch yesterday turned out to be an attack on her intestines," he paused then said, "and her stomach."

Rhea's response was without emotion. "I guess she should've remained at school and eaten the hog shit as she called it."

Luther Richmond looked at Milestone uncomfortably then turned and acknowledged, "Please come in, Ms. Michaels."

Upon entering Richmond's office, Rhea immediately waved her hand as she observed his display of the battle at Gettysburg during the American Civil War. "You've been busy. When did you add Lee's surrender to Grant at Appomattox?"

"Once I finished the battle at Bull Run, I was hooked. And that's why I had to move to this office. The other one was closing in on me."

Floor-to-ceiling glass doors opened to a second-floor veranda. Today, scaffolding towered outside where carpenters were repairing certain sections of the roof after the snowstorm.

The once-plantation home had been purchased by the Eaton County Board of Education in 1960. Since then, there had been many necessary repairs, but for most members of the community, the building was a reminder of historical divisiveness, causing hostilities to erupt periodically.

"Please have a seat, Ms. Michaels." Luther Richmond lowered himself behind his desk. "What can I help you with today?"

Luther Richmond had always been a hefty man with his body shaped like a jumbo egg. But today, he was gaunt.

The contrast from old to new was more than phenomenal. Richmond's previous gray hair had turned completely white with strands falling down the nape of his neck onto the collar of his light green shirt.

It seems Richmond's fascination with the Civil War has definitely shifted to another level.

Rhea wanted to observe Richmond's countenance, so she paused, sighed, then said, "It was terrible about Deborah Halsey, wasn't it?"

Richmond nodded. "Yes...Yes, it was."

"Mrs. Halsey came to see me the morning the same day she died."

Richmond's visage revealed puzzlement. "You never know when it'll happen. One second here then the next second there—wherever there might be."

Rhea decided to be cautious concerning Halsey's instructions concerning Richmond's actions or his lack thereof. "She delivered some items to me, but just before she left, Mrs. Halsey's said, 'I need for you to go and speak to Luther Richmond. Ask him about the 20 percent raise teachers were supposed to receive over a period of three years.'" Rhea eyed Richmond directly. "Mrs. Halsey then said, 'Observe his reaction.'"

Richmond twisted his chair to the left then to the right only to return it to its original center position. "I don't understand. I really don't know to what Mrs. Halsey was referring."

Rhea nodded her agreement. "I didn't either, but since the legislature has failed to give teachers—even retired teachers—a raise in years, it made me think Mrs. Halsey might be correct with her assumption. I haven't been to ask you before today because it's been one thing after another not only at home but also the high school."

"Yes. Peter Anton's death"—Richmond's visage revealed angst—"was terrible. But the pay raise to which Mrs. Halsey was referring—it must've been before my time."

Rhea remembered her vision and Richmond's vehicle bucking like a wild horse. *You did do something with the money that was meant for teachers' salaries.* "No, Mrs. Halsey was resolute concerning her request."

Richmond tapped his fingers on his desk as if he were playing the keys on a piano. "Well, if there's nothing else, it's closing time."

Rhea ignored Richmond's suggestion to leave. "I need to talk to you about what I really came to discuss." Rhea pushed a sheet of paper in front of Richmond's eyes. "This is a description and an analysis of the educational consultants at the high school. After you read it, I want you to think about whom you've hired."

Richmond eyed the paper lying beneath his gaze. "Ms. Michaels—"

"Things don't add up concerning those two." Rhea watched Richmond fidget in his seat. "You should hear the comments from the faculty and students. Eventually, strife will break through the door, and we're all in trouble."

Luther Richmond avoided Rhea's eyes. "I really don't know what you're talking about."

"Jules Herman and Dee Burke—Milestone said you hired them."

Luther Richmond's face turned beet red while saliva formed at the corners of his mouth. "I didn't—"

"If you didn't, then who did?"

"Ms. Michaels, I—ah, well, I—ah, well, they came well-recommended."

"All I can say is they are an insult to the pedagogical community."

Richmond huffed. "You…you—"

Rhea ignored Richmond's interruption and continued her dialogue. "There's also something I need to say before I go because I might not have another opportunity—"

"And what might that be?"

"During my tenure, it has been obvious politicians or, should I say, legislators don't care about education. They just use it to fluff their political campaigns. It's also obvious not only politicians but also people in positions of authority in school systems have had the misfortune of contracting a virus."

Richmond coughed then exclaimed, "Virus! What are you talking about?"

Rhea smirked then warned. "The virus known as plantation overseer and ivory tower syndrome. Those individuals in administrative positions, and I mean all, have a superiority attitude—the high I and the low you—focused downward and toward teachers. But what the plantation overseers and ivory tower inhabitants don't realize is they wouldn't be in their padded positions or receive their lucrative paychecks without the lower-paid teachers and vulnerable students."

"How dare you! Rhea Michaels! How dare you!"

"Oh, I dare all right, Mr. Richmond. That's been my experience. And I'm sure I'm not alone. There's no respect for teachers. If you're a teacher, you're on a ship, and the captain tries everything possible to ensure the teacher walks the plank." Rhea paused then continued, "Another analogy involves an apple tree."

"Apple tree?" Richmond shook his head then repeated, "Apple tree?" After huffing, he exclaimed, "Really!"

Rhea's visage revealed she was not amused by Richmond's response. "The trunk of the apple tree represents the teachers and students. While it's alive, the apple tree's trunk supports the branches, leaves, and fruit—plantation overseers and ivory tower inhabitants. But when those rotten apples who represent the plantation overseers and the inhabitants of the ivory tower fall and pile up and choke the tree, it dies. The school loses teachers, and students will leave and enroll in other systems."

Richmond huffed. "I never."

Rhea rose from her chair, walked toward the door, and then stopped. "Before I leave, I want you to know my presence in the Eaton County School System has been precarious—like a double-edged sword."

Richmond huffed. "You're not making any sense!"

"The overseers wanted and want to destroy me. In fact, I was even warned the first year of my career how much the administration despised me. However, over the years, they realized I—as others—was needed to ensure the system's state tests' scores remained in the upper percentiles. That's why they gave me every subject for which I am certified. But at the same time, they hoped I would fail, so they would have an excuse to fire me."

"I don't know what you're talking about."

Rhea smirked. "Oh, you know exactly what I'm talking about. You as well as others are behind the scheme. So when I leave the Eaton County School System, what do you think will happen?"

"Uh...I...uh...I don't know."

"Well, you think about all those times I was attacked, set up, mocked, and ridiculed—even received death threats." After Rhea remained silent momentarily to act as if she were thinking about her next revelation, she then said, "I've been told you're extremely gifted in your mockery of me."

"Ms. Michaels," Luther Richmond hissed, "I want you to know the very second you walked through the door you were filmed and recorded. Every threatening word you said to me is recorded."

"No, Mr. Richmond, you're mistaken. As soon as I walked through the door, the cameras and recording system ceased to operate." Rhea paused. "I know now why Deborah Halsey encouraged me to speak to you about the 20 percent raise."

Richmond huffed. "You...you—"

Rhea ignored Richmond's interruption and continued, "But now, I return to the cameras and recording system you have in your office. You see, I know about the cameras and recording system in my classroom. I also know there are more involved with those who are trying to kill me."

Richmond huffed. "Cameras and recording system in you classroom—I don't know what you're talking about." He attempted to laugh. "And somebody is trying to kill you!" Richmond appeared to be nervous. "Give me a break."

Rhea eyed Richmond intently as she asked, "How many death threats have you received?"

Richmond paused to think about what Rhea had just asked then said, "Ah—I—ah. None."

"Of course you haven't because you're like so many others in positions of authority—you don't have the guts to stand up when you're being threatened to engage criminal activity." Rhea hissed. "Some morning you will walk through the main office door, and there will be no electricity, no lights, no filming or recording, no computer accessibility."

Richmond's chest swelled. "Backup system, Ms. Michaels. Backup system."

"Afraid not. You've been warned." Rhea looked at the miniature battlefields. "Mr. Richmond, you need to check the authenticity of your displays. I believe you need to rearrange some of the soldiers and cannons. Their positions are incorrect. Believe me, I know." Rhea's laughed sinisterly as she walked out the door of the superintendent's office.

*****

Frowning at her mnemonic review of her encounter with Richmond, Rhea slammed the door to her car. Fluffy flakes of snow kissed her face, but just as she was about to ascend the steps of her deck, Rhea noticed a light in Turner Ashton's garage. "Hmm…" She scanned the lawn. "No one seems to be home. Good time to conduct a reconnaissance mission."

After entering Ashton's lawn, Rhea's solar plexus activated. *But what's going to be my excuse?*

Rhea's mental reply was swift. *You need to wait.*

Listening to her mental warning, Rhea retraced her steps to her deck, scanned her back lawn, and noticed a couple of black plastic bags lying next to the vineyard's gate. Rhea analyzed the depth of the snow and experienced a chill then acknowledged to herself. "I'll get them later, or maybe, they'll blow away on their own. They flew here, so they can fly into another lawn."

Upon entering her kitchen, Rhea grabbed the remote to her television, opened a soda, and then prepared herself a roast beef sandwich. "If I weren't so tired and disgusted, I'd go to Ariel's for dinner."

But while Rhea was talking to herself and thinking about what she was going to do the remainder of the evening, the local news anchor announced, "There's been a robbery in Will's Store, Kentucky, this afternoon. Two suspects walked into Henry's Diner and held the proprietor at gunpoint while they directed the waitress to unload the register and the patrons their cash. No one was harmed, but the waitress was taken to Eaton County Memorial Hospital because of chest pains. Kentucky State Police are asking anyone with any information to contact them immediately."

Rhea grimaced with a slight shift of her facial features. "There'll be more."

*****

William Shepherd and Gabriel Hall watched as Ira Abbott poured three glasses of scotch.

After Abbott handed the glasses to Shepherd and Hall, he then opened a humidor and offered each man a cigar. Once the sticks' caps had been cut, the cigars lit, and all three men inhaled and exhaled,

Abbott asked, "So what's the latest concerning Rhea Michaels—even Max Hastings? How are Mason and Christopher working out?"

Hall responded, "Mason and Christopher are fitting in nicely."

Abbott nodded. "I thought they would." He took a sip of scotch. "Now, to the situation or, should I say, situations at hand."

William Shepherd looked at Gabriel Hall then asked, "Have you read what we sent to you?"

Abbott replied, Yes."

William Shepherd warned, "You know Max Hastings continues to asked questions about our intentions and why he's being involved concerning Rhea Michaels."

Abbott nodded and walked to the window. "What do you tell him?"

Hall responded in a flat tone. "Basically, all in good time."

"I see." Abbott continued to gaze out the window toward the streetlight. "Does Hastings know about me?"

Hall interjected, "Once, we mentioned Ivar."

"What was his reaction?"

William Shepherd volunteered, "Ira Abbott remains unknown to Hastings."

"And what about Rhea Michaels? What does she know?"

Hall replied, "During our recent conversation with her, she did not mention you specifically." He took a sip of scotch. "But that doesn't mean she doesn't know who you are. Remember the descriptions of herself."

Abbott nodded and replied, "Yes."

Silence blanketed the room. No one spoke but continued to drink their scotch and smoke their cigars.

Then Hall broke the silence and warned, "She is demanding the delta nine invite her to a meeting. And from listening to her, the entity who exists in Rhea Michaels's form means business. So whatever you can do to encourage that invitation, I suggests you do so promptly." Hall then played the entity's directives for Ira Abbott.

After the message ended, Ira Abbott seated himself in a chair, took another sip of scotch, then a draw from his cigar, and upon exhale said, "I think there needs to be a meeting in a neutral zone."

William Shepherd interjected, "Whoever you send, even wherever you send them, I'm sure the entity who inhabits Rhea Michaels's form is already preparing for the encounter."

Ira Abbott remained silent.

Gabriel Hall smiled. "She observes."

After flipping ashes from the tip of his cigar into an ashtray, Abbott replied, "I see."

Hall eyed Abbott and warned, "I'm afraid you don't. When you engage in a conversation with her, I'm sure you'll understand she means business on many levels."

"Yes," Ira Abbott revealed his thoughts. "I have a lot to think about—we all do."

*****

Once Shepherd and Hall had left Ira Abbott's residence, Hall asked, "Do you think he listened to us?"

"That remains to be seen, doesn't it?" Shepherd replied. "But somebody somewhere needs to listen." He frowned. "It looks like Abbott wants others to meet her before he makes additional contacts."

Hall nodded. "Seems that way. I just hope he doesn't do anything extraordinary. That might not be the path he needs to walk. There could be repercussions from multiple sources, and ones I don't even want to consider."

Shepherd nodded in agreement then said, "Talk later."

Hall replied, "Yeah, probably sooner than later."

Both men went their separate ways and disappeared into the darkness.

*****

Ira Abbott opened the desk drawer, retrieved a device, pressed numbers, and then waited for a response. When he heard acknowledgment, he said, "She demands to speak to us."

Abbott listened to the other party's response then said, "We need to consider what the options are, but first, I think a secure zone needs to be in play."

Abbott listened then said, "The entity is tired of being ignored. She doesn't like our lackadaisical attitude concerning multiple themes. So I'll be in touch."

*****

Max Hastings looked at his watch as horns from his cell phone forced him to check his ID. "Rhea."

"Mr. Hastings, I apologize for calling you at this late hour, but I need to meet with you as soon as possible."

"That's quite all right, but I thought we's on first-name basis."

"I guess I'm like the cliché, 'old habits die hard.'"

"I understand. So you don't want to talk over the phone?"

"No. I believe I need to speak to you in person."

"I have trials this week—both district and circuit."

"Then I'll check with you next week. I have a feeling something else might happen, so maybe it's best our meeting be postponed until later. But I'll tell you this much, there's going to be more murders—even attempts."

Hastings lowered his recliner and leaned forward, stood, walked to his refrigerator, opened its door to search for something to eat. Seeing nothing he wanted, Hastings looked at the clock and thought, *Still time*. He then continued his conversation with Rhea. "Do you have any idea who they are, or where they will occur?"

Rhea was silent momentarily then replied, "Multiple incidents."

"What about your neighbor, Ashton?"

"I started to snoop around this afternoon when I arrived home, but my solar plexus warned against it. I've learned from experience I need to listen to its warnings. Manipura has saved me many, many times."

"I guess a lot of people would be better off if they paid attention to their own Manipuras in general."

"I didn't realize you were aware of Manipura, Mr. Hastings." Rhea smiled then congenially replied, "I mean Max."

"I've learned a few things during trial and error. Are you sure you don't see when the murders will happen or who's involved?"

"No, but I'm really concerned."

After her phone conversation with Hastings ended, Rhea decided to conduct an automatic writing.

> Cosmic Mother—
> I need speech to give me clues of what's to be.

When Rhea finished writing, she analyzed, "The verses are similar to *The Man* yet different. But the repetition is obvious. Every time, the message is written—it is the same."

*****

Hastings tried to relax before he retired for the evening. But once he went to bed, his dream journey was troubling. He was at Eaton County High School searching through the individual rooms for someone to direct him to the problem. But not finding anything extraordinary, Hastings left the premises. *I'll wait and see what happens.* He then shifted to another scene.

14

Hastings observed two contentious, elderly men blowing their horns at each other when different horns from his cell phone blasted throughout his bedroom. Not awakening immediately, Hastings watched the elderly men shoving their fists at each other as he listened to the stopping and starting, stopping and starting, stopping and starting of horns reverberate in his bedroom.

But as the line between sleep mode and the awakened state materialized, Hastings understood it was his phone and not an altercation between two elderly men. "Hello."

"Max, Ross here. Sorry about calling so early, but Owen Lawrence and Leo Lovelace need a warrant to search Emery Rafter's and Daniel Rafter's premises."

"Ross, I'm barely awake. What time is it anyway?" Hastings looked at the digital clock on his night stand. "Damn it, Ross. I've not been in bed very long."

Jackson revealed the urgency of his request. "I understand, but we need to talk before there's too much traffic."

Hastings rubbed his face. "Give me a minute. You'll be able to see when I unlock the door, but bolt it back when you enter."

Jackson replied, "Okay. We'll be watching…"

Hastings looked into the mirror while he brushed his teeth. "I guess I can wait to shave."

Once he entered his office, Hastings prepared the coffee maker then unlocked the door. After returning to his inner office, he seated himself and waited for Jackson and the detectives to arrive. Wanting to calm himself, Hastings lit a cigarette. Then after taking a couple of draws with deep inhales and exhales, he extinguished the tip, realizing none of the three men smoked. He looked at the jars of candy.

"I need to buy more chocolate bars—maybe even some jelly beans and cinnamon pieces."

When Jackson, Lawrence, and Lovelace entered the main office's door, Hastings rose from his desk, walked toward them, and in a flat tone said, "Coffee's ready. Would you like a cup? I certainly need one."

"Yes" was acknowledged by all three men.

While waiting for his cup to fill, Jackson volunteered, "I haven't been to bed yet."

Hastings looked at the clock on the wall. "I must say, it's early."

After taking a sip from his cup, Detective Lawrence volunteered, "We apologize, but we need a warrant."

"Have a seat." Hastings then reseated himself. "So Emery Rafter—what about him?" Hastings eyed the three men and, while he observed their visages, said, "So Emery Rafter's death is suspicious?"

Jackson responded, "When I first arrived at the scene, it was chaotic. Lilly was screaming, 'He shot himself! He shot himself!' But the longer I scanned the room, the scene didn't appear to be the way it should if Emery committed suicide." He nodded toward the detectives. "Owen and Leo showed up and determined it couldn't be suicide."

> HASTINGS. So who found Emery?
> JACKSON. Lilly.
> HASTINGS. What about her?
> JACKSON. Lilly went to the store and saw some people she hadn't seen for a while. Time got away from her, and when she returned home, Emery was in the chair. But it was Vance Kelby who called 911. He heard Lilly's screams and went to check on her.
> HASTINGS. So Kelby didn't hear the shot?
> LAWRENCE. He said the shot must have happened when a truck backfired.
> HASTINGS. Seems convenient. But what about Emery?
> JACKSON. He couldn't have pulled the trigger.
> LOVELACE. The gun was in his left hand. His right hand was clasped tightly to the arm of his chair.

JACKSON. And he was right-handed.

HASTINGS. So whoever murdered him didn't know Emery was right-handed.

LAWRENCE. Correct.

HASTINGS. What is Daniel's alibi?

LOVELACE. Said he's with Oscar Wheels, and Oscar backed him up.

HASTINGS. Oscar would. If Oscar ate onions, Daniel could easily burp them up.

JACKSON. And Daniel is acting strange—worried, angry, even frightened. I really can't put my finger on it. But…

HASTINGS. And no one saw anything out of the ordinary?

JACKSON. I asked Mr. Kelby, but he couldn't remember if he did or not.

HASTINGS. How did Mr. Kelby and Emery get along?

JACKSON. Kelby seemed upset—even vomited at the scene.

HASTINGS. Emery had a vintage Winchester. See it anywhere?

JACKSON. According to Lilly, Emery's Winchester was stolen.

While Hastings wrote the warrant, he said, "I'm stating any and all evidence, which may lead to discovery of anything relevant to the commission of Emery Rafter's murder, be seized."

Detective Lawrence nodded. "So Emery Rafter's murder may lead us into unchartered territory?"

"Yes," Hastings replied, "and this warrant will give you leeway to do what you need to do without having to return for another warrant." Hastings looked at the clock. "I believe Ariel should be open by now. I could use some pancakes and bacon."

Jackson nodded. "I could handle breakfast." He looked at the detectives. "How about you two? Do you want to come along?"

Lawrence and Lovelace accepted Jackson's invitation because they had not eaten anything since the previous evening, and they too were hungry.

*****

Rhea Michaels read and followed signs from nature and used them daily. As an avid researcher of ancient keys to wisdom, Rhea engaged comparative analysis of their practices of divination. And while her interest lay in advancing her knowledge of cultural, historical, and technological aspects of ancient civilizations, she believed ancient texts and their coded messages were sources for her own armor. Symbolism and prophecy within the ancient lines were guides for Rhea to use during her ongoing existential conflicts and interdimensional cosmic battles.

One of Rhea's favorite literature examples for her students to understand ancient divination through nature was the omen predicating a catastrophic event in Book XII of *The Iliad*.

Hector, during a battle attacking the Greeks, urged his men to cross a trench. An eagle carrying a serpent, writhing in its talons, flew across the battlefield.

While dancing in the eagle's claws, the serpent struck the eagle on its breast. In pain, the eagle dropped the serpent among the Trojan troops. When Polydamas, a Trojan, saw the serpent lying among the Trojan warriors, he urged Hector to withdraw from battle. Polydamas understood the prophetic omen from nature's own, not only for that battle but also for the eventual end of the war. Polydamas predicted the Trojans, like the eagle, would think they were defeating the Greeks; but it would be the Greeks, like the serpent, who would be the victor.

Rhea thought often about the analogous significance between the scene in *The Iliad* and her enemies. While she believed neither she nor they could be compared to the Greek and Trojan warriors, she did feel a connection of spirit with the two creatures—the predator and the prey—whether they be the eagle and serpent or the serpent and eagle.

Rhea laughed as she entered the main doors of the high school proper. "Like the eagle, I shall fly, and like the serpent, my fangs shall strike my prey when they think me to be the most vulnerable."

*****

Two days earlier, Rhea had discussed divination from two cultures—the Norsemen and the Romans. "While the Norsemen cast pieces of wood with the symbols of their alphabet, the runes, to read and determine the warriors' prowess and whether they would be victorious in the forthcoming battle the next day, the Roman general ordered an animal to be eviscerated. After the cavity was opened, a soothsayer read the viscera to inform the generals to engage battle or wait for a more favorable revelation.

Students had listened intently with some admitting they were curious and intended to conduct research about other cultures' divination rituals. "Good idea for our semester projects, Ms. Michaels." Many had decided.

*****

"Hey, Rhea, what're you doing here so early?" Etta Smiley had just entered the main entrance and was about to unlock the teachers' lounge.

"I thought I'd rearrange my room before everyone arrives. I'm tired of students cheating. I'm tired of cell phones being more important than the subject matter. I'm tire of vaping. I keep smelling mint, and I know it's not candy or gum. And I'm tired of finding tobacco and chew spittle in paper cups under desks. In fact, I'm stopping food and drinks period."

"You're making me tired just talking about it." Etta shifted her book bag from one arm to the other. "I have the same problem. If what you do works, let me know. But I think you're wasting your time."

Rhea laughed and nodded in agreement. "I probably am. Sometimes, I like to watch the surprised expressions on their faces when they walk through the door. I immediately see their cranial cavities plotting their plans to outwit me."

"But you already know you're fighting a losing battle with those cell phones."

Rhea acknowledged Etta's analysis of the situation. "I know I am because they're everybody's pacifier—adults included."

Etta looked at her watch. "I need to check my mail. I'll see you in a few minutes. If you need any help with moving furniture, I can after I start the copy machine. I'm giving a test today."

After ascending the second flight of stairs, Rhea looked at the darkened corridor. *This might not have been such a good idea, old girl. You never know what's lurking and waiting to pounce.* But it was the fetid odor attacking her nose that made her stop and pause.

Rhea flipped the switch to illuminate the hallway. She then paused to look toward her classroom. "Oh!"

The carcasses of two malnourished dogs lay with their backs pushed against her classroom's door. Twisted viscera protruding from their abdominal cavities splayed over the floor with their blood spreading toward Shirley Bass's classroom. The stench from the decaying flesh and viscera pierced the weighted air.

Dropping her book bag, purse, and keys, Rhea braced herself against the wall. Clasping her hand to her mouth to control the infinite scream pushing to the surface, Rhea stared at the intentional desecration lying before her eyes. *This is a threat.*

Knowing she was the first person on the floor and Etta was just behind her, Rhea rushed down the steps in search of Rip Freed.

Etta Smiley saw Rhea running toward her. "What's wrong?"

"Upstairs!" Rhea gagged. "I need to find Rip. The hallway is covered in blood." She visualized the bloody scene again and rushed to the restroom, bent over a commode, and released her breakfast, feeling heat rise from the depths of her being.

Etta pulled paper towels from the wall dispenser, wetting the entire two sheets from the basin's spout. "Here," Etta offered, "pat your face with these." While Etta waited for Rhea to calm herself, she thought about what Rhea had said then asked, "Blood—what do you mean by blood?"

Rhea continued to pat her face with the paper towels. "There're dead dogs in front of my door, and blood is running down the hallway. And I mean everywhere."

"What's the matter?" Rip Freed stood beside Etta. "What's all the ruckus about?"

Etta responded while Rhea continued to pat her face with the wet paper towel. "Rhea says there's two dead dogs in front of her door."

Freed was visibly shocked. "No way!"

"Yes, I'm afraid—way." Rhea had stabilized herself. "And it's bad. We need to call the police."

Freed replied stubbornly, "I'm going to check things out first."

"I'll go with you," Etta supported. "You don't need to go by yourself."

Rhea looked at Freed and Etta standing in front of her. "You don't need to go by yourselves."

With their mouths and noses covered, the three returned to the scene. "Who would do something like this?" Rip Freed inched cautiously down the hall.

Etta suggested, "It could be anybody." Then Etta asked Rhea, "How has Calendar been acting lately?"

"I presented a lesson on ancient forms of divination, and the Romans happened to be one of my examples."

Etta shook her head then sighed. "So you think somebody's trying to be cute?"

Rip Freed stood in the front of Shirley Bass's door and looked inside her classroom. "I don't think they were trying to be cute at all—whoever it was."

"What do you mean, Rip?" Etta eased toward Bass's door and looked inside. Instantaneously, her screams reverberated throughout the corridors of the high school. She jumped up down, up and down, up and down. Etta then bent over and moaned only to repeat jumping up and down, up and down, up and down. Finally, she leaned against the wall and scooted downward and seated herself on the floor.

Rhea had frozen in disbelief as she watched Etta's reaction to what she had seen in Bass's classroom. "Etta, stop it. You're going to hyperventilate!" Rhea then decided to look into Bass's classroom herself, and what lay before her eyes was worse than her initial sighting of the dogs' carcasses. Shirley Bass was sitting in her desk's chair, but it was obvious she was dead.

Rhea listened as Rip Freed called the police, fire department, EMS, Luther Richmond, and Zachary Milestone. "School needs to be called off before anyone else arrives. I'm sure the police don't want to deal with the mayhem like they did when Anton was discovered."

Rhea watched Freed while he listened to the other party only to relate, "It's Ms. Bass. She's dead. And from the looks of things, it's like Anton's murder to a degree, but at the same time…different."

Another round of silence then Freed responded, "I've already called the authorities. And I think I'm safe in saying school won't be in session for at least a couple of days—if not more. There's a lot here—in the hallway and Ms. Bass's room."

Now, Rhea could hear the other party speaking but could not decipher what was being said then Freed described, "Dogs' carcasses are in the hallway. Blood is everywhere, but one heavy vein flows toward Ms. Bass's door. Looks like a message of sorts, but what kind of message, that's for somebody else to figure out."

*****

Hastings, Jackson, and the detectives were in the middle of their breakfast when Jackson's radio notified the men about the incident at the high school. He looked at Hastings. "Are you coming with us?"

Jackson and the detectives walked out the door without paying for their meals, so Hastings opened his wallet and handed Ariel enough cash for all four meals plus a gratuity.

"You don't have to do this, Max."

"I do."

"Thanks, Max. I appreciate it."

"And I appreciate you, Ariel."

*****

Rhea's cell phone buzzed. While reading the text, Rhea realized she would not be permitted to leave the premises. And now, she had to think just how much she intended to divulge to the authorities.

Waterfalls rolled down Etta's face and neck. "Here, Etta, wipe your face with this." Rhea offered wet paper towels from the restroom. "It looks like it's my turn to help you."

"I don't think there'll ever be any help for me after seeing what I just saw." Etta thought about Bass's corpse. "But you warned her, didn't you? You warned Shirley what could happen to her."

"I did, but I didn't think she'd end up being murdered."

EMS arrived, administered care, and then transferred Etta to Eaton County Memorial Hospital where she had momentary relapses of visualizing Bass's death scene.

Unlocking her car's door, Rhea seated herself and touched her cheeks and forehead with the back of her right hand. Leaving the door ajar, Rhea faced the windshield with her feet set firmly on the floorboard. As she leaned her body backward against the seat, Rhea inhaled the morning's cold but fresh air. After taking a sip of water from an almost empty bottle, she closed her eyes and reviewed the scene, experiencing the scent of blood permeating her nasal cavity.

Talking to herself, Rhea analyzed the scene. "The dogs were at my door, but Shirley was the one tortured and murdered. So is it a warning for me, or were the dogs placed at my door for the blood to flow to Shirley's door? But why Shirley?"

"Maybe you were right about your warnings to Shirley. Maybe she was on somebody's payroll, then maybe it's for you" was Rhea's mental reply.

"Maybe?"

"Maybe what?"

Rhea jumped at seeing a figure standing at her door. "Oh, Sheriff, you've just about scared me into a heart attack."

Jackson responded, "I'm sorry. I thought you saw me walking up to your car."

"No, and I've had enough surprises today to last me a lifetime."

"I understand, but we have questions."

Rhea nodded. "Yes, I know. But please give me a minute, and I'll be there."

"Can I get you anything?"

"No. I just need a minute to calm myself."

Jackson then suggested, "Don't take too long. We need a statement."

Rhea nodded her understanding of Jackson's demeanor and persona.

15

When Rhea returned to the main office of the high school, Ross Jackson, Owen Lawrence, Leo Lovelace, Max Hastings, Jules Herman, and Zachary Milestone were waiting in the principal's office. With his hands placed flatly atop his desk, Milestone looked at Rhea then nodded toward Lawrence and Lovelace. "These gentlemen need to ask you a few questions."

Rhea received Hastings's telepathic warning when they eyed each other.

Milestone coughed as he continued to focus his attention on the detectives. "I'm sure Ms. Michaels will tell you everything you need to know." He then looked directly at Rhea. "Now, won't you, Ms. Michaels?"

Rhea's reply was almost inaudible. "I'll try."

LAWRENCE. So you were the first one in the building this morning.
MICHAELS. Yes.
LAWRENCE. Are you sure?
MICHAELS. As far as I know, at least on second floor. I had to turn the light on.
LAWRENCE. And you didn't see anyone else in the hallway?
MICHAELS. No.
LAWRENCE. Retrace your steps from the time you entered the building until you discovered Ms. Bass.
MICHAELS. I didn't discover Shirley. Rip Freed, the custodian, discovered her.
LAWRENCE. Oh, yes. It was Mr. Freed.

Rhea realized she was being tested and waited until Lawrence was ready to continue with his interrogation, but she was shocked when the detective turned toward Milestone and asked, "Do you have cameras monitoring the halls?"

Jules Herman leaned backward against the wall, folded his arms, and appeared nervous but smiled when Milestone confessed, "We did, but they were damaged, and we haven't replaced them yet."

Rhea interjected, "There are cameras in my room."

> LOVELACE. You have cameras in your room? Why in your room and nowhere else? That doesn't make sense.
> MICHAELS. True. But there are cameras in my room.
> LOVELACE. Mr. Milestone, if one of those cameras is facing the door, we might be able to identify the culprit who left the dogs. If we discover the dogs weren't a practical joke, then we have the murderer or murderers.
> MILESTONE. Ms. Michaels is crazy. There's no cameras in her room. She's talking all the time about this and that.
> MICHAELS. Look at my sketch then check for yourselves. You will discover I am telling you the truth.
> LOVELACE. We will. But now, we need for you to retrace your steps.
> MICHAELS. Before I saw anything, the stench overpowered me. I guess it was curiosity which encouraged me to flip the light switch.
> MILESTONE. You know curiosity killed the cat. What if the murderer had still been up there?
> MICHAELS. When I saw the dogs carcasses and the blood, I panicked and ran down the steps. It was not until Rip Freed, Etta, and I returned to the scene that Shirley's body was discovered.
> HERMAN. Ms. Smiley has said bad things about and to Ms. Bass.
> MICHAELS. Etta was still downstairs. When we three returned to the second floor, and Etta looked into Shirley's classroom, she became hysterical.

LAWRENCE. And you, Ms. Michaels, did you become hysterical?
MICHAELS. I became nauseated.
LAWRENCE. I see, but not hysterical.

Rhea looked at Hastings and asked, "Is that all? I need to check on Etta."

Hastings nodded. "That's all for now, but we'll be in touch."

Lawrence started to ask another question, but Hastings shook his head in negation.

The detective nodded. "Okay, Ms. Michaels, that's all for now."

As Rhea walked out the door, she heard Herman's accusation. "I believe Ms. Michaels knows more than she's letting on. She didn't like Ms. Bass, and Etta Smiley's hysterical act could've been just that—a hysterical act."

Rhea was not surprised when Milestone remained silent.

Ross Jackson interjected the discussion. "Neither one of those women could've had enough strength to overpower Ms. Bass, and what about those carcasses? Do you honestly think those two women killed those dogs, hauled then to the second floor, and set them against Michaels's door?" Jackson then answered himself. "No way."

"Maybe that was part of their plot to kill Ms. Bass," Herman suggested, "to throw you off."

Rhea then heard weighted silence permeate Milestone's office.

Once Rhea returned to her vehicle and opened her car's door, she vomited again, releasing water and gastric acid. After wiping her mouth, she said to herself, "I've got to calm down." Then another visual and olfactory flash hit her. "But now, before I can take care of myself, I have to go to the hospital."

*****

Once Rhea arrived at Eaton County Memorial, she discovered Etta had already been admitted and was in a private room. As Rhea was about to knock on the door, it opened, and a nurse almost bumped into her. "I'm here to check on Etta."

The nurse smiled. "Ms. Michaels, it's good to see you. Ms. Smiley is resting, but I think it'll be okay if you go in."

"Thanks."

The nurse repeated amiably. "It's good to see you again."

"And it's good to see you, but I wish under better circumstances." Rhea then acknowledged to her former student. "I'm glad you became a nurse."

Rhea's former student nodded her acceptance of Rhea's compliment. "Me too."

Upon Rhea's entering the hospital room, Etta opened her eyes. "Rhea."

"I wanted to come by and check on you before I go home."

"I think they're going to keep me for observation. My blood pressure is sky-high."

"I can see why."

"Rhea, why aren't you upset?"

Rhea paused to plan how she would acknowledge her paranormal warning. "Etta, I believe I's warned about today—I just wasn't able to read the signs."

"You and your signs and feelings." Etta looked toward the door. "Have you seen Haldan?"

"No," Rhea replied then asked, "Has anyone called him?"

"They say they have, so I guess he'll be here soon." Etta adjusted herself in the bed. "If you thought something was going to happen, why didn't you tell me? Maybe my blood pressure wouldn't be through the roof."

Rhea frowned. "When I do warn you about something going to happen, you mock me—as does everyone else."

Etta grasped the top of her sheet and blanket, pulling them closer to her face. "I'm sorry. I'm scared. I can't seem to calm down. But what was the warning?"

"It was a dream."

"Tell me."

"Etta, are you sure you want to hear it?"

"I'm sure. Maybe I'll be able to make sense out of this morning."

Rhea pulled a chair next to Etta's hospital bed and seated herself. "I's walking down the hallway toward my room when I noticed a wreath of red hydrangeas hanging on a door." Rhea paused thoughtfully to analyze. "But now, while I'm describing the scene, I realize the wreath wasn't on my door but the one across the hall. Anyway, I opened the door and discovered someone had been hired to help me with students. But the new staff member had completely taken over, changing my desks and chairs."

Etta lifted her head. "Are you hearing yourself?"

"Yes, but anyway, when I entered the room, my desk had been moved to the opposite side of my classroom. The staff member had decorated the walls with a mathematical chart as a border to the ceiling, which completely circled the room with 3.14159."

"That's strange."

"I know, but that's not the end. I became disgusted and stomped out of the room, walked down the hallway, only to stop and return to my room to arrange the desks and chairs the way I wanted them to be."

"Rhea, this is weird."

"Yeah, but I'm not finished. When I entered the room the second time, it was filled with trees, shrubs, and vines. In fact, the vines blocked my path to my desk. Finally, I became frustrated and left."

"That's it?"

"No. There's more. I then went to the teachers' lounge downstairs where students had taken over, occupying all the seats. When I asked them to leave, they just laughed and became belligerent. One boy walked to the vending machine hit it with his fist, breaking the glass."

Etta interrupted, "Those machines don't have glass."

Rhea responded to Etta's interjection of her tale. "I know they don't. Remember, I was dreaming."

"Oh, yeah," Etta replied. She was becoming drowsy.

"Etta, do you want me to finish or not?"

"Yes. I'm sorry I interrupted you."

"Anyway," Rhea continued, "shards splattered across the floor. But when I started to pick the pieces up, they transformed into knives."

"What do you think the part about the lounge means?"

Rhea shook her head. "I don't know. I hope it's not another confrontation with Norma Preston or Richard Calendar, but it could be anybody."

Etta gasped, "Rhea, your eyes."

"My eyes. There's nothing wrong with my eyes."

"Yes," Etta uttered. "They're…they're—uh—they're…yellow."

"Yellow? What do you mean yellow? Etta, you're confused. I need to leave and let you go to sleep."

Etta stuttered, "No…no, it's your irises."

"What about my irises?"

"Rhea, I tell you—they're yellow!" Etta's body shook as she repeated, "Yellow."

"Don't be ridiculous, Etta." Rhea rose from her chair and walked to a mirror attached to the wall." She saw nothing different about her visage. "It must be the medicine they've given you. There's nothing wrong with my eyes."

Etta tugged on the sheet and blanket. "Rhea, you need to look into the mirror again. I promise you—your eyes are yellow, but now, their shape has changed."

Rhea laughed. "Etta, really? And just what shape might that be?"

"They're ovals, Rhea, vertical ovals."

"As I said, your medicine is kicking in. You need to go to sleep."

"Listen to me, Rhea. Your eyes are yellow, vertical ovals. In fact, your face is different."

"Etta, I'm going to leave now. I need to calm myself down too. I'll talk to you tomorrow."

Opening the door to leave, Ross Jackson, Owen Lawrence, and Leo Lovelace were waiting to enter, so Rhea warned, "Etta is seeing things—hallucinating. I doubt if she could answer any of your questions at present. And her blood pressure is dangerously high."

"Ms. Michaels," Detective Lawrence looked into Etta's room, "do you have any idea who'd want to torture and murder Ms. Bass?"

"Shirley Bass was constantly antagonizing people. If it were not one person, it could be two, even three. She was nosy and a braggart.

But she must've made somebody terribly angry for him or her or them—and it's probably them—to cut her tongue out and place it back into her mouth. That is a significant clue."

Lawrence started to speak, "Ms. Michaels—"

"I'm not finished. She either talked too much, or she didn't accomplish a deed for which she'd been paid." Rhea eyed the three men. "Shirley Bass was always bragging about getting something for nothing—money or moonshine—any number of things."

Lawrence attempted to ask another question, "Ms. Michaels—"

"I'm not finished. I need for you to listen to what I have to say. You want to know, do you not?"

Lawrence nodded affirmatively.

"You can forget about what Jules Herman said about Etta and me. Our altercations were always verbal and usually an attempt to protect ourselves from Shirley's attacks. And for what it's worth, Jules Herman is a troublemaker."

Detective Lawrence interjected, "Maybe the two of you got tired and decided to shut the verbal attacks up once and for all."

"I need to go home." Rhea looked at Etta who had fallen asleep. "It seems the sedative they've given Etta has kicked in. You'll just have to wait and interrogate her later."

*****

When Rhea entered her driveway, Tobias Harding was standing at its edge, appearing to be waiting for her. And when she opened her car's door, Rhea asked, "Tobias, what can I do for you today?"

"Just wondering if what I heard is true."

"What have you heard?"

"The Bass teacher went and got herself murdered."

"Yes, Tobias. Shirley Bass did go and get herself murdered."

"Know who did it."

"There's an investigation."

Tobias paused, looked around Rhea's lawn, then returned his focus to her, and said, "So do you know who killed her?"

"No, Tobias. I don't know who killed her, but when the murderer is caught, I doubt I'll be surprised."

"I tell you what, all these people getting themselves killed, and none of them solved. People are scared. I tell ya, really scared."

"If people would stop kissing up to the drug people and stop accepting bribes to do whatever the drug people want and pay to be done, done then maybe people wouldn't have to be so scared now, would they?"

"Are you saying Bass was dealing drugs."

Rhea focused her attention toward the street. "No, Tobias, but it wouldn't surprise me if somebody involved with the drug people murdered her." She paused. "Why don't you go to the authorities and tell them what you know about drug people?"

"I ain't telling nobody nothing 'cause I don't want to get myself killed."

"Then don't complain about the murders not being solved."

Harding turned and stomped toward his house, talking to himself. "Can't get a damn thing out of that damn bitch. All she can do is talk, talk, talk and say nothing. Bitch! Wouldn't be surprised if she doesn't end up dead before it's all over—not surprised at all."

Rhea turned to walk down her driveway. "That's what you think, asshole."

"Ms. Michaels…Ms. Michaels."

Rhea stopped and watched an elderly lady enter her front lawn. "Yes."

The woman carried a paper bag with her.

"How can I help you?"

"I'm Esmeralda Blake, and I just moved into the house on the corner." Blake handed the paper bag to Rhea. "I've heard about the incident at the high school. I thought I'd bring you a little something to help you calm down."

Rhea looked inside the bag. "Ms. Blake, how kind of you. Thank you."

"Oh, call me Esme. Everyone does. It's peach brandy. The bread is homemade." Blake laughed. "Well, the peach brandy is homemade too—if you know what I mean."

"And I'm Rhea." She smiled while looking at the brandy. "This is very thoughtful of you. Rhea realized she needed to return her new neighbor's kindness. "Would you like to come in?"

"No. You need to rest."

Rhea smiled. "I really appreciate this, but it should be I delivering you a welcome gift to the neighborhood."

"The circumstance does alter the case, does it not?" As Esmeralda Blake turned to walk away, she said, "Enjoy the brandy and the homemade bread."

"Again, thank you, and I assure you I will." Rhea talked to herself as she entered her kitchen. "What a nice lady. I'll definitely need to repay her kindness."

Gigi greeted Rhea with a meow.

"What's wrong, baby doll? You shouldn't be hungry. Oh, you missed me, didn't you?" Then Rhea answered herself, "I know that's not the case."

As Rhea prepared herself a cup of tea, her cell phone interrupted her thoughts. Looking at the ID, Rhea sighed. "Max, I'm surprised to hear from you so soon."

"I thought I needed to check on you."

Rhea remained silent momentarily to think about her next sentence then warned, "Max, I need for you to tell those detectives to leave me and Etta alone. You know we didn't kill Shirley Bass."

"I know we discussed waiting about a meeting, but this murder changes things. So I'll write you in for a four o'clock appointment."

Rhea thought about her new neighbor. "Esmeralda Blake brought me some homemade bread and peach brandy. She said the peach brandy was homemade like the bread."

Hastings acknowledged, "It's rare Esmeralda Blake gives peach brandy away. So enjoy."

After their conversation ended, Rhea collected her cup of tea and carried it to the sofa. As she eased downward onto the soft pillows, Rhea thought about Death's next capture.

16

Oscar Wheels was eating breakfast when his doorbell demanded attention. "Irma, get the door!"

The bell rang again, but this time the visitor kept his or her finger on the button. "Irma, would you please get that damn door! I'm half-naked! I can't imagine anyone visiting this time of day."

Irma rushed to the door. "Come in." She led the visitor into the kitchen. "Oscar, it's Daniel." Irma looked at Rafter and asked, "Would you like a cup of coffee, even breakfast?"

"Nah, don't have much time." But when Rafter saw Oscar's plate, he changed his mind and accepted Irma's offer. "Yes, I would like one of your famous biscuits, a little gravy, and coffee."

"Coming right up." Irma turned toward Wheels. "Oscar, I need to run some errands. If I receive any packages while I'm gone, just leave them in the hallway. I'll open them later." She set Rafter's plate in front of him. "Daniel, I've added caramelized apples to go with the biscuit and gravy." Irma then realized she had not mentioned Emery Rafter's death and offered her condolences. "Have you made arrangements yet?"

"There ain't gonna be none. Uncle Emery always said, 'Once I leave here, it should be as if I never existed. So no funeral for me.'"

"If that's what he wanted, then you're right to respect his wishes." Irma observed Wheels as he continued to eat his breakfast. "Oscar, Edna, and I are going on a shopping trip. If we can't find what we need locally, then we'll have to drive until we do."

"Whatever, Irma. I'll expect you when I see you walk through the door."

"If you don't need anything else, I need to finish getting ready."

After scraping gravy over a biscuit and taking a bite, Wheels looked at Rafter and smirked. "What's got you out so early this morning?"

"Those damn cops! That's who!"

"What're you talking about?" Wheels looked into the den. "You might want to tone it down a notch. Irma is still in the house."

"Okay, okay, but those damn cops searched mine and Emery's houses, barns, buildings. They went everywhere."

Wheels took a sip of coffee. "Did they find anything that could cause us problems, or should I say your problems?"

Rafter shook his head. "No, but they know Uncle Emery's death wasn't a suicide."

"Did you shoot him up with anything?"

"No."

Wheels opened a biscuit. "They asked me if you were with me."

"And you told them I was, didn't ya?"

Wheels's tone was flat. "I did."

"I have an alibi then."

"Yes." Wheels took a bite of his biscuit and gravy then caramelized apples.

Rafter confessed, "I shot Emery up sometimes, but not that evening." Rafter took a bite of his biscuit and gravy then said, "Oscar, I'm afraid somebody is after us—all of us."

"Yeah, me too, and who could be next? It looks like one of us wants everything for himself."

"I know." Rafter sighed. "Have you talked to Samuel lately?"

Wheels nodded. "I let him call me."

"I see. Well, the reason I'm here so early is I need to run something by you."

"There's something else?"

"Afraid so." Worried lines formed on Rafter's forehead as he asked, "What're we gonna do about Caleb?"

Wheels shook his head and sighed. "I really don't know. I've thought about talking to Ashton about Caleb, but I haven't decided when to do it or what I'm gonna say when I do."

Rafter saw a bottle of bourbon. "I need to spike my coffee."

"Whatever, but don't you think it's a little early?"

Rafter ignored Wheels's negative response and added the liquor to his coffee. "I'm not sure I trust Ashton. There's something about him—something eerie."

Wheels opened another biscuit then spread butter and Irma's homemade blackberry jam on the bottom half only to slap the top half over it. He then took a bite with some of the jam forming at the corners of his mouth. "I think Ashton is the only one who can do anything with Caleb."

Daniel Rafter's cell phone interrupted his and Wheels's conversation. "Hello." He listened to the message then asked, "What do you mean?" He rose from his chair. "I'll be right there." Rafter returned his phone to his pocket. "Those damn sons of bitches!"

"What's going on, Daniel?"

"Those fucking detectives are asking more questions. I tell you, Oscar, Max Hastings is gonna get a piece of my mind, and maybe even one if not both of my fists. I ain't gonna take this shit!"

"Daniel, you need to calm down. Don't go and get yourself in any more trouble than you already are. We can't afford it." Wheels's tone became sinister as he grabbed Rafter's arm. "That's an order. Don't go blowing off steam and give them any more ideas than they already have. You hear me!"

"Yeah, yeah, I hear ya." Rafter jerked his arm away from Wheels's hand.

Then both men heard Irma slam her car's door.

"Fuck!" Wheels exclaimed. "I hope Irma didn't hear anything." He rushed out the door and into the garage.

Irma had already started her car when Wheels tapped on the window. She lowered her window. "What is it, Oscar? I'm in a hurry."

Wheels tried to read Irma's visage. "Did you hear our conversation?"

"I wasn't listening, Oscar. I have better things to do. I don't listen to any of your conversations. If you don't think I'm smart enough to work in your business, then why would I listen to you talk about your business?"

"I just thought I'd check. Daniel is up in the air about Emery's death. There's a controversy."

Irma continued to press on the brake while she suggested, "Oscar, you need to stop worrying about everybody else. I know you think you need to take care of everybody, but you need to start thinking about yourself. I'm sorry about Emery's death and Daniel's plight, but you have enough worries of your own."

With the corners of his mouth turning upward, forming a smile, Wheels replied, "You might not believe what I'm about to say, but I appreciate you—more than you know." Wheels hit the side of Irma's car door with a grateful pat. "You and Edna have a safe trip."

"And remember, I don't know how long we'll be. I'll call or text when I have a chance."

After Irma turned onto the highway, she thought about Oscar's demeanor because there had been a strange woman walk up to her in the strip mall's parking lot and warned, "If you don't know what your husband is doing, you need to be finding out. It could save your life and maybe even your friend's life."

Rafter opened his truck's door. "Oscar, I'll fill you in on details after I find out what the cops want."

"Okay, Daniel, and remember what I said about jumping on Hastings."

"Yeah, I hear ya."

Wheels then returned to his den to watch the morning's news broadcasts. While flipping the remote to find his favorite morning show, Wheels heard the doorbell ring. "Now what?" He then saw who was standing at the door. "Turner, come in. Would you like a cup of coffee, even some breakfast? Irma outdid herself this morning. There's plenty left."

"Thanks, but just coffee."

While Wheels poured the coffee, he nodded toward a chair. "Have a seat." As he set the mug in front of Ashton, Wheels asked, "What's so important that you'd drive all the way out here to talk? You could've seen me at the dealership later."

"It's too public. I didn't want anyone to see me at your business. The second reason is I need your undivided attention. The third reason is I's in the neighborhood and thought it'd be a good time to stop since your wife just left."

"So talk."

Ashton hesitated then said, "I've been thinking. Your numbers are depleting with Calvin, Race, Eldon, and Emery being dead."

"So you've heard."

Ashton nodded. "Yeah, sad, ain't it?"

"Law says he's murdered. There's a hold on the body."

Ashton acted shocked. "Murdered—really?"

Wheels nodded. "Yeah, and they're giving Daniel the third degree."

Ashton scanned the kitchen then focused on the refrigerator. "How is Daniel handling the situation?"

"He's pissed. And I'm afraid he's gonna say or do something stupid putting all of us in jeopardy."

"Do you think Daniel killed his uncle?"

"Nah. No way. Daniel thought the world of Emery. It had to be somebody else. Maybe there was a robbery, and Daniel and the authorities haven't discovered what's been taken."

Ashton eyed Wheels intently. "I see. But now, I need to discuss why I'm here. I's wondering if you might want some new blood. And I wanted to mention it to you first before I brought it up to the rest of the members."

Wheels scowled. "Like who?"

"Benjamin Stillwater."

"Hell, that son of a bitching con artist."

Shocked at Wheels's abrupt response, Ashton was silent momentarily then said, "I just thought I'd ask because a lot of people really think he's something special."

"He's special all right. Stillwater will steal from you then turn around and try to make you think you stole from him."

Ashton shook his head. "Really?"

"Yeah, really. And he's a liar."

"So, Oscar, you don't think much of Benjamin Stillwater."

"It goes beyond not thinking much—I hate him."

"Strong language, Oscar."

"Maybe." Wheels huffed. "I'm surprised you haven't picked up on how dangerous he is."

"Oscar, Benjamin Stillwater is exactly what you and the others need right now." Ashton paused to consider what his next statement needed to be then said, "Stillwater and Rhea Michaels aren't on the best of terms. I saw their exchanges during Eaton County's Fall Festival. He'd be perfect if and when you attempt an attack—even set Rhea Michaels up with whatever."

"If you want to use Benjamin Stillwater in your plots and plans to harass and antagonize Rhea Michaels, go for it. But for him to become involved with us, the answer is no. I have enough problems with the others and their attitudes concerning Rhea Michaels and their reasons for attacking her."

Ashton paused thoughtfully then asked, "So you don't care if I use him?"

"Keep Stillwater away from us." Wheels shook his head. "I guess it's obvious you're not going to heed my warning, but you really need to reconsider your plans concerning Benjamin Stillwater."

Ashton laughed. "I'll take my chances." In a sinister tone, he then warned, "Nobody wants to feed me any crap."

"Suit yourself, but you won't be able to say I didn't warn you. And if you ask any of the other members, they'll tell you the same thing." Wheels realized an opportunity had just landed at his table. "Turner, what about Caleb? His mental state since Calvin's death is off the charts. None of us knows what to say or do when he's around. He bursts into tangents declaring Calvin's not dead."

"I hear ya. He's the same with me." Ashton looked at his watch. "I've got to go. I'm already late for an appointment."

*****

Irma Wheels and Edna Norton had not been driving very long when they heard the siren and saw the flashing light behind Irma's vehicle.

Irma huffed as she hit her steering wheel and exclaimed, "Damn it! Damn it! Damn it! I know I stopped and had my turn signal on. Shit! Shit! Shit!"

Edna sighed as she unhooked her seat belt and turned her entire body around to see who had stopped them. "We'll never be able to do all we need to do today. And you half-stopped like you always do."

Irma frowned. "Damn it! But when there's no one in sight, why bother is what I say."

Edna's reply was direct. "And where did it get you today? Stopped."

Irma sighed. "Maybe I can talk him out of a ticket."

Edna shook her head. "I wouldn't try that either."

Irma laughed. "You never know. Sometimes it works."

Jackson walked to the driver's side of Irma's vehicle. "Hello, ladies. Where are the two of you headed in such a hurry?"

Irma attempted joviality. "Ross Jackson. How are you?"

Ross Jackson warned, "Irma, somebody's broken your taillights."

Irma was shocked. "What? What're you talking about?"

Jackson suggested, "Come and see for yourselves."

Following Jackson's instruction, Irma and Edna immediately opened their car doors, stepped out, and walked to the vehicle's rear. When they saw the broken taillights, Irma moaned. "I can't even think of a day or time when somebody would've had an opportunity to smash my taillights."

"It could've happened somewhere else, but you need to get these repaired and soon, or you'll be stopped again."

"We've planned a shopping trip."

Jackson shook his head negatively to support his warning. "Irma, I wouldn't risk it—not in this vehicle. These lights need attention as soon as possible."

Jackson looked at Edna and smiled only to return his focus to Irma. "Let me see if Sanderson can do something about them." While Jackson pressed numbers on his cell phone and waited for an answer, he said to Irma but eyed Edna, "Sanderson should be able to take care of the damage."

While the three waited, Edna made a point to return Jackson's smile. She liked Ross Jackson, and she hoped Ross Jackson liked her.

When Jackson heard Sanderson respond, he said, "Abner, Irma Wheels needs her taillights fixed. Both are shattered. Looks like vandalism to me."

Sanderson's tone was flat. "Tell her it'll take a while."

Irma smiled in gratitude. "Thanks, Ross. I appreciate it."

Edna interjected, "We both do."

Jackson wanted to take this opportunity to extend the meeting with Edna, so he focused directly toward her and asked, "Edna, how's Caleb doing?"

"Not very good, I'm afraid. He's up one minute and down the next. Refuses to go to the doctor." Edna nodded toward Irma. "We're planning something to boost his spirits. That's why we're out today. But I really don't think anything is going to help Caleb."

Jackson frowned. "I see."

Edna sighed, eyeing Jackson intently. "Have you discovered anything new about what happened to Calvin and the other two who were with him?"

"I'm afraid not." Then Jackson offered, "But we're still investigating."

"Do you think the person who killed Calvin and the other two people with him are responsible for the other murders as well?"

"We're checking all leads, Edna. That's all I can say right now."

Edna nodded. "I understand. And I appreciate everything you're doing."

While Jackson, Irma, and Edna discussed the vandalism and Calvin's death, Turner Ashton passed in his truck and saw their verbal exchange. He laughed. "It doesn't get any better than this." As Ashton's laughter rescinded, he sent a text to both Oscar Wheels and Caleb Norton.

> Guess who has your wife stopped—none other than the local sheriff. And they seem to be having an informative conversation.

Ashton then changed his voice and called Oscar Wheels. "You need to watch that wife of yours—especially the business you're in."

"Okay, ladies, Abner is expecting you. And you know how contentious he gets when things don't go to his liking."

"Yes, we know." Edna looked directly at Jackson and said, "Thanks, Ross, for all your help."

*****

When Edna dropped Irma off after their shopping trip, Irma's house was completely dark. Before the women delivered Irma's vehicle to Sanderson's, they had gotten Edna's car to continue their trip. "Do you want me to help you with your packages, Irma?"

"I'll be all right. Talk to you tomorrow."

After Edna left, Irma attempted to flip the light switch in the garage, but it remained dark. "Don't tell me the electricity is off."

As Irma grabbed her phone from her purse, it was knocked out of her hand, and she was shoved against the wall only to be punched in her back and stomach. When she fell to the concrete floor, another round of punches and kicks rammed her body. "Oscar! Oscar!"

But the only response Irma received was a forceful kick into her abdomen. Drawing herself into the fetal position, Irma lost consciousness.

When Irma awakened, she was in a hospital room at Eaton County Memorial with Wheels sitting beside her bed. "Oscar." She placed her hand on her bandaged head then asked, "What happened?"

"You were attacked."

"Who?"

"I don't know. I found you lying on the garage's floor. The doctor says you're lucky, but you've got to take it easy. You have a concussion plus some fractures." Wheels paused then said, "And bruises. I don't want you to be too shocked when you look into a mirror. Your bruises are bad."

"I don't remember."

"It's probably better that you don't."

"What time is it anyway?"

"Two o'clock. And I'm gonna go. You need to rest. I'll be back in the morning—well, later this morning—but it'll be after the doctor makes his rounds. I should know then whether you can go home or will have to stay another day or two."

Not understanding Wheels's attitude toward her, Irma asked, "What's wrong, Oscar? You don't seem yourself. Do you know who did this to me?"

"You're still dazed. So try to get some rest. I'll see you later. Right now, I need to check on the house."

Irma repeated her question. "What's wrong?"

Oscar Wheels kissed Irma on her forehead then walked out of her hospital room, leaving his wife confused and worried.

Bradford Wainwright's Review 2

Wainwright stood and stretched. "Sitting and reading too long without a break isn't good for this body, but especially mine, Mina Sille. But what I need is something to eat. It's read, eat, digest, excrete, and then another round. But what else is there to do this cold weather?" He looked around his apartment and answered himself, "Well, nothing."

While thinking about the pizza and groceries he had ordered, the doorbell rang. "I hope this is food." When Wainwright opened the door and saw his wish had arrived, he exclaimed, "Ah! Just in time."

The delivery man apologized, "Sorry, Dr. Wainwright. I'm running a little late, but the roads are treacherous."

After collecting the groceries and pizza, Wainwright started to tip the delivery man five dollars. He then remembered Hastings paying for his, Jackson's, and the detectives' meals plus a gratuity and handed the delivery man a twenty-dollar bill. "I appreciate your making two different stops for me under these treacherous conditions."

"Dr. Wainwright! Thanks!"

As Wainwright closed the door, he warned, "Take it easy out there!" Wainwright immediately unloaded his groceries and reheated two slices of pizza in his countertop convection oven.

After finishing his quick meal, Wainwright grabbed a beer from the refrigerator, flipped the tab, and then returned to his reading assignment. "I guess I need to do a little review before I continue the remainder of this particular manuscript. So Mina Sille or Nicholas Moon, chapters 9 and 10 shift back and forth from Rhea Michaels and Max Hastings eating dinner at Ariel's and Rhea's home to the cartel conducting a business meeting in a bunker where cannabis and cocaine are being processed for distribution.

"Chapter 9 begins with Hastings and Rhea discussing Turner Ashton as they are waiting to be served their meals at Ariel's. The chapter then shifts and ends with the cartel arguing about what to do or not to do concerning their plots against Hastings and Rhea. During their arguments, Caleb Norton bursts his denial of Calvin's death. The chapter ends with the members entering the bunker's cafeteria.

"Chapter 10 opens with a return to Hastings and Rhea discussing Jules Herman and Dee Burke. Ross Jackson appears, orders dinner, and enters the conversation. The chapter shifts to the cartel continuing their conversation in the cafeteria. The reader is presented with more details concerning Oscar Wheels's sinister persona. The chapter ends with Elmo Thornton revealing he has seen a shadowy figure following Rhea Michaels as if he's protecting her. I believe the introduction of the shadowy figure is to be foreshadowing of its role in later chapters—maybe even the next installment in the series. If I made a bet on that assumption, I'd win."

Wainwright turned the page. "Now, in chapter 11, Hastings drives Rhea home from the restaurant, but when they arrive, Turner Ashton appears to be introduced to Hastings. Rhea invites Hastings into her home where she takes him on a tour of her house and reveals not only its paranormal activity at present but also its being a portal to other dimensions. The chapter shifts to Turner Ashton peeping through his window and sees Rhea is returning his observation. The chapter returns to Rhea and Hastings where Rhea *lifts the veil* on who she is, whom she needs to meet, and her cosmic age. The chapter ends with Rhea going to bed and entering a dimension only to fall through space-time to the coldness of her bedroom.

"Chapter 12 starts with Rhea at the high school. She, Etta Smiley, and Shirley Bass are complaining about returning to school on a Friday. The chapter shifts to Hastings and his having to go to the dentist where he observes an interaction between Turner Ashton and Caleb Norton. The chapter then returns to Rhea in her classroom and hallway where she is threatened by a student who dislikes the sack lunches. The chapter ends with Hastings returning from the dentist and going to his apartment for the remainder of the day.

"At the beginning of chapter 13, Rhea is at the Eaton County Board of Education where she confronts the superintendent about missing monies for teachers' raises and his hiring Jules Herman and Dee Burke. When she arrives home, she prepares a sandwich and listens to the news and hears a robbery has occurred in Will's Store. The chapter shifts to William Shepherd and Gabriel Hall meeting with a new character, Ira Abbott, who appears to be their superior."

Wainwright paused then said to himself, "But is he? I wonder what role he'll play in future chapters. I'm sure Mina Sille or Nicholas Moon didn't introduce this character and his not being significant in later chapters even manuscripts." Wainwright sighed. "The chapter ends with Rhea calling Max Hastings to express her need to speak to him in person. She also warns about future incidents. But they end their conversation deciding to wait and see what happens. Their conversation is a foreshadowing of two murders in subsequent chapters.

"Chapter 14 begins with Hastings being awakened by a phone call during a dream he is having about two elderly men blowing their horns at each other. The phone call is from Ross Jackson. He and two KSP detectives need to meet with Hastings concerning a warrant to search Emery Rafter's and Daniel Rafter's premises after the supposed suicide of Emery Rafter but which at present has been determined to be a murder.

"The chapter shifts to Rhea entering the high school earlier than usual to rearrange her classroom. After talking to Etta Smiley, Rhea ascends the steps to the darkened second floor where she encounters a fetid odor. Being curious, she flips the light switch to discover the carcasses of two dogs lying against her door and blood covering the hallway. Immediately, Rhea returns to the first floor where she informs Etta and Rip Freed what she has seen. When the three returned to the scene, Rip Freed discovers Shirley Bass has been murdered.

"There is a shift to Hastings, Jackson, and the detectives at Ariel's eating breakfast when they are notified of the incident at the high school. The chapter ends with Rhea sitting in her car when

Jackson appears to inform Rhea she is expected to return to the principal's office.

"Chapter 15 opens with Rhea in Milestone's office. She and Hastings communicate by telepathy, and she is careful with her responses during her interrogation. After she leaves the high school, Rhea visits Etta at the hospital where she undergoes a shift in front of Etta. As she leaves, Jackson and the detectives arrive, but Rhea informs the three men Etta is unable to speak to them. When Rhea returns home, Tobias Harding is waiting to interrogate her about Shirley Bass's murder. Their verbal altercation ends with Harding calling Rhea names as he walks away. Esmeralda Blake appears to offer Rhea homemade bread and peach brandy. The women's conversation is pleasant. The chapter ends with Rhea drinking tea and thinking about Death's next appearance.

"Chapter 16 opens in Oscar Wheels's kitchen where he is eating breakfast. Daniel Rafter arrives and declares his plans to confront Hastings. After Daniel and Irma leave the house, Turner Ashton rings the doorbell. He wants the cartel to accept Benjamin Stillwater as a member since the membership has depleted from all the deaths. Wheels refuses. After Ashton leaves Wheels's home, he sees Irma and Edna talking to Ross Jackson. Ashton immediately texts the women's husbands. The chapter ends with Irma being attacked in the garage when she returns from her shopping trip."

Wainwright placed the manuscript on the table. "Just eight more to go, and if they're anything like the sixteen I've just read, I need to prepare myself for another roller-coaster ride. But now, time for a break."

After going to the bathroom and grabbing a bottle of water from the refrigerator, Wainwright twisted the cap and took a drink. When he reseated himself, Wainwright set the bottle in a holder within the arm of his recliner. "My throat is sore from all this reading. I need to make sure I keep hydrated." He collected the remaining chapters of *Lifting the Veil* and said to the open space of his apartment, "Let's see, Mina Sille or Nicholas Moon what you have for me in these final chapters—if there are any surprises." He then started reading chapter 17.

17

Irma Wheels watched Oscar as he carried a food tray with chicken noodle soup, crackers, and a soda toward her. Cherry gelatin and sugar cookies nestled against the upper-right corner.

Wheels placed the tray over Irma's lap. "This should help you feel better. Is there anything else you need before I make some phone calls?"

Irma shook her head. "No, I'll be all right, but I need to know if there's any leads concerning my attacker or attackers."

Oscar Wheels avoided Irma's eyes as he suggested, "There's been a slew of home invasions."

Attempting to make herself more comfortable, Irma shifted her body in her chair. "Was there anything taken?"

"Doesn't seem to be, but I've had all the locks changed on the doors, and I'm thinking about making the windows more secure."

"Oscar," Irma replied, "whoever attacked me will be able to enter this house regardless of what you do. Somebody broke the taillights on my car. If Ross Jackson hadn't stopped and warned Edna and me, we'd been stopped later on." Irma looked at the food on her tray. "I've tried to think when the taillights could've been smashed. But nothing is registering with me."

Wheels looked out their living room windows and shook his head.

"Where were you when I's attacked? I called and called for you to help me. I even begged them to stop."

Wheels's response was quick and to the point. "At the shop. I'd gone back to make sure I'd locked the place up. I had to leave early, so I wasn't sure I'd set the alarm. I guess whoever it was had been watching the house. I guess I should've thought about installing a security system here."

Tears rolled down Irma's cheeks. "Could you have made somebody angry?"

Wheels continued to gaze at their front lawn. "I don't know what to say. I just know I'm glad you're alive." Wheels looked at his watch and sighed. "I really need to make those phone calls then go into town. Will you be all right if I leave for an hour or two?"

Irma's response revealed her irritation. "Yes…Yes, of course."

As Wheels leaned over to kiss Irma's forehead, he whispered, "I won't be long."

*****

When Addison Haslett entered Max Hastings's office, he noticed Patty and Bessie were not seated behind their desks, and the two young men he heard talking seemed to be in the conference room or library. So Haslett grabbed a couple of paper cups and walked directly into Hastings's office.

"So, Ad, what's happening this sunny day in Bell City, or is it Eaton County that's the problem?"

"Roads and money, internet and money, complaints and money. And I think one maybe two of the magistrates will be running against me for judge executive."

"Really?"

After opening his can of chew and performing the dipping ritual, Haslett set the chew between his right gum and cheek. "I's hoping you'd find out for me." He offered Hastings his can of chew. "You're in the know."

Hastings accepted the chew. "I got into my great-grandfather's tobacco twist when I was seven years old. I can't remember when I was as sick. Talk about turning green. It seemed like I vomited for two days." Hastings paused as he eyed the can. "But it's been awhile."

Haslett was anxious. "So will you help me?"

Hastings held the can tightly between his fingers, set his wrist and fingers in motion slinging and snapping, slinging and snapping, slinging and snapping the packed chew. After he gave one final tap with the knuckle of his middle finger atop the can, Hastings removed the lid.

Once the lid was opened, Hastings squinted and contorted his face as his fingers pulled a portion of the chew and set it between his gum and lower lip.

Ad Haslett lifted the paper cup to his mouth and spat then said, "I've even heard there may be one from Will's Store. Looks like the slate will be full." Then he asked, "Would you at least try to find out for me?"

With his lower lip protruding, Hastings knew Haslett would not like his response. "Ad, I'm swamped. I've got all I can say grace over. If you knew what's facing me, you would know I don't have time—even need—to get involved. Whoever is elected, I have to work with him or her. So you're on your own."

Haslett spat into the paper cup again then said, "There's something else."

Hastings mimicked Haslett's ritual. "What?"

"What's going on with Ross? He's seems to be preoccupied."

"I guess he's like all of us and has a lot on his mind."

"Whatever it is, it's not good for him or anybody else for that matter. He's the sheriff."

Hastings spat in his cup a second time before he said, "And you want me to talk to him?"

"Yeah, more or less." Spittle tipped the corner of Haslett's mouth. "There are others who have the same concern, or maybe I should say complaint. It's like he's not paying attention to anything or anybody."

"I guess it's time I talk to Ross about what's bothering him, but it will be when the opportunity presents itself—and not before."

Haslett rose from his seated position and hit the back of the chair. "Talk later. I've got to start campaigning."

As Hastings watched Haslett walk out the door, he spat the last remnants of his chew into his paper cup, opened a bottle of water, rinsed his mouth, and repeated the spitting ritual again before he threw the paper cup into the trash can. Returning his focus to the papers lying beneath his gaze, he said to himself. "Now back to the grind."

*****

Irma Wheels's cell phone awakened her from a short nap. "Yes." She looked at the ID. "Oh, Edna, what's going on?"

"I wanted to check on you. See how you're doing."

"I'm sore, but lucky to be alive. I've thought and thought, but I still can't figure out why anyone would want to harm me. At first, I thought it could be a robber, but Oscar says nothing's missing."

"Irma, I think I know what happened, but you can't let on I've told you anything."

"Edna, what are you talking about? Do you know who did this to me?"

"Somebody saw you and me talking to Ross Jackson."

"So what difference does that make?"

"Irma, somebody texted Caleb and Oscar about our talking to Ross."

Irma's response revealed a lack of understanding of Edna's innuendo. "Again, so?"

"Caleb and Oscar got pretty pissed when they received the text."

"How do you know all this?"

"Caleb jumped me. And the jump happened when he was at himself and not in one of his foggy states. He really gave me a whyfor and where-when."

Irma sighed. "What did you do?"

"When I told Caleb about the broken taillights, he turned as white as a sheet."

"Really!" Irma did not want to believe what she was hearing, so she said for verification. "So, Edna, you're telling me Oscar was so angry we were talking to Ross Jackson that he attacked me and made it look like a home invasion."

"Yes, that's what I'm saying. But do not—and I repeat do not—mention what I've told you to Oscar…not yet anyway. I'm bringing you some dishes. So we'll discuss what I know in more detail when we talk person to person."

"All right. But I can't believe Oscar would attack me. I just can't."

Edna repeated her warning, "Remember, Irma. You are to say nothing to Oscar about what I've told you."

After her conversation ended with Edna, Irma attempted to visualize in her mind's eye the scene, but the pieces of the puzzle did not form a whole. When they did, Oscar Wheels would be surprised at his wife's ability to plot his demise.

*****

Patty Parks had just returned from the courthouse when Daniel Rafter barreled into the office. "Where's Hastings? I need to talk to him. And now!"

Mason and Christopher rose from their seated positions behind their computers then Mason asked, "May we be of assistance, Mr.... Mr...."

"I'm Daniel Rafter, boys, and I'm here to have a word with your boss."

Mason braced himself. "Mr. Hastings is busy at the moment. If you would like to wait, you can have a seat. If you don't want to wait, you can check with Ms. Parks and make an appointment."

Daniel Rafter smirked. "And who put you in charge?"

"Right now," Mason replied sternly, "under the circumstances, I'm placing myself in charge. So I repeat, you can have a seat or make an appointment. Check with Ms. Parks, and she'll let you know if anything is available."

Rafter's shouted at the four. "Hellfire and damnation! Tell Hastings I've been here, and I'll be back, and it'll be this afternoon." He shoved the door open, but as he stomped out, Rafter continued his tirade. "Worthless piece of shit! Yeah, a worthless piece of fucking shit!"

Hastings opened his door. "What's going on?"

Patty sighed. "Daniel Rafter is demanding to see you today."

"Do I have an opening?"

"You have an appointment with Rhea Michaels after school."

Hastings realized he would have an opportunity to observe Rafter's encounter with Rhea. *Perfect.* "When Rafter returns, make sure he stays. Tell him it'll be a few minutes."

Patty paused then said, "You might want to brace yourself for an impact. He's ripe."

"I'll be all right. "Hastings looked at the stack of folders and asked, "So what do I need to check first?"

Patty handed the folders to Hastings. "They're in order."

"I'd better get started and accomplish as much as I can before Rafter returns and Rhea Michaels shows up."

*****

After taking a drink of water to prepare herself for a discussion about guilds during the Middle ages, a knock on Rhea's classroom door interrupted her in midsentence. She scanned her students and said, "Excuse me. It seems I'm having a problem getting started this morning." When Rhea opened the door, she was shocked. "Mr. Milestone!"

"Ms. Michaels, I need to speak to you in the hall."

"Of course." Rhea closed the door behind her but stood where she could observe her students. "What do you want?"

"I know you're upset with me."

Rhea decided to set her visage to reveal puzzlement. "Why would you think I'd be upset?"

"It's about the morning Ms. Bass was murdered."

"What about it?"

"I want to apologize for what I said to you."

Rhea smirked. "You meant what you said, so why apologize?"

"I…I just think—well, I knew you, Ms. Smiley, Ms. Bass had differences, so I just thought I needed to…"

"You thought because Shirley Bass antagonized and attacked us every day Etta and I would torture and kill her."

"I…I just—"

"You just what!" Rhea focused her eyes directly on Milestone's own. "Now you need to think—and I mean really think—about what I'm going to say to you. Apologies are overrated. People think they can do and say whatever they want, when and where they want, and all they have to do is say, 'I'm sorry.'"

"Ms. Michaels—"

"I'm not finished, and if the person attacked refuses to accept the apology, the burden of the wrongdoing is placed on the victim who had been abused or bullied in the first place. The victim receives a double whammy. Apologies add insult to the injury when the physical—even verbal—attack is intentional. So, Mr. Milestone, do you want to know what I think of your apology?"

Milestone trembled in anger. "No. Can't say I do, but I'm certain you intend to tell me anyway."

"People need to think before they speak, act, even react. Furthermore, people—you included—need to realize some attacks can never be forgiven."

Milestone huffed. "The Bible says."

"Stop! Don't go there. I know more about what's written in the Bible than you do!" Rhea smirked. "And for what's it worth, the churches I've been in, I doubt if the prayers made it above the seats of the pews!"

Milestone jumped.

Rhea placed her hands on her hips. "Anytime somebody wants to commit an atrocity and get away with it, he or she uses a quote from the Bible or some religious reference to support or defend the attack on the intended victim. And I can assure you, Mr. Milestone, that's not the right path to walk. Many books have been left out of the biblical anthology—important ones."

Milestone's eyes transformed into beads. "And how would you know that?"

"You'd be surprised what I know about a lot of things. There is such a thing as weighing of the soul."

"You and your hogwash."

"There's also something to the phrase 'until hell freezes over.' Of course, hell isn't going to freeze over. It's going to shift from fire to ice. And those souls who land in that dimensional plane need to understand what's to be their empta dolore docet experientia."

"What?"

Rhea laughed. "It's Latin and means 'experience purchased with pain teaches effectively.' And to translate even more simply, your ass will burn. Whether you're sitting on a plane of ice or on a burning precipice, you're still gonna feel the pain."

"Are you threatening me?"

"I don't threaten. I don't have to threaten, but for what's it's worth, I just want you to know where you've landed after your soul has been weighed." Rhea continued to focus directly on Milestone's eyes. "Because that's where you're going for the crimes you have committed against me."

"Ah…ah…ah."

"There's no point to saying 'ah.' You came to smooth things over. It hasn't worked." As Rhea turned the knob on her classroom's door, she said, "Apology not accepted."

Upon entering her classroom, Rhea looked at the clock on the wall and said to her students, "It's almost time for the bell. I'll finish this lesson tomorrow."

*****

Daniel Rafter entered Hastings's office. "I'm back. Hastings has to be here. It's two thirty."

Patty rose from her desk's chair and walked to Hastings's inner office, "Daniel is here. And he's still ripe."

"I heard him. Tell Daniel I'll be a few minutes. It'll be about five when I open my door."

"From the way he was acting earlier," Patty warned, "you need to expect anything from him."

"I'll be all right. He just needs to let off some steam."

"Max, I hope steam is all it is."

When Hastings walked to the front office, Mason and Christopher were at their individual computers while Patty and Bessie looked at their screens. Daniel Rafter was seated but looked out the window, appearing to be anxious.

"Daniel."

Rafter jumped. "Hell, Hastings, it's about time."

"Follow me, Daniel. Tell me what's going on."

"Hell, Hastings, you wrote a damn search warrant on mine and Uncle Emery's properties when there was no need—no need at all." Rafter paused then said, "They searched everywhere."

Hastings motioned for Rafter to be seated as he said, "I guess we have some clearing up to do, but you go first, and I'll listen. But when you finish, I have something to say, and you're going to listen to me."

Rafter smirked. "You don't scare me none."

Hastings paused momentarily for effect then replied, "I'm not trying to scare you. What I'm trying to do is give you an opportunity to say what you want to say."

Daniel Rafter's response was an interrogative exclamation. "Who in the fucking hell do you think you are anyway? Huh, I'd like to know!"

Hastings remained silent.

"Okay, then, I'll play your game!" Rafter sneered. "You made it look like I killed Uncle Emery. I loved Uncle Emery. I'd never do anything to hurt him."

Hastings lit a cigarette, inhaled, and then upon exhale replied accusingly, "Looks to me like you'd want the murder weapon found."

Rafter's response was a whimper. "But to search through my things. People are talking."

Hastings flipped the burned tip of his cigarette into the ashtray.

Rafter exclaimed, "Do you know where they searched?"

Hastings took another draw, eyed Rafter pointedly as he asked upon exhale. "Are you finished, or do you want to foul up the air some more?"

Rafter huffed. "Hell, I've said what I fucking need, but I won't ever get over or forget what's been done to me."

Hastings placed his cigarette into the ashtray then leaned backward in his chair. "Okay, Daniel, whatever you think or however you feel, I want you to listen to me carefully. And after I've finished, you might understand why I wrote the warrant the way I did."

"You can talk and explain, but I won't accept any fucking excuse from you or your buddies."

Hastings leaned forward and returned Rafter's stare. "Well, what I have to say may save your life because Emery was tortured before he was murdered. And you know it."

Rafter slumped his shoulders as tears rolled down his cheeks.

"It was obvious your uncle was taunted and teased, but the physical attack was much worse. Your uncle urinated and defecated prior to his death. We had to search everywhere because we were looking for the switchblade, which was used to carve Emery's torso."

Rafter moaned. "But he was shot?"

"He was dead before he was shot, Daniel." Hastings paused then said, "There's similarities to other crime scenes."

Rafter stared at Hastings then asked, "Race's and Eldon's?"

"I can't say who or what in case something else happens."

"Okay, I'll back off, but people are looking at me funny."

"People are people, Daniel." Hastings then shifted his tone. "We intend to solve these murders regardless of what we have to do to solve them. I know you understand what I'm saying."

Rafter nodded his acceptance of Hastings's revelation. "Yes, I understand."

"If there are more murders like the ones already committed, how things look is the least of your worries." Hastings rose from his chair. "I've said all I need to say for now."

18

While Rhea waited patiently for Hastings to open his door, Patty Parks inquired, "Ms. Michaels, would you like a cup of coffee or tea? Max shouldn't be much longer."

"Thank you. I believe I will. That wind cuts right through my clothes. It doesn't make any difference how many layers I wear."

Parks nodded in agreement. "You'll find everything you need at the beverage station."

As Rhea prepared her drink, Hastings's office door opened, revealing Daniel Rafter standing within its frame.

Rhea paused as her mind warned, *Prepare yourself.*

When Rafter saw Rhea, he jumped. But as he walked toward the main entrance, Rafter attempted joviality to hide his angst and exclaimed, "Rhea Michaels! Haven't seen you in ages. What brings you out on such a cold afternoon?"

As she held her cup, Rhea transformed her visage to reveal sympathy. "Daniel, I'm sorry to hear about your uncle. How's your aunt?"

"She's trying to cope, but it's been difficult."

"When you see her"—Rhea eyed Rafter with pathos—"tell her I send my condolences."

Rafter appeared not to know how to respond and rushed out the door.

Hastings then acknowledged Rhea. "Ms. Michaels."

Once Hastings and Rhea were inside his inner office, he offered, "Please. Have a seat." After reseating himself and opening a jar of miniature chocolate pieces, Hastings asked, "Would you like a couple of these?"

"Thank you, but this coffee is exactly what I need."

Hastings pulled a couple of the miniature chocolates from the jar. "I believe we need to begin with Shirley Bass."

"Etta and I didn't murder Shirley Bass, and I spent a large portion of a class period this morning telling Milestone off. He made an attempt to apologize for his verbal attacks against Etta and me. But he's not very good at playing psychological games, especially with me. I know what he's going to do before he says, does—even approaches me."

Hastings pulled two additional chocolates from the jar. "Do you have any idea who the murderer or murderers could be?"

Rhea nodded. "I do, but I've been trying to decide if it be one, two, or three. I've considered the possibility that one knows the two, and they are together. However, it could be the two are unknown to the one."

"You're not making any sense."

"I know how I sound, but it's complicated. I may need to conduct an automatic writing to verify what I'm sensing."

"And when do you think you'll be conducting this writing exercise?"

Rhea's answer was noncommittal. "Soon." She took a sip of coffee then acknowledged, "I've conducted one already, and the message was repeated from a previous writing. If the message is repeated a third time, then what's written will be revealed."

Hastings nodded his understanding as he unfolded the wrapper of the piece of chocolate. "Tell me about Etta Smiley?"

"Etta's angst is in overdrive. She's afraid she's next on the culprit's list, but I've told her more than once—if anybody is next, it'll be me."

Max Hastings placed the lid on the jar of chocolates then set it aside. "Do you want to take your paintings today?"

"Not today. That is, if they're not in your way. Ashton stole my paintings, so I don't want to give him another opportunity to steal them again."

Hastings nodded. "Your paintings are safe here until you decide what you want to do."

"Thank you." Rhea took a sip of coffee. Sighing, she then said, "I need to confess something to you before we continue."

"Do I need to brace myself?"

Rhea smiled. "No, but my real reason for coming here today was not to discuss Shirley Bass, Etta Smiley, or my paintings."

Hastings nodded. "I see. So I guess I do need to brace myself."

Rhea ignored Hastings's response. "I have the visions I told you about." She handed the envelope to him. "They describe activity around the courthouse, the bank, and the *Messenger Budget*."

Hastings accepted the envelop as he replied, "So the cliché 'forewarned is forearmed' is in play." He then began reading silently.

> A man is crouching over a cloth in the bell tower of the courthouse. He is fumbling with the cloth beneath him, lying on the wooden floor. Some pigeons and doves sit on the brick ledge while others waddle around him. Sparrows are resting in the trees beneath the tower.
>
> The man appears to be cursing under his breath because he scoots his shoe through the splatter while attempting to focus on his target. But the droppings are too slippery, and he falls backward against the wall. He makes an attempt to rise from the floor but fails.

After reading the first two paragraphs, Hastings stopped momentarily, stared at the page, looked at Rhea, then returned his focus to the description.

> By now, the birds are surrounding the man, and he appears unable to decide what to do. The birds' presence is making it difficult for him to position himself for the shot. He's facing a conundrum regardless of what he does. If he moves too much, the birds will give his position away. If he

does nothing, the birds will crowd around him, prohibiting the shot.

Hastings spoke more to himself than to Rhea. "The man could point his rifle in any direction and have a clear shot to any quadrant of the town." He looked at Rhea and analyzed. "Like so many towns in this area, the Eaton County Courthouse is in the center of town." Hastings reread the last sentence. "When did you write this?"

"I don't know. Again, it was a three o'clock writing. Regardless of the birds' blockage of the assassin's attempt, you need to heed the warning. I don't know anything about guns," Rhea confessed, "but if a person is hit with a bullet or bullets from an assault rifle, it would be the end of the clay form's existential experience on this planet."

Hastings was shocked at Rhea's response. "Your analysis is somewhat cold."

A slight shift in Rhea's eyes occurred when she replied, "But factual. Please continue with the second description."

Hastings turned the page again reading silently.

> The woman is looking at displays in store windows. She seems indecisive whether to enter the store or just observe from the outside. Her brown dress is old and dirty. Her shoes are also brown and dirty. The woman's hair is gray with a single braid descending down the back of her dress.
>
> While she walks the streets, the woman identifies all landmarks.
>
> The distinguishing characteristic about the woman is the dagger she carries with her. The hilt is inlaid with mother-of-pearl. When the woman enters the building, the dagger's hilt glistens in the sun.

Hastings raised his head from reading the description. "So is the second vision for you or me?"

"This particular vision is for me, but when and where I have no idea. I think the bank represents another building."

"The school, you think?"

Rhea smiled. "Possibly. But when, that's still a mystery."

Hastings rose from his desk. "I need something to drink. Would you like another cup?"

"Yes, I have more revelations before I leave today."

*****

While sitting and waiting in Oscar Wheels's office of his used car lot, Daniel Rafter thought about his dialogue with Max Hastings as he observed the cartel members arrive for their meeting. He wanted to take this opportunity to relate concerns and reveal Hastings's warning.

Wheels had called the meeting because Samuel Meadows had made contact concerning their collective business interests.

"Gentlemen, we need to get started." Wheels seated himself behind his desk. "And while we're waiting for Samuel to arrive, Daniel has the floor."

Rafter stood. "There's something Hastings said to me today that's got me to thinking."

"You went to see Max Hastings," Caleb Norton hissed. "Bullshit! You stupid ass."

"Shut the fuck up, Caleb. And listen because I think you're behind these problems we've been having—you and your buddy."

"Now, you listen to me, Rafter. I ain't behind nothing!" Caleb Norton shouted, "And before you shoot any more shit from that mouth of yours, I think Turner needs to be here, so you can attack him too!"

Daniel Rafter's reply pierced the air. "That's just it, Caleb. Turner Ashton is never here. I believe I've seen him once or maybe twice at a meeting." Rafter paused for effect then said, "Oh, I forgot about the once or twice he showed up as the meetings were ending. So, Caleb, what kind of fools do you think we are?"

Other members nodded affirmatively while they eyed Norton intently.

"What do you mean?" Caleb Norton trembled. "I don't know what you're talking about."

Daniel Rafter replied vehemently, "I'm talking about Turner Ashton—a character you brought in just to cause us problems. Since he's appeared, it's been nothing but chaos and a lot of deaths. If you haven't been keeping count, there's four of us dead. And I guess it'll be a toss-up on who's next."

"Now, you wait just one fucking minute," Caleb screeched. "You don't need to accuse me of…of…of…"

"Of what, Caleb?" Rafter knew he had Norton where he wanted him. "You need to take another look at your so-called friend and business partner. He may be using you to promote his own business activities, and where does that leave you? Maybe in a hole where no one knows where you are."

"Hell! Rafter, you're—you're wrong. I tell ya. You're wrong!"

Daniel Rafter scanned the other members. "Do any of you want to support me?"

There was a heavy blanket of silence with each member's thoughts considering what Rafter's warning meant for each of them.

Huffing, Rafter eyed each member present. "None of you will be able to say I didn't warn you."

The bell jingled on the entrance door to Wheels's showroom. "Let me see who that is." But as Wheels rose from his chair, Samuel Meadows appeared in the office's doorframe. "Samuel, I'm glad you're finally here. We's just winding up, so you've got the floor."

"This won't take long." Meadows hoped the men would cooperate, so he did not have to remain in the area any longer than necessary. "I've set up four accounts. Everything you have—both individual and membership—will be transferred to these accounts."

"I say, let's sign and get it over with," Clay Kearney interjected, eager to end the session before there were any more interruptions.

Daniel Rafter shook his head. "I don't know about this. It seems too sudden. We need to have more discussions before we sign anything." He looked at Meadows and offered an apology. "No offense,

Samuel," he then asked, "but what are the names of the accounts, and where are they located?"

With his body stiffening and his voice mechanical, Meadows revealed, "Star, Horizon, Well, and Oasis. They're located in banks in different archipelagos to ensure secrecy."

Percival Brody nodded toward Kearney. "Clay's right. We'd better play it safe and sign."

"But what if something goes wrong?" Daniel Rafter was not convinced and argued, "We're talking about everything."

"That's what I'm talking about, Daniel, but if it does, our assets are safe." Kearney was exasperated and continued with his argument. "Remember what I said about Strife. I think our signatures on one of these accounts is the only way Strife doesn't come knocking on our doors—probably the only way."

Elmo Thornton attempted to be peacemaker. "Couldn't some of us sign now and others sign later?"

Samuel Meadows shook his head. "It needs to be all of you at the same time. I don't need a lot of traffic on these accounts. I don't care what bank it is or the island where it's located."

When Oscar Wheels realized there was a stalemate, he interrupted the debate. "Okay, I see we need to think about this a little longer, but eventually, we'll have to sign our names to one of these accounts and the sooner the better." He looked at Samuel Meadows. "I'll be in touch."

After Samuel Meadows left, Wheels rose from his seat and ordered, "Meeting's over. I need to check on Irma. I can't leave her alone for very long. She might hurt herself."

*****

Hastings had reseated himself, and after both had taken sips of coffee from their individual cups, Rhea said, "I need to tell you about a dream I had. I think it's a revelation about the town and maybe the county."

Hastings acknowledged, "Okay. Let me hear it because I've been having some weird dreams too."

"I was standing in front of your office when four horses pulled a hearse in front of me. There was no evidence of wheels or driver."

"Hmm…" Hastings attempted to camouflage his reaction to the omen.

Reading Hastings's visage, Rhea analyzed, "If it helps, I don't think the hearse had anything to do with you or me."

Hastings lit a cigarette. "Then who?"

"The hearse circled the courthouse once then turned toward the west and disappeared."

"And your interpretation is what?"

"Symbolic—the courthouse is the symbol of the county proper. I think it's a warning of what will be happening throughout the county, not just to you or me. The murders, which have already occurred, are just the beginning. There'll be more deaths." Rhea then suggested, "Now, I'm ready for the question or questions you have for me."

"What makes you think I have questions?"

"I know you have questions."

Hastings sighed then paused. "I didn't ask you when I drove you home from Ariel's because we discussed other topics, so I've been wondering where you were or went when no one knew your whereabouts."

Rhea smiled. "I's traveling."

Hastings leaned forward. "Where did you go?"

Suddenly, Rhea's form was discarded and cast backward and against the chair as it had during previous appointments.

With a quick inhale and exhale of air, Hastings pushed his chair backward and against the bookcase, gripping the sides tightly.

The entity communicated by telepathy. *I traveled over the Pacific Ocean, circled Africa, projected myself across Asia then eastern and western Europe, traversed the Atlantic Ocean, dipped to South America then returned to North America. I stopped at specific latitudes and longitudes. Walking and swimming and flying across this planet was definitely an adventure. It's a beautiful planet, and it's sad Homo sapiens sapiens are not respectful of their habitat and other species' right to live here.*

Hastings did not want to reveal how frightened he was. "During your journey—"

The genus Homo sapiens sapiens is causing air, land, and water pollution. The species is at fault for overpopulation of its genus at the expense of other genera. While there have been cycles of climate change, seafloor spreading, magnetic displacement, axis shifts over millions and millions of years, the at-present conditions are caused by humans. The constant wars over land boundaries, religion, ethnicity, and race have to stop. Political and theological leaders' domination and subjugation of their peoples and other countries' peoples for self-glory and greed have to stop.

Hastings started to speak but decided to remain quiet and listen.

The inhumanity against humanity has to stop.

The form paused as she shifted in her chair then continued telepathically. *The extinction of flora and fauna just for fun and greed has to stop. I could split this planet in half faster than the speed of a thought. As I mentioned to you earlier, when you drove Rhea Michaels home from this restaurant, there are both terrestrials and extraterrestrials who need to stop ignoring my presence. I realize some are fearful of me because I am female, and as you know, females are not treated well in many countries. They are subjugated, enslaved, abused, and controlled. They are not considered equal. But those, both female and male, who want to place chains around females at all levels of society need to think how they are being manipulated. Once the female is controlled, the male gender is next. I assure you I know what I am revealing to you. It has happened in other star systems. One gender has no right to control the other gender whether the gender is male or female. So those who think I will give up—because I will not—need to meet with me. I have suffered horrors beyond your imagination during multiple incarnations because of political and theological control.* There was a pause then the entity continued. *"But in this time frame, the planet will be saved one way or the other.*

Hastings's question was almost inaudible. "And its inhabitants?"

That's up for debate for both terrestrials and extraterrestrials. If they really care about the planet, even their survival on it, they'll listen to me. But since you mentioned inhabitants, I need to make this statement—artificial intelligence is beneficial to a point, but when it is allowed to take complete control—again, both genders are endangered. It's happened in other star systems. I assure you I know. Nature or the natural order needs to be maintained.

The entity then read Hastings's next question.

It doesn't make any difference how much you tell yourself you're seeing an aberration—you are seeing who I am. I've shifted to different forms and races in order to convince you that Rhea Michaels is my host. Her form is my way to traverse this existential plane. While other genera communicate within their genus, I needed to utilize the humanoid form to relay my message. And that is the way it is. I am from another dimension. As I've revealed previously, the umbrella of all other dimensions.

Hastings paused momentarily to plot his next sentence.

The entity leaned backward into the chair to encase and reclaim Rhea Michaels's form. "I need for you to show me the palms of your hands."

"Why?"

"Just show me."

Hastings opened his palms.

Michaels examined Hastings's palms then said, "I see." Rhea paused and returned her gaze to Hastings's visage and said pointedly, "Now I need to discuss Ross Jackson again."

Hastings placed the palms of his hands flatly atop his desk and set his shoulders. "I'm listening."

"Ross Jackson is in love with a married woman. He loves this woman beyond sensibility, and he doesn't know what to do or which way to turn concerning his feelings for her." Hastings shook his head. "I don't need—"

"The outcome of two different scenarios in the stream will determine whether he betrays you or not. If one scenario plays out, and Jackson saves her, he won't betray you."

Hastings sighed. "And the second?"

Rhea eyed Hastings intently as she replied, "By the way, this woman loves him as much as he loves her."

Hastings relaxed his arms and shoulders. "Really?"

"Yes." Rhea's reply was a repeat of Hastings. "Really. Remember, I warned you about the betrayal when you drove me home from

Ariel's. I'm telling you now, the scenario involves the life or death of this woman."

Hastings lit a cigarette. "There's always something else for me to worry about. It never ends—never."

Rhea waved her hand in front of Hastings as she spoke. "Even though I've lifted the veil and revealed to you who and what I am, your conversations with William Shepherd and Gabriel Hall will continue to be testy as they have been in the past. And so it is—and so it be."

Hastings sighed as he suggested, "We need to stay in touch."

"Of course, we have a lot in common. Our enemies are still after us, but I can play any game to ensure my enemies reveal what's hidden behind their masks."

Hastings took a draw from his cigarette, inhaled, then exhaled only to extinguish its tip inside the mound of its brothers and sisters. "Masks?"

Rhea smiled. "Everyone has a mask to hide who they really are. And while I've said that, I need to warn you about something else before I leave."

"You've already given me a lot to worry about."

"I may decide to have a cousin of mine to come for a visit."

"Really?" Hastings pulled another cigarette from the pack. "So why are you telling me about your cousin? Is there something—"

"I may contract the flu, so she'll need to help me around the house. She's always been mischievous, so I expect her to play the same role when she arrives for a visit."

"And will I be introduced to her?" Hastings sighed. "I need to know what to expect."

"It depends. She'll play her role to ensure I remain undetected." Rhea eyed Hastings intently then said, "Her name is Aila—Aila Murrah." Rhea frowned as she pulled an envelope from her purse. "This is another verse similar to *The Man*. Please hold it until William Shepherd and Gabriel Hall return. I'll be in touch when they arrive." She paused then said, "I hoped you analyzed Jules Herman when you had the opportunity."

As he accepted the envelope, he replied, "I did." Hastings then said, "Shepherd and Hall want to wait to draw others out, but I think—"

Rhea nodded affirmatively. "Right now, I believe Shepherd and Hall are correct. We need to discover who has purchased their services."

*****

After Rhea Michaels left, Max Hastings looked at the paintings of the Native Americans. "It looks like my war continues." He turned the light off but continued his dialogue. "And on more than one front. Grandma, how I wish you were here."

Hastings then heard a voice in his head repeat a warning from the past. "Remember the apple tree. Be a good apple and remain on the tree."

Hastings replied to himself and the aether in his office. "There's a lot who are shaking the tree, Grandma, and I don't know how much more I can endure before they destroy me."

"Resoluteness is the key," Hastings heard. "And you will defeat your enemies."

Hastings sighed as he looked at the chairs in front of his desk then the door. "I hope you are right, Grandma. I really hope you are right.

*****

After Rhea left Hastings's office and she was sitting at the stoplight, she had a quick intake of air. *Did I see who I thought I saw?*

"I need to make a phone call."

19

Rhea sat at the stoplight waiting for the light to turn green. She had driven to Henry's Diner in Will's Store and gotten his today's special. After a hectic day at school, Rhea wanted to drive somewhere to calm herself, so Will's Store had become her focused stop for her return home.

The occupants in the car to her left watched—even stared—at her physical, rhythmic movements to the song playing on her car's radio. She realized the occupants were mocking her, but she continued her mime. Now as the instrumental solo bridged the vocals, Rhea thought about how dangerous it was to be driving alone these days, but for her, driving alone had always been perilous.

*****

One afternoon on her return home from a lecture at a college campus, a man played a cat and mouse, road hog game. He speeded up when Rhea attempted to pass him only to slow down to a crawl when curves aided his blockage. When they finally arrived in a small town with only one stoplight, both stopped. While waiting for the red light to change, the man opened his door, stepped out of his car, and walked to Rhea's vehicle.

Rhea rolled down her window just enough to listen to what the man had to say.

Smiling broadly, the man looked to his left then to his right only to return his gaze toward Rhea and ranted, "Bitch! Whore! Thought you's gonna pass me." He sneered, "Well, you fucking didn't now, did ya!"

While she listened to the road hog's verbal assault, Rhea's visage transformed as she hissed. "Now you listen to me, you lowlife. Get out of my face and go to hell. And the sooner the better. In fact, you may find hell is just straight ahead. All you have to do is continue through this stoplight, and there's a curve waiting for you."

The man stepped backward, and his smirk changed to horror.

Stabbing the man's eyes with her own, Rhea waved her hand back and forth beside the window and hissed. "Now after you hit that curve, you'll be driving and driving and driving. There'll be no place to stop or pull off the never-ending, winding road."

The man remained frozen in his stance.

Observing the man was unable to move, Rhea continued her curse. "You'll become thirsty, even need the restroom, but there'll never be a rest area appear along the roadside. You'll look and look and look, but there will never be a place to stop. Never."

The man remained transfixed unable to remove his eyes from Rhea's own.

"And"—Rhea smiled revealing her sharp, white teeth—"while you're continuing your trek, there'll be a moment when you remember your encounter with me. And to your horror, you'll realize your attack on me was the biggest mistake you ever made in the short time you contaminated this planet with your breath."

The man's response was almost inaudible. "What?"

Rhea waved her hand back and forth beside her window again, releasing the man from his position. "Now you return to your car and be on your way to meet your destiny—your own personal hell."

The man looked up and down the street to see if anyone had heard Rhea's response to his attack, for he had never—in all the years he had antagonized women on the road—encountered a retaliation from a woman like what he had just experienced. He had misjudged, and he sensed he was in trouble. The man rushed to his car, jumped in, and drove away, just missing a pedestrian walking across the street.

Rhea hit her wheel. "Poor woman—who carried and birthed you—poor woman!"

A few moments later, the man hit an embankment in a curve. His car flipped against the side of a hill, and he did not survive the car's crash into the curve.

*****

As she walked up the steps to her back door, Rhea continued to think about the attack, which channeled her thoughts to other attacks she had experienced, setting her mood in a downward spiral.

Rhea's phone buzzed in her purse. Pulling it from its niche and seeing the caller's ID, Rhea acted shocked. "Charlotte, I must say I'm surprised."

Charlotte's tone revealed irritation. "Rhea, why haven't you answered your phone?"

Rhea's response was forceful. "I just stepped into my kitchen, Charlotte."

"I've spent the past fifteen minutes trying to get in touch with you. I made sure it was after school dismissed, so you'd be able to talk."

Rhea huffed. "Fifteen minutes—really. First, I went to get something to eat. Second, my phone was in my purse. Third, I was listening to a song during my drive home, and it was loud. I've been bingeing on rock and roll."

"I bet your neighbors get tired of your bingeing."

"Charlotte, I don't give a damn what my neighbors like or dislike or love or hate—even think or don't think. If I thought my musical binges would push Tobias Harding and the Ashtons away, I'd play rock and roll as loudly as I possibly could 24-7."

"Rhea, for heaven's sake. What's wrong? What's got into you?"

Rhea repeated Charlotte's question. "What's wrong?" She then admitted, "Well, I'll tell you what's wrong. I can't breathe. And what's got into me has always been inside me."

Charlotte realized she had hit the wrong chord. "Please—for heaven's sake."

"I'm not finished, Charlotte. I'm tired of listening to lies when I can read what people are thinking. I'm tired of setups. I'm tired of people playing games with me—trying to kill me—I am tired of everything!"

"Rhea, calm down."

"Charlotte," Rhea shouted, "I don't want to calm down!"

Attempting to placate Rhea's accusatory outburst, Charlotte answered, "All right, I apologize, but what's happened to put you in such a foul mood?"

Rhea inhaled deeply then exhaled. "You name it, and there's another problem to solve."

Charlotte acknowledged Rhea's admission. "It's been chaotic here too."

"By the way, Charlotte, is Samuel there?"

"No. Why?"

"I think I saw him here. At first, I thought I was seeing things, but now, the longer I've had time to think about it, I'm sure it was Samuel."

"It couldn't have been Samuel, Rhea. He's on the West Coast."

"Charlotte, are you sure?"

"Positive." Charlotte laughed. "You probably saw a phantom."

"Phantom, really, Charlotte?"

"Yes, really. Do you remember after Miss Pearl and Miss Maggie died? You thought you saw them in their car driving north on the four-lane while we were driving south. You turned around and you tried to chase them down."

"Yeah." Rhea laughed. "Their car disappeared after they ascended a rise in the road."

Rhea wanted to end her conversation with her sister. "Charlotte, I need to go, but tell Samuel I said hi, and he must have the ability to be in more than once place at a time."

"I will, Rhea. Talk to you soon." But before their conversation ended, Charlotte suggested, "You know you could call us once in a while."

"Maybe I'll surprise you one day."

"Okay, Rhea. Bye for now."

"Bye, Charlotte."

As soon as Rhea placed her phone, dinner, and purse on the counter and her schoolbag in the barstool, she was greeted by Gigi. "So, my friend, what have you been up to today?"

Gigi purred then scampered down the hallway.

Thinking about her conservation with her sister, Rhea talked to herself as she removed her dinner from its box, set it on the counter, and then prepared herself a soda. "I guess I was a little mean to Charlotte, but she's never listens to me. She doesn't have any idea what is thrown at me day in and day out."

Another buzz from her phone drew Rhea's attention from her dinner. "What now?" Then the bell at the back door rang. "For heaven's sake! Give me a break!"

Rhea walked to the door as she checked her phone. "Etta, can you hold a minute? I need to see who's at the door."

Etta's tone was upbeat. "Sure."

I suppose she wants to talk about today. Let a male appear, and Etta is raring to go. Rhea saw who was standing at the door. "Megan! What's the problem?"

Megan appeared worried. "Have you seen Turner?"

"I just got home." Rhea pretended to think before she replied, paused, and then said, "The last time I saw Turner was when he wanted to know who Max Hastings was. And I might add, very rude at the time."

Megan trembled, but she ignored Rhea's negative attitude and response. "He called and gave me his dinner order, but now, he's not answering his phone."

Rhea's reply was curt. "Why don't you check with Tobias? He and Turner are big buddies." Rhea continued to block Megan from entering the door. "Or it seems that way to me."

"What're you saying?" Megan Ashton stepped backward and leaned on the banister of Rhea's deck. "What's wrong with Tobias?"

Rhea raised her eyebrows. "Tobias Harding is for Tobias Harding, and Turner Ashton is for Turner Ashton. Furthermore, Turner expects everybody to be at his beck and call, and Tobias is a stubborn old coot who wants to see how many people he can harass."

Megan Ashton frowned. "So you're saying Turner is a…a… what is that word? I can't remember."

Rhea knew she was being tested and stared directly into Megan Ashton's eyes. "A narcist, and now if you'll excuse me, I have someone who has been waiting on the phone to talk to me." Rhea then realized she had just had an opportunity land at her doorstep. "Turner."

Megan appeared surprised. "What?" Then realizing she may have been compromised, Megan turned to scan her back lawn. "Turner? Where's Turner?"

Rhea straightened her back. "Megan, before you go, I need to say this about Turner. I don't give a damn where Turner is or what's he's doing. I've had a terrible day, and tomorrow will probably be worse than today. I'm tired. So if Turner has gone and gotten himself lost—fallen down a shaft, met with a loan shark, drowned in a lake, even stumped his toe—I don't give a damn."

"Rhea! I can't believe you're talking this way."

"Well, you really don't know me, Megan. Nobody knows me. But nobody knows anybody else. Everyone wears a mask to hide his or her true nature. And that goes for you and Turner."

"What do you mean by masks?"

"Oh, hell, Megan, I mean people have faces for the world to hide their true natures—their inner personas."

"I still don't understand what you're talking about. I just came over here to ask if you had seen Turner."

Rhea ignored Megan's excuse because she knew Megan had an ulterior motive for knocking on her door and that was to snoop. "And since I've belched what I've belched about Turner, I'll say this—I'm sick and tired of people thinking I'm some stupid bitch who doesn't have a clue as to what they're trying to do to me."

"Wow! You are pissed!"

"I'm more than pissed, Megan. So I need to go inside and not be in contact with anyone the rest of the evening, and if Turner has gone missing, I suggest you call the police and file a missing person's report."

Tears welled in Megan's eyes. "I'm sorry if I got you at a bad moment. I really am."

"That doesn't change my attitude right now about life," Rhea screamed, "and humans! Humans! Humans!"

Megan jumped backward, almost falling down the steps.

Rhea closed the door. "Now I have to change my clothes."

"Rhea!"

"What Etta? What do you want, if I may ask? Wait a minute. I know. You want to talk about the new guy."

"No. I called to see if you wanted to go to the basketball game tonight."

"So you can goggle-eye the new guy."

"Rhea, that's not my intention at all, but I must say he looks a hell of a lot better than Bass now, doesn't he?"

"Etta, listen to yourself. Of course, that's the reason, and all you want me for is to tag along in case somebody says something to Haldan."

"Rhea! What's wrong?"

"I'm pissed at the world, Etta. That's what's wrong."

"You do need to get out. You know they're always making comments about teachers not attending enough extracurricular activities, especially sports events."

"Etta, I'm really not in the mood. The past two days have been hell. I have a very bad feeling tomorrow will be even worse. So I'm sorry, but the answer is no. Besides, I'll just be in the way during your attempt to lasso the new hire."

> SMILEY. One thing is certain. He's good to look at.
> MICHAELS. Remember how people talked about you and Peter Anton.
> SMILEY. Rhea, Peter, and I were just friends, and you know it.
> MICHAELS. Everybody else had another idea about you and Anton, and it wasn't platonic.
> SMILEY. But…but—"
> MICHAELS. No buts about it.
> SMILEY. Oh, yes, there's a butt about it. He's got the sexiest butt I've seen in a while.

MICHAELS. I have to admit. His butt is sexy.
SMILEY. You know, I think Zebadiah Garner is about the best-looking man I've seen, especially around here. I mean, Greek or Trojan warrior.
MICHAELS. Or a warrior prince. What about warrior shaman?
SMILEY. Listen to yourself.
MICHAELS. You started it.
SMILEY. Come on. Let's go.
MICHAELS. What if he's not there?
SMILEY. We leave.
MICHAELS. I was right. Shame on you.
SMILEY. Shame on me. But I can't help it. And I know I don't have a chance, but that doesn't change the fact he causes things astir in me. And you may not admit it, but he does something to you too now, doesn't he?
MICHAELS. He certainly is intriguing. I will give him that for sure.
SMILEY. Okay, I'll pick you up.

*****

Hastings pushed the button on his intercom and informed Patty. "I'm calling it a day. What is on the book for tomorrow?"

"Otis Borden and Rudd Dewey want a few minutes."

"I wonder what they're trying to take now. Has to be a problem about a line. That's all they think about is land and as much as they can steal."

"Max, I've heard they're trying to move on Alma Whirs again. They've even built a pond on her. They've torn down a fence and set trees beyond what was the fence line. Just thought I'd give you a warning before they arrive. The subject might be something entirely different, but you have background in case Alma Whirs's name is mentioned."

Hastings lit a cigarette. "You're probably right. I've already warned them about Alma Whirs's being fire and the flame—blue. People have always underestimated her." Hastings paused as he took a draw from his cigarette. "But it seems people are underestimating one another a lot lately. Never know what's going to happen. Right place, right time, the prey can become the predator."

Patty's response revealed her knowledge of the conflict. "Alma may be little, but she's tough, and you're right—even mean. If Otis and Rudd are harassing her, they may be surprised at how she responds."

Hastings extinguished his cigarette. "I guess I'll find out tomorrow. Patty, you have a good evening."

"You too, Max."

*****

When Rhea and Etta entered the gym's main entrance, Richard Calendar's mother greeted the women with a snide remark. "Well, what a surprise. What made you two decide to walk into strange territory such as the gym?" Calendar's mother stood behind the concession stand, arranging a line of chips and candy bars. "Wonders never cease."

Rhea looked at Etta and said, "Rotten apples don't fall far from the tree. It's no wonder Richard acts the way he does."

Etta giggled. "She may hear you."

"I don't give a damn."

Calendar's mother blurted, "What did you say, Ms. Michaels?"

Looking directly toward Calendar's mother, Rhea projected her voice. "I said that Richard is just like you. He never knows when to talk or when to keep his mouth shut."

Etta jerked Rhea's arm as she ordered, "Gym! And now!"

Richard Calendar's mother retaliated, "I see why Richard doesn't like you."

Rhea paused before she entered the gym's doors, turned toward Calendar's mother, and said, "For what it's worth, Richard doesn't like anybody, including himself. And if you realized what he says about you, I doubt very much if you'd defend his bullying nature. But if your son doesn't like me, I suggest you get him transferred to another class. I assure you, it won't hurt my feedings the least bit."

Calendar's mother turned away, but Rhea heard her verbal expletive. "Bitch! Bitch! Bitch!"

As Rhea entered the gym's door, she felt a slight flip on her coat, but when she turned to see who had touched her, no one was there.

"Okay, Rhea." Etta pointed to a section where most of the bleachers were vacant. "Scan the bleachers to see if he's here."

"Etta, calm down. What makes you think Zeb Garner will be at this basketball game when he has just been hired, and the season is almost over?" Rhea conducted the scan then said, "There's no way he's here. I'm sure he's trying to find a place to live."

"Live, of course. Rhea, don't you have an apartment over the garage?"

"Etta Marie Smiley, you wait just one minute. Don't even think about going there."

Etta giggled. "I already have."

"You what! You didn't!"

"Oh, yes, I did." Etta continued to smile as she confessed, "I told Zeb if he couldn't find what he wanted, I knew about a place already furnished."

20

While sitting in her recliner, Irma Wheels pressed the television remote and shifted from news channels to shopping channels back and forth until she became tired of the monotony.

The doorbell buzzed, released, buzzed, released.

"Just a minute!" She limped cautiously toward the door, but when she saw who was waiting patiently, she exclaimed, "Edna! Come in!"

"I thought I needed to check on you." Edna extended the boxes she held in her arms. "And I've brought you a few prepared dishes and baked goods."

Irma looked at the boxes. "Ah, donuts! And my favorites." She motioned toward the kitchen. "If you don't mind, set the desserts on the table. Get a couple plates, two cups of coffee, and we'll sample." Irma then thought about the other dishes. "And please put the other containers in the refrigerator. As you can see, I can't do much lifting."

While Edna placed the food containers in the refrigerator, prepared their donuts, poured their coffees into mugs, she asked, "Are you any better?"

"A little," Irma replied then confessed, "but if I start to do anything, spears and arrows pierce and shoot throughout my body, making me experience my attack—both physically and mentally—all over again. After I calm down, I then try to visualize the scene to help me see my attacker."

When Edna returned to the living room, Irma observed Edna's distraught visage and decided to change her dialogue. "But anytime I have a choice of chocolate, caramel, or glazed donuts, I'm more than happy to indulge."

"Are you doing therapy?"

"Yeah, they come to the house. There was no way I could go to someone's office."

Edna placed Irma's snack on a table beside her chair, collected her own cup and snack, then seated herself in a chair beside the fireplace. "I can see why. You're still bruised. And how long has it been—a week or more?"

After taking a bite of her caramel donut, Irma replied, "My entire body is bruised—not just my face. I have broken ribs. I wonder if I'll ever be any better." She looked at the mantle over the fireplace. "Well, it's more like worry than wonder."

"Are you taking any pain medication?"

"Yes, over the counter. Oscar's afraid I'll get hooked on something stronger."

Edna took a sip of coffee then set the mug onto a coaster already placed on the end table. She remained silent, focusing toward the fireplace.

IRMA. What's on your mind?

EDNA. Have you thought about our conversation and why you were attacked?

IRMA. Yes, but why would Oscar care about our talking to Ross Jackson?

EDNA. I think it's time you and I accept some cold hard facts about our husbands.

IRMA. I remember the warning a strange woman gave me in the strip mall's parking lot. I thought it was a hoax at the time, but now, not so much. I've asked myself more than once what this woman—whoever she is—knows that I don't. I also think she was warning you because she said—your friend.

EDNA. How does Oscar act toward you since the attack?

IRMA. He's very attentive, but he can't look at me.

EDNA. Whatever our husbands are involved in, we have to find out.

IRMA. How do you propose we do that?

EDNA. We could invite the other members' wives to a brunch.

IRMA. Or we could crash one of our husbands' cooperative meetings.
EDNA. We could have the lunch catered.
IRMA. What about some snooping?
EDNA. Brunch first—I don't think you're able to do a reconnaissance mission.
IRMA. But we can plan.
EDNA. Plan it is.
IRMA. And we need to start immediately.

When Irma's cell buzzed, she looked at the ID. "It's Oscar." She then pressed the speaker.

Oscar's voice appeared cautious. "Hey, hon, just checking in. How are you feeling?"

"Edna's here. She brought some dishes and your favorite, donuts."

"Good. Save some for me." There was a long, silent pause then Oscar said, "Well, I just thought I'd check in. See you later."

Irma nodded toward Edna and smiled. "Talk later. Be careful on your way home."

"Love you."

Irma returned her phone to the table. "Oscar has told me he loves me, since my attack, more than he ever has."

Edna remained silent as she thought about what hers and Irma's next steps needed to be.

"So Oscar knows who did it." Irma spoke to herself more than Edna. "Or is he really the one who attacked me? Either way, he's at fault and afraid of my finding out." Irma sneered, "So I'm going to make him squirm—make sure his bowels remain in an uproar."

Edna sighed. "I have an idea. You may not be healed, but maybe you don't need to be completely. People need to see your bruises and your need for a wheelchair."

IRMA. What are you suggesting?
EDNA. February fair. I've heard it may be moved to the first week in March because of the winter we've had—maybe

will still have. The committee members are arguing about the date. But when they decide, it'd be perfect for you to be out and about. After all, you've been cooped up in the house.

IRMA. There's no way.

EDNA. Yes, there's a way. It's being held in Bell City this year. I've heard it has something to do with the park and recreation center.

IRMA. Really. Why the change?

EDNA. More space—I think is the reason.

IRMA. Maybe you're right. I'll work a little harder during my therapy sessions.

EDNA, *thoughtfully*. But even if you heal completely, you need to pretend frailty.

IRMA, *yawning*. But now I need to take a nap.

EDNA. I'm sorry I've stayed too long.

IRMA. It's not that. I just seem to get sleepy suddenly, and when I do, I have to give in and doze for a while.

EDNA. Okay. I'll see myself out.

After Edna left, Irma Wheels grabbed a notepad and began writing remembrances concerning her husband's actions and conversations. When she finished the exercise, she did not like the pattern revealed on the page.

*****

Max Hastings escorted two elderly men from his inner office then stopped at Patty Park's desk and said, "Call, Ad Haslett. Tell him I'm sending two gentlemen to talk to him. They're on their way now." As Hastings watched the two men walk across the street, he continued his directive. "And tell Ad not to send them back to me. Their concerns are his problem, not mine."

As Hastings turned toward his inner office, Otis Borden and Rudd Dewey entered the door. "Hastings, we need a word."

"How many, Rudd?"

"How many what?" Dewey stared at Hastings and realized he and Otis had caught Hastings at a bad time. "A few."

"I thought so. So more than one. I only have a few minutes."

Otis Borden huffed. "You always only have a few minutes."

Pretending not to listen to the men's verbal exchange, Patty Parks pressed numbers on her phone to call Ad Haslett.

When the men entered Hastings's inner office, he said, "It's the nature of the office, Otis, but have a seat. What have you two been up to lately?"

Dewey stepped backward, for Hastings had caught him off guard. "What do you mean, what have we been up to lately?"

Borden grabbed the back of a chair.

Hastings motioned for the men to be seated. And as he seated himself, he declared, "Just a greeting, but your response means I hit a note—a sour note. So what kind of mess have you gotten yourselves into this time?" He pulled a cigarette from an half-empty pack while he eyed both men. "Well, I'm waiting."

Rudd Dewey spoke first. "We need for you to do something about Alma Whirs. We've asked you time and time again to do something about her, but it seems you've ignored our requests or she's ignored you."

Hastings shoved a stack of papers to the left side of his desk. "What's the problem?"

The two men exchanged glances then Otis Borden turned toward Hastings and said, "Alma Whirs is messing with our equipment."

Hastings lit the cigarette, paused, and then replied, "Really."

"And just doing aggravating stuff to us in general," Rudd Dewey supported.

Hastings responded, "This fight with Alma Whirs and the two of you has gone on long enough. I've told you repeatedly. If the conflict among you three doesn't stop, one of you—if not all three—will get hurt. Maybe dead. So my suggestion is to stop antagonizing her."

Borden answered, "We're not."

Hastings continued. "I've heard differently—cutting her trees, destroying a fence row, building a pond on her property. That's been going on for months. So you had to be felling trees and destroying her fence when you came to see me last fall."

Dewey attempted to speak. "She's…she's—"

Hastings interrupted, "Ms. Whirs doesn't bother anybody unless somebody bothers her. So think about what you've done to her, and maybe, you'll understand why she's retaliating—if she is. Remember: trees, fence, pond."

Borden and Dewey looked at each other then Borden blurted, "I told Rudd it wouldn't do any good to come and talk to you." He turned his head toward Dewey. "Let's get out of here."

Hastings set the tobacco stem in his ashtray. "If it'll calm you down, I'll call Ms. Whirs. Get her side of the story. But if I find out her actions are a return of what you've done to her, then don't come back in here and waste my time."

*****

When Irma heard Wheels's car enter their driveway, she listened for it to stop. She then waited for the car's door to open and close only to follow each step her husband made until she heard the kitchen's door open. "Oscar."

"Just a minute, Irma. Bathroom calls." Once he entered the room, Wheels looked into the mirror and prepared himself for another round of his wife's interrogative tactics.

As he opened the bathroom's door, he heard Irma's suggestion. "Oscar, grab a couple of donuts and a cup of coffee."

Wheels walked into the den with his snack. "Irma, before you begin, I just talked to Ross Jackson, and there's still no leads."

"There won't be any leads, Oscar. My attack is just like everything else that's happened the past few months."

As he set his plate on a table and eased himself into his recliner, Oscar avoided eye contact with his wife. "I've check on things myself, but nobody knows anything."

"I don't understand why they didn't steal anything. It appears the attackers were after me. I don't think I'll ever be the same—physically, emotionally, psychologically." Irma shrugged, then reacting to a piercing arrow of pain, she moaned. "Oh!"

Wheels jumped. "Irma!"

"I'm okay." Irma shifted her body cautiously into an alternate position. "But whoever did this to me could've mistaken this house for someone else's. I just happened to be at the wrong house at the wrong time."

Wheels shook his head. "Some time, huh."

"Yeah, but I've decided to make a change. What do you think about—when I get better—Edna and I invite the wives of the new members of your farmers' cooperative to a brunch? Edna said she'd help me. Of course, it'll have to be catered."

After taking a sip of coffee, Oscar replied, "I don't think that's a good idea, Irma."

"Why?"

"The new members' wives are younger. I don't want to hurt your feedings, but I think you and Edna need to forget about a brunch."

"What does mine and Edna's age have to do with anything? We're in our forties."

Wheels stood from his seated position. "I said *no*! And I want it left at that!" He realized he might have overreacted, so Wheels reseated himself and attempted to make amends. "Irma, I don't mean to be hateful about it, but you and Edna haven't offered to meet with the new members' wives before now."

"Edna and I discussed it. We don't want them to think we're snobs."

Oscar grabbed his plate and cup, walked to the kitchen, and while he set the empty dishes into the sink, he said, "Irma, I need to check on something, but I'll ask the new members if they think their wives would attend yours and Edna's brunch." He leaned around the corner of the door's frame. "Will that satisfy you?"

"Yes, Oscar, that will satisfy me."

"Is there anything else you need before I leave?"

"No. I'll be fine, Oscar. Be careful."

"I will. Love ya."

After Wheels walked out the door, Irma huffed. "That went to the shit pot. But I know now there's more to the farmers' cooperative—if that's what it really is. So my next move is to dig a little deeper." A sinister smile tipped the corners of Irma's mouth as she pressed numbers on her cell then waited for a response. "Edna."

"Irma, what's wrong?"

"Talked to Oscar."

"And?"

"Oscar said we might not have anything in common with the new members' wives. It's our age. Evidently, his excuse is that we're too old."

Edna laughed. "Really?" She then responded arrogantly. "So the brunch is off."

"Yes. Your suggestion about a brunch gave me the ammunition I needed to see Oscar's reaction, and now that I have, I know there's more to my attack than what I wanted to admit to myself." Irma moaned from pain. "How's Caleb?"

"Caleb cursed me because he couldn't find some papers he misplaced. We had words."

"Words?"

Edna sighed. "Caleb threatened me like he always does, but when he found the envelope where he had placed it, I was off the hook." Edna stopped speaking as if she had had a revelation.

Irma waited for Edna's response, but when there was a long pause, she asked, "What is it, Edna?"

"I've decided Caleb may be acting like he's losing it—just to throw me off and maybe others, especially Turner Ashton." Edna Norton paused thoughtfully then said, "I think Turner Ashton knows something and is not telling Caleb."

Surprised, Irma asked, "Why do you think that?"

"It's just a feeling I have." Edna was silent then said, "I've observed their countenances when they don't know I am. So maybe Caleb knows something, but he can't prove it. Acting is his way of finding out what he wants to know."

Irma replied, "I see."

Edna paused then confessed, "Irma, I'm tired of this life. I can't take much more. I'm ready to call it quits."

Irma shook her head. "Not just yet, Edna. I need to find out for certain if Oscar attacked me, and I need your help."

"All right, I'll help you, but as soon as you discover the truth, I'm leaving Caleb."

Irma smiled. "Good, but now, we plan for the February fair. We'll then decide our next move."

Edna laughed. "Sounds good to me," she then warned, "but we need to be careful."

Irma attempted to calm Edna's angst. "If we're careful, we'll discover what we both want to know. After what's revealed, we'll decide what actions to take concerning the downfall or, should I say, demise of our husbands."

Edna was shocked at the change in Irma's attitude. "Don't you think demise is dramatic?"

"It was my demise that seemed to be my attacker's goal." Irma paused then said, "But don't worry, Edna, you and I have a lot of reconnaissance missions to plot and engage. I want verification that Oscar was my attacker. I want to be sure. And however long it takes, what I have to plot, even do, I will."

"Okay," Edna replied. "We need to start plotting—the sooner the better."

"Agree." Irma Wheels placed her cell phone on the end table and smiled.

21

Rhea collected her lunch from the refrigerator beneath the table behind her desk. While she was opening the container and withdrawing its contents, Etta Smiley walked through the door with her own lunch and exclaimed, "What a morning! If Dee Burke asks me another stupid question or butts in where she has no business, I'm going to scream as loudly as I possibly can in hopes she pees so much it runs down her legs."

Rhea's tone was flat. "Tell me about it."

Etta seated herself at a student's desk then asked, "What has Burke bitch done to you?"

Rhea placed her sandwich atop the container's lid. "My morning with Richard Calendar was one from hell, but you go first. My anecdote about Calendar will take longer—a lot of descriptive details."

Etta wondered about Calendar but wanted to release her frustration. "Burke tested me again. Brought up Bass then eased into what I thought about the new hire, Zeb."

Rhea smiled because she knew Etta's encounter might give her a release from the tension she was experiencing at the moment. "Exactly what did Burke want to know about Garner?"

Etta flipped the tab on her soda. "Where Zeb came from, and why he would choose to come to a place like Bell City."

"Did you ask Burke where she and Herman came from, and why they came to a place like Bell City?"

Etta shook her head as she checked her sandwich. "Of course not. I was too pissed when she asked me about Zeb in the first place."

Rhea laughed. "Now, why would Burke's asking you about Garner piss you off, Etta?"

"Because Burke started talking about Zeb's physique and how handsome he is. And it just pissed me off."

Rhea looked out her classroom window then returned her focus toward Smiley. "Etta, I hope you didn't give yourself away. Burke will use it against you. So cool it. Don't give her or Herman an excuse to set you up or me for that matter."

"All right, Rhea, I hear ya. So tell me, what did Calendar do this morning that he hasn't already done?"

Rhea remained silent momentarily then asked, "Are you sure you want to hear the gory details?"

Etta started to laugh, but when she saw Rhea's visage, she admitted, "Probably not, but surely it's not worse than anything he's already done a thousand times to all of us."

Rhea took a drink of soda and directed her focus to the wall behind Etta. "It started with his usual bouncing golf balls, and yes, he had two this morning." Rhea sighed. "After a couple of rounds of up and down, Calendar teased, 'Ms. R, do you like my balls? I got new ones.'"

Etta shook her head. "He plays with those damn balls all the time—not just in your classroom."

Rhea ignored Etta's attempt to placate Calendar's actions and continued. "Calendar then asked, 'Would you like to play with my balls?'"

Etta's eyebrows raised. "Richard Calendar did not ask you that. Surely not. What did the others students say, even do?"

"Stella Morris told him it was obvious he had an inferiority complex."

Etta looked at the remaining portion of her sandwich. "Did you write him up for disrespect?"

"No. You know it wouldn't do any good. Besides, what he said and did has already waved throughout the school. I'm surprised you haven't already heard about it."

Etta took a bite of her sandwich.

"I told Richard to put the golf balls up or I'd take them."

Etta laughed.

Rhea frowned. "Calendar looked around the room and said to the entire class, 'Hey, everybody, Ms. R is going to take my balls.'"

Etta acknowledged, "I can see and hear his reaction, 'Ms. R, if you want my balls, come and get them,' then he continues to bounce away."

Rhea grimaced. "Not exactly. Calendar sat down, stretched his legs out, crossed his shoes at his ankles, then appeared to change his mind, rose from his seat, and stood beside his desk."

Etta was not prepared for Rhea's description of Calendar's actions when she inquired half-heartedly. "So what was the finality this time?"

Rhea's response was almost a whisper. "I thought I had experienced every attack a teacher could possibly experience before this morning, but I was wrong. This morning was the worse. I doubt if what was done to me—has ever been done—will ever be done to another teacher. If it has, teachers are an endangered species. No wonder there's a shortage."

When Etta saw the expression on Rhea's face, she asked, "What did he do, Rhea? For heaven's sake, what did he do?"

"Still standing, Richard Calendar projected his scrotum and said, 'This is for what you said about me to my mother.' He then unzipped his pants, undulated back and forth, back and forth, back and forth." Rhea looked out the window as she said, "Calendar then turned around and pulled his jeans and briefs down."

"He didn't!"

"Oh, but he did."

Etta began laughing hysterically, and with tears rolling down her cheeks, she exclaimed, "You've got to be kidding me!"

"Not kidding—not making it up."

"Oh, Rhea, I've heard it all."

"No, you haven't heard it all. I'm not finished. Calendar bent over, placed his forefingers at his crack, pulled his cheeks apart, then pushed them back and forth three times. After that part of the dance was completed, he twisted his butt back and forth as if he were doing a striptease, but he had already stripped."

Etta attempted to hold her laughter because Rhea's visage worried her. "Rhea, I don't know what to say. I really don't. It's unbelievable. I've just heard a description of an action that goes beyond disrespect, yet with Richard Calendar, anything is possible."

Reliving the scene, Rhea whispered, "A line was crossed. Everything is different now. Nothing will ever be the same as it was—how I act, how I react, how I speak, how I plot. I am forever changed—maybe even my ability to empathize."

Etta nodded. "I can understand why. Calendar went too far."

The fire alarm blared, and as the two women walked from the building, Rhea warned, "Etta, you're my witness if they try to accuse me of pulling the alarm."

"And, Rhea, you're mine. Good thing we were eating lunch together today."

*****

Max Hastings had sent for carryout from Ariel's because he wanted to call Alma Whirs during the noon hour. After taking a bite of his pimento cheese sandwich, he pressed numbers on his office phone and waited. When Whirs did not answer immediately, he stirred his chili then took a bite. But after five rings and no response from Whirs, Hastings started to return the receiver to its cradle. But it was then Hastings heard Alma Whirs's acknowledgment.

> HASTINGS. Ms. Whirs, it's Max Hastings.
> WHIRS. I can see. I have caller ID. Let's me know if I want to talk or ignore the person at the other end. Really handy this caller ID.
> HASTINGS. I usually can't ignore my calls, but it does help if I need to return the call at a later time.
> WHIRS. I don't think you called to chat about caller ID, so what can I do for you on this cold, sunny day?
> HASTINGS. All right, Ms. Whirs, I'll get to the point. Otis Borden and Rudd Dewey are complaining about your vandalizing their machinery.

WHIRS. I haven't touched their damn machinery, but I just might now.

HASTINGS. You don't need to do anything rash.

WHIRS. They could've damaged their damn machinery to make it look like I did it. You can't put anything past those two lowlife, heathen criminals.

HASTINGS. Do you own a rifle?

WHIRS. Shotgun that I keep handy. And a pistol, but I'll have to find it.

HASTINGS. Do you have an assault rifle?

WHIRS. A what?

HASTINGS. They use them in the military. But a lot of civilians have them too.

WHIRS. I don't. And anybody who says I do is a liar. If those heathen criminals are saying I do, they're trying to set me up and take my land.

HASTINGS. Ms. Whirs, I need for you to calm down and stay away from Borden and Dewey.

WHIRS. They need to stay away from me and off my property. Of all the heathens to be adjoining my property, it's those two assholes.

HASTINGS. You're not listening to me.

WHIRS. You name it, and they've done it to me. And what you know is just part of it. What you don't know is worse. So you know the old saying, the straw that broke the camel's back.

HASTINGS. I've heard it all my life.

WHIRS. Well, it's gonna be true in this case. Attack after attack, then suddenly, there you are—the moment of retribution has arrived. The predator becomes the prey.

HASTINGS. I don't want you to be put yourself in a position where you're on the opposite side of the courtroom from me.

WHIRS. What will be, Max Hastings, will be. I've accepted my role. But you know as well as I do, it'll be Morris Rhines who'll be sitting across the courtroom from me.

>   And we also both know how the Commonwealth attorney is now, don't we?
> HASTINGS. I want you to know, Mrs. Whirs, I'll be calling to check on you. See that you're okay.
> WHIRS. No need to bother yourself. You've never checked on me before now, so why start?
> HASTINGS. I don't want anyone to get hurt, especially you.
> WHIRS. Dewey and Borden are criminals. So if you, the law, can't do anything about them, I guess it's left up to me. I'm on my downhill swing anyway, so what happens, happens. I won't start it, but if they come after me, I'll defend myself.

As Hastings returned the receiver to its cradle, he exclaimed, "Damn it! Damn it! Damn it!"

When Patty Parks heard Hastings's expletives, she walked to his office. "What's wrong, Max?"

"Alma Whirs, Otis Borden, and Rudd Dewey are going to send me to my grave. Their feud is going to a dark place. And it doesn't seem I can do anything about it." He looked directly at Patty and asked, "Have you seen Ross today?"

"No. Do you want me to call him?"

"I will." Hastings pressed on his cell then waited, but when Jackson did not acknowledged him, Hastings suggested in a subtle tone, "Ross, when you've got a minute, I need to talk to you. Another crisis is in play." Hastings frowned then said, "Or more like chaos is knocking on the door. It's Alma Whirs, Otis Borden, and Rudd Dewey again."

*****

While everyone was waiting to return to the building, Etta nodded toward Dee Burke and whispered to Rhea. "Look at that whore."

"Shhh…someone will hear you, Etta."

"I don't care. Watch how she's making over Zeb."

Rhea shook her head. "There you go again. You need to watch yourself."

Etta huffed. "I hate that bitch. I hate her more than I hate Herman and Milestone. And I consider them vermin."

"There's not one thing you can do about Burke flirting with Zebadiah Garner."

"Watch me."

"You're going to get into trouble."

"I'm just being pleasant, but look at him. He's a hunk, and he's in Bell City."

Rhea watched Burke flirt with Garner. "I know your pleasantries, Etta. You flirt. You flirt when you don't even realize you're flirting."

Ignoring Rhea's warning, Etta waved her right hand toward Dee Burke and Garner then yelled, "Zeb! Zeb! Rhea and I need to talk to you!"

Garner excused himself and walked toward Rhea and Etta.

Dee Burke placed her hands on her hips then huffed and stomped. After thinking about her next move, Dee Burke decided to follow Garner to where the two women waited.

Etta smirked at Burke, turned toward Garner, smiled, and asked, "Zeb, have you found a place to rent yet?"

Dee Burke interrupted before Garner could answer. "Oh, I'm gonna show him around after school this afternoon." Burke eyed Garner for verification and asked, "Right, Zeb?"

"Well, I—"

Annoyed, Etta interjected, "Zeb, you don't need Burke to help with your search." She turned toward Rhea. "I know the perfect place." Etta nodded toward Burke. "Besides, she's not from around here. She doesn't know anything about Bell City. She's just acting like she does. What she really wants is to get into your pants. That's obvious."

Burke retaliated, "You're out of line, Etta Smiley. Really out of line."

"You're the one out of line, Burke." Etta focused her attention again toward Rhea and Garner. "Zeb, Rhea has an apartment over her garage. Remember, I already told you about it."

Garner nodded as he smiled. "Rhea, it sounds like the perfect place. Would you care if I check it out?"

Etta motioned for Dee Burke to step away from Rhea and Garner. "We need to talk."

Dee Burke sneered, "What about?"

Etta motioned for Burke to move away from the crowd. Once they were out of earshot of students, Etta hissed, "I'm really tired of you and that thing that hangs on to your tail. And I bet if your friend, Jules baby, finds out you're flirting with Zeb, he won't be too happy about it. Might get real pissed—even piss on you."

"You wouldn't."

Etta forced her laugh. "Oh, I not only would, but I will. So my advice to you is if Jules baby isn't satisfying you, then find someone who can." To irritate Burke further, Etta continued her verbal attack. "It's obvious Jules baby doesn't have what it takes, but you're wasting your time with Zeb." Etta scanned the lawn and crowd again to ensure no one could hear her warning. "So back off. Leave Zeb Garner alone."

Dee Burke stepped backward and hissed, "Just wait until I tell Jules and Milestone."

Etta laughed. "Tell them what, Dee? You're not going to tell them anything because if you do, I'll tell Jules baby and Milestone more than what I've already said I'd tell them."

Burke pointed her finger at Etta. "You've just made the biggest mistake of your life, bitch! You have no idea what I can do."

Etta retaliated without hesitation. "Bring it on, bitch. However tough you think you are, you have no idea what I can do. So back off and stay the fuck away from me. I've put up with you and that thing you're with as long as I'm going to. So stay out of my business, stay away from my classroom, stay away from me—period."

Burke repeated her threat. "Like I said, you've made a mistake."

Etta then repeated her warning. "And you heard me, bitch." Etta then returned to where Rhea and Garner stood and asked, "Well, what have you two decided?"

Zebadiah Garner nodded. "Yes, I think Rhea may consider to let me rent the apartment."

Etta looked at Rhea. "Good. I'm glad you decided to help Zeb out."

As they returned to the building and Garner and Burke walked in front of them, Etta suggested, "Who knows, Rhea, just how important Zeb Garner could be."

"Etta, really?" But Rhea smiled as she watched Garner walk into the building.

"So when is he coming to check the apartment?"

"I think tomorrow after school."

Etta confirmed, "With the neighbors you have, you need someone close by. I do believe Zeb Garner's physique would deter anyone from crossing him verbally or physically."

Rhea smiled. "You could be right, Etta. I can see the expression on Turner Ashton's face now."

22

Patty had just reseated herself at her desk when Bessie Waite and Ross Jackson walked through the main door, talking and laughing. "Ross, Max needs to talk to you."

"Yeah, I got his message. It's one thing after another."

Patty smiled. "And you're probably about to receive even more."

Jackson's visage revealed he already knew what to expect. "Yeah, I thought so."

After seating himself and pulling his left boot over his right knee, Jackson looked directly at Hastings and asked, "So what is it with Whirs, Borden, and Dewey now?"

Realizing the sheriff needed to vent his frustration about other issues, Hastings grabbed the jar of chocolate pieces sitting atop his desk and offered it to Jackson as he asked, "What's wrong, Ross?"

Jackson waved his hand in negation, remained silent momentarily, looked around Hastings's office, and then replied, "It's the same old fucking shit. I'm tired of being asked, 'Any leads on all those murders, Ross? I tell ya, Ross, I'm worried—just don't know what's gonna happen next, do ya?'"

Hastings nodded his understanding of Jackson's anger. "Comments are made to me too."

"I can't say I blame them, but it's hard not to be able to say something. It's even worse not to have solved at least one of the crimes."

Hastings removed the paper from his piece of candy. "Maryann Colbert was found. That's at least one. And she was alive, not dead. So don't give up just yet. There's clues. If you stop to think, it's not been that long—the fall."

"Max, it started in July. Remember, the park in July." Jackson coughed. "Give me a second." He then grabbed a handkerchief from his pocket and held it over his mouth as he sneezed. Phlegm released from his nasal passages landed in his mouth. He rose to go to the restroom. "Again, give me a second."

After dumping additional chocolates atop his desk, Hastings closed the lid.

When Jackson returned from the restroom, Hastings asked, "You okay, Ross?"

"Allergies. I forgot my medication this morning, so I'm paying for it now." Jackson eyed the jar of chocolates. "I'm worried about what else can happen before we hit the one-year anniversary."

Hastings unwrapped another chocolate piece. "Eventually, somebody will see something, and if we're lucky, they may even talk. There'll be a break. The culprit or culprits will mess up. How and when, I don't know. But eventually, we'll have an answer to everything."

"I hope you're right because it's wearing me down."

Hastings offered Jackson the jar of chocolates again as he warned, "And we can't let our adversary or adversaries sense a weakness in us. And you know that without my having to tell you." Hastings wanted to show Jackson his support. "So stop blaming yourself."

Jackson accepted the jar of chocolates and dumped three pieces into his left palm. "Do you think they're all connected—the same person or persons committed all the crimes? If you ask me, they have a serial label." Jackson paused. "Have your friends made any headway with their investigation?"

"I haven't talked to them recently, so I don't know. But now, we need to discuss Alma Whirs, Otis Borden, and Rudd Dewey. That's why I called you in the first place."

"Yeah, so what have they done now?"

Hastings frowned. "It's what they might do."

"I see." Jackson removed the paper wrappings from one of the chocolate pieces. "Okay, let me hear the latest, so I can prepare myself for war."

"And war it might be with all three ending up dead."

After throwing the piece of chocolate into his mouth, Jackson said, "But before we jump into that mess, I need to mention the attack on Irma Wheels."

"I've been wondering about her. How is she?"

Jackson shrugged. "Whoever attacked her meant to kill her. It's a miracle she's still alive."

"Do you think it's somebody sending Oscar a message, a robbery gone awry, or something else entirely?"

"Not sure. I's talking to Irma and Edna Norton that morning. Irma's taillights had been smashed." Jackson experienced another round of phlegm erupting in his mouth. He rose from his chair and went to the restroom. When the sheriff returned to his seat, he said, "Damn. I'm gonna have to go home after I leave here and take my allergy medicine. I actually believe I'm allergic to something in my office or the building in general."

"You were talking about Irma Wheels. Do you have any ideas about her attacker?"

"You won't believe my theory."

"Tell me."

"I think Oscar attacked Irma."

Hastings straightened in his chair and set his shoulders. "Really?"

"Yes, but it's a wait and see. Edna Norton told me that Oscar is really being attentive to the point he's out of character."

"I see. Maybe you need to delve a little deeper into that situation."

"I'm already on it, Max, but now, back to Otis, Rudd, and Alma Whirs."

"Otis and Rudd were in here yesterday accusing Alma Whirs of tampering with their machinery."

Jackson repeated, "Machinery? So what did Alma Whirs do to their farm machinery?" Jackson paused then revealed his thoughts. "Weren't they spinning that yarn last fall?"

Hastings nodded. "Now that you mention it, I believe they did."

"Hell, Max, I must say they've got nerve."

"I agree."

Jackson coughed, but this time, he grabbed a handkerchief from his right pocket of his uniform pants and wiped his mouth. "Last fall, Borden and Dewey also accused Whirs of telling her cattle to stomp their corn crop." He stopped and smiled. "Now that's possible because she does talk to her cattle. She even sings—"

Hastings interjected before Jackson had time to finish his sentence. "I asked Alma about an assault rifle."

Jackson frowned. "Seriously? What did she say?"

"Denied having one."

"Do you think she's lying?"

Hastings shook his head. "She's pissed. And I mean really pissed."

Jackson acknowledged his immediate role. "And you want me to go check on her."

Hastings nodded. "This conflict could mushroom, so yes, today if you have time."

Jackson rose from his chair. "I'll go now, and my excuse will be her fried apple pies. She makes the best. Hers are like what my grandmother made."

*****

Rhea was locking her classroom's door when Etta Smiley joined her to leave the school's campus for the weekend. "Is Zeb coming today to check the apartment?"

"I believe that's the plan. So I'm kinda in a hurry."

As they cleared the exit, Etta smiled as she suggested, "It's Friday. You'll have the weekend to get acquainted."

"Etta, you're being ridiculous." Then Rhea confessed, "But I must say he is a hunk."

Etta laughed. "So you finally admit to me what I've known since the first day you focused your eyes on that body."

Rhea and Etta were walking to their vehicles when Jules Herman yelled, "Smiley and Michaels! I want a word with both of you!"

"You're not being very respectful, Jules. After all, we're still on school property." Etta had stopped and set her body for both defense and offense. "So it's Ms. Smiley and Ms. Michaels."

Herman ignored Etta's antagonistic response. "You two need to listen to what I have to say."

"It's Friday. We're leaving." Etta paused as if she were thinking then continued her barrage. "But I'll bite. What is it you want to say, Jules?"

Rhea remained silent.

"Dee was telling me how you talked to her yesterday during the fire drill. And I just want you to know, Smiley, I don't like your attitude." Herman huffed. "I never have." He focused toward Rhea. "And the same goes for you, Michaels. So both of you had better watch yourselves."

Etta Smiley giggled. "I bet Dee didn't tell you she's flirting with Zeb Garner now, did she?"

Jules Herman huffed. "I don't believe you. She said you made fun of her."

Rhea interjected before Etta had a chance to respond. "Maybe we don't like the way the two of you have treated us. You've lied about us and tried to set us up with one thing or another."

Herman shouted, "And I'll cause you a lot more! Dee's been crying because of what you said to her."

Etta mocked, "Boo-hoo." She then looked at Rhea and said, "You know, Jules here has just threatened us."

Herman exclaimed, "I warned you!"

"Warn and threat are synonyms—so same thing!" Etta shook her body but continued her verbal assault. "Look, Jules, I'm convulsing because I'm so scared." Etta's visage then completely changed as she threatened, "Now you listen to me you lowlife. I have friends in high places, and all I have to do is make a call, and guess what will happen."

Herman froze. "What?"

Etta laughed. "Those friends of mine in high places will be here so fast your head will spin—maybe even off that body of yours."

"You're lying."

"You want to bet, Jules?" Etta stepped closer to Herman. "Jules, they're already checking on things, and you want to know why?"

"Why?"

"You made the mistake of accusing Rhea and me of killing Shirley Bass. And now you're in over your head." Etta stopped and placed her forefinger and middle finger toward her eyes then pointed to Herman's own and hissed. "I'll be watching you very, very closely."

Herman attempted to regain the advantage. "You're bluffing!"

"How much do you want to bet?" Etta smirked as she pretended to think about the outcome of a wager. "If we bet, and it's revealed I'm not bluffing, where will that leave you and Dee the crybaby, huh?"

Rhea listened in disbelief to Etta's verbal attack while she observed Herman's body language.

"So you don't need to be threatening anybody, especially me." Etta continued her verbal barrage. "But what you need to do is think before you open that mouth of yours."

Herman had regained a semblance of courage. "And why would I do that!"

"My, my." Etta looked at Rhea. "Jules doesn't realize—"

Herman asked smugly. "What is it I don't realize?"

Etta giggled. "Oh, Jules, you are a jewel. You don't realize every time you open your mouth diarrhea flows. You have halitosis—bad breath. The blend of your breath and the words you speak almost knocks a person down. So shit is the only word that can accurately define what erupts from your oral cavity."

Herman stepped backward. "What!"

"It stinks. Just like you, and you know why you stink?" Etta did not wait for an answer. "You stink because you're full of shit! So don't threaten me again. You won't like the results."

Zeb Garner walked up to Herman, Smiley, and Michaels. "Rhea, is it still all right for me to check the apartment today?"

Shocked by Etta's verbal assault, Rhea remained focused toward Etta and Herman. "Rhea," Zebadiah Garner repeated.

Rhea turned toward Garner and replied, "Yes, yes, of course."

"Good."

Rhea smiled as she looked at Garner. "I have to stop for dinner, and I'll have enough for you. If I'm not there when you arrive, I won't be long."

As Garner walked away, he smiled. "See you then."

After Garner left, Etta continued her verbal attack. "You know, Jules, I understand why Dee would be after Zeb. Comparing or, should I say, contrasting the two of you, well, we both know Zeb would win every time."

"You think you're smart." He pulled out his cell phone and said, "I've got every word you've said."

Rhea decided to interject. "Better check. I bet you had it turned off and didn't know it."

Herman checked his phone. "Fuck!"

Rhea smirked. "See, you don't need to be bragging about something you have when you don't. Not smart at all."

Pretending to think, Etta placed and pressed her forefinger on her cheek and then challenged, "By the way, my contacts have informed me you and Burke bitch are the ones who killed Shirley Bass. And I must say—if that be true—you certainly were messy." Etta laughed. "Now you think about that, Jules."

As Rhea and Etta walked away, Etta bragged, "Guess I got his blood to freeze."

"What has gotten into you, Etta? I've never. What do you mean by people in high places?"

Etta inhaled deeply then exhaled.

Rhea looked at Etta pointedly. "You didn't answer my question."

Etta remained silent momentarily then answered, "Rhea, you know I can't say anything. So don't ask. I just did what I was told to do." While she opened her car's door, Etta suggested, "Rhea, we need a mental health day—go shopping, but we'll have to wait until after the February fair."

Rhea shook her head. "It's more work to prepare for a sub than it's worth."

"We'll pick a day when there's a lot of trips."

"At least give me a warning."

"I will, but now, you'd better go. Zeb is waiting."

Rhea looked at her watch. "Yes, he probably is. You have a good weekend, Etta."

"You too, Rhea." Etta smiled. "See you Monday."

As Rhea drove from the parking lot, she said to herself. "I need to make a phone call. Somebody has gotten Etta involved, and she doesn't need to be."

*****

Alma Whirs was walking toward her barn when Ross Jackson entered her driveway. Once she saw it was the sheriff's vehicle, Alma stopped and waited until Jackson turned off the ignition and opened his truck's door. "Max Hastings sent you, didn't he?"

"Thought I'd come by for some of your dried apple pies."

"Sure you did."

Realizing he was not getting anywhere and might as well present the reason for his visit, Jackson said, "Some of your neighbors are worried about you, so I thought I'd come and check on you."

"Sure, neighbors. Max Hastings sent you. And don't tell me he didn't. Hastings thinks I'll get my hands bloody from a killing. Ain't that right, Sheriff?"

"Your neighbors are concerned. More than one has come to see me."

"I don't believe you. My neighbors don't give a shit about me, especially those two heathen criminals bordering my property. And don't tell me that's not why you're here. You are checking on me because you're worried about what's going to happen to those two buzzards."

"They're saying—"

"They're saying I got one of those assault rifles after them and destroyed their corn with my cattle last fall. Well, let me tell you, it wasn't me. I's gone to visit relatives in Virginia. And for what it's worth, when I got back home, my barn had been vandalized. And you know who I blame? I blame those two heathens, that's who."

Jackson wanted to laugh and tried to set his facial muscles so Whirs would not think he was laughing at her. "Now, Ms. Whirs—"

"Call me Alma. I's married five times, and all five were shits."

"All right, Alma. I'm here in an attempt to stop something before it gets started and out of control."

"Then, go talk to those two assholes who's trying to steal my property from me." Alma Whirs looked into the fields beyond the fence row. "You know why they want my land, don't ya?"

"No, can't say I do."

"They want my land to grow their pot"—Whirs eyed Jackson sternly—"because it's away from everybody, and there's fields and fields where they can plant their pot. In fact, I—"

"You what, Alma?"

"Nothing…nothing at all."

Realizing he was not getting anywhere with Alma Whirs, Jackson warned, "I'll be coming back to check on you, but if you need me before then, you call me or Max. And this is anytime—day or night. And don't be going on Dewey's and Borden's property. You hear me?"

"I hear ya. But you remind Max Hastings I have no intention of sitting in the courtroom opposite him or Harry Rhines for that matter. I'll make sure that never happens. You tell him that, ya hear."

Not wanting to reveal his understanding of Whirs's declaration, he replied, "I will, but for now, I need for you to go on about your business and let me and Max take care of Dewey and Borden."

"I will unless they come after me."

"Again, if they harass you, call me."

As Jackson was leaving Alma Whirs's property, the sheriff had a terrible sensation is his solar plexus—one he knew was a warning.

*****

Later, Jackson sat at a table in Ariel's when Hastings walked through the door. "Over here, Max!"

After Hastings seated himself at Jackson's table, he asked, "Is Whirs still pissed?"

Jackson nodded. "She's fiery, all right."

"Do you think she listened?"

Jackson knew Hastings would not like his response but replied, "Not to one word."

Hastings shook his head. "So we're to expect the worse."

"Yes, but she gave me an idea, Max. She opened the door for me to observe Dewey and Borden, even make a pest of myself."

Hastings smiled. "It's a great opportunity."

Jackson then revealed. "And Alma may have a case. I didn't tell her that, but she said she was visiting relatives in Virginia when she's accused of pointing the semiautomatic at Borden and Dewey."

"Ross," Hastings revealed his thoughts, "if it wasn't Alma, then who?"

Ariel walked to their table. "Gentlemen, what can I get for you?"

Jackson ordered first. "Ariel, bring me the special. And whatever dessert is left, I want that too."

"I'll have the same, Ariel." Hastings looked toward the street. "We've talked about Whirs, Borden, and Dewey, but I feel more is to come and not just from them. It's just when and where."

Jackson nodded in agreement. "And how."

23

As Rhea closed the door to the garage, which led to the apartment, she thought about Zeb Garner. "I need to watch myself. I can't let myself fall for this man. I don't know where he's from, what his intentions are, why he's here. Yes, why would Zebadiah Garner come to a place like Bell City to teach?"

You need to give him a chance.

"Of course, I'll give him a chance. He looks like he's walked through space-time from a battle field of ancient warriors."

Remember the message during your night travel. You need to remember the message.

*****

A couple of nights earlier, Rhea had awakened suddenly at 2:30 a.m. and knew she had been driving a truck on a country road in Eaton County. It had been completely dark and difficult for her to see what lay on each side of the road.

With her hands gripping the steering wheel and her head leaning forward for a better view, Rhea attempted to see beyond the minimal light projecting from the headlights' beams.

Suddenly, another vehicle appeared in front of her, blocking the road completely. Not being able to pass, Rhea stopped and stepped from her truck, walked to the driver's side of the vehicle, and then stood and waited.

The vehicle's body and windows were black, making it impossible for Rhea to see inside the craft. It was a new car—futuristic—shaped for aerodynamic speed and flight.

After Rhea had stood at the side of the vehicle and waited to be acknowledged, the window of the vehicle finally lowered automatically. Not waiting for Rhea to speak and without hesitation, the man in the vehicle warned through telepathy, *I'm here to prepare you for the tests.*

The man wore a gray military uniform. The cap covering his head was round and stiff with a prominent square brim.

Although she was standing outside and the man remained in the vehicle, Rhea's face and eyes were level with the man's own visage.

*****

Now analyzing the specific details, Rhea talked to herself, "The man's vehicle was hovering—it had to be. I was standing, he was sitting, and his face was level with mine."

Thinking about the man's facial features, Rhea continued to verbalize her experience. "The man's complexion was so white it was almost transparent. His eyes were large and very white, but his irises were yellow. His beard was curved, but it didn't completely cover his cheeks."

Rhea remembered her reply to the man's warning. "You can't help me with tests. I have to pass them on my own."

The man turned toward the passenger's side and encouraged Rhea to focus to that space of the vehicle. Rhea now remembered and said to herself, "The driver was encased in the vehicle. There was no open space for another occupant. The driver of the vehicle then returned his focus to me, and when he smiled, he had large white teeth."

Rhea looked toward the street and continued her conversation with herself. "I was so mesmerized by his teeth I didn't listen to what he was telling me. I couldn't remove my eyes from his teeth. His mouth moved, but I don't remember what he said. Damn it! Somehow—someway—I have to remember his warning. I need to remember what he told me, but that wasn't the end. I was then transported to a kitchen."

Rhea inhaled then exhaled as she remembered the scene. "I was washing dishes as I looked out the window. The moon was so bright it seemed like day. I stopped and absorbed the moon's beams permeating my body. The beams caressed, fed, and calmed me. But then, the stone figures appeared in the field. I thought about the possibility of moving them with my mind, so I focused."

Rhea unlocked her back door. "I focused, waited, focused, waited, and then hoped if I concentrated long enough, I could make the stones move. Finally, after projecting my control of the figures, they moved toward me but stopped in front of the window." Rhea smiled from her memory. "I was proud of my accomplishment. I felt empowered. So what does this dream mean? Was I in an alternate universe? I really need to remember what the extraterrestrial told me." Rhea sighed. "I really need to remember before I have to pass those tests."

"Remember what, Rhea? You're talking to yourself?"

Rhea jumped. "Turner Ashton, you really have a knack for scaring me out of my skin."

Ashton laughed. "I wonder what you'd look like then?"

"Really?" Rhea huffed. "Really, Turner?"

"What's wrong, Rhea? You seem to be in deep thought."

"Good grief. Now you're asking me what I'm thinking. Give me a break. I've got a lot on my mind, and I'm tired of people butting into my business."

"Wow! Sorry, I stopped." As Ashton walked away, he said, "We'll talk later when you're in a better mood."

Rhea observed Ashton as he walked across the street to Tobias Harding's property. "I need to conduct another reconnaissance mission. But when is the question."

At that moment, Benjamin Stillwater entered Harding's driveway. "So the three miscreants are meeting. Tobias and Turner are bad enough, but adding Stillwater to the mix stirs an aggravating concoction—maybe even deadly—for somebody."

*****

Party Parks had just locked the door for the day when William Shepherd and Gabriel Hall appeared. "I'm sorry, gentlemen, I didn't mean to be rude."

"No problem, Ms. Parks. We waited until we saw you at the door. We didn't want to interfere with Max's scheduled appointments. Is he still here?"

"Yes, I'll let him know you've arrived."

"No need, Patty." Hastings had just walked into the main office. "It's about time, William." Hastings looked at Patty and asked, "Would you go to Ariel's for me?"

Patty smiled. "I'll get my notepad."

Once inside his inner office, Hastings spoke immediately. "Michaels came to see me with additional revelations."

"Really?" Hall seated himself.

Shepherd remained standing. "We know we should've returned sooner, but we've been busy since the last time we were here."

"I'm sure Rhea Michaels would be happy if you followed through with her requests." Hastings eyed his visitors. "But I believe they were more like demands, wouldn't you say?"

Patty entered Hastings's inner office. "What would you like from Ariel's?"

"Whatever the special is," Hastings interjected then looked at Shepherd and Hall. "How about the two of you?"

"Max always knows best, so I'll have the same." Shepherd seated himself.

Patty looked at Hall. "And you?"

"I'll have the same as Max and William. I have to admit, I've missed Ariel's menu."

"Patty," Hastings suggested, "have Mason and Christopher help you. Also, I'm buying yours, Bessie's, Mason's, and Christopher's. Tell Ariel to fix a tab, and if she doesn't care, send me one of her pies if she still has one."

"Will do, but don't you want dessert now?"

"If you can carry it, bring whatever she has. I'm hungry."

"What about drinks?"

Looking at Shepherd and Hall, Hastings offered, "I have drinks here, but if you want something different, now's the time to speak."

Shepherd volunteered, "We're fine with whatever."

*****

Rhea heard Zeb Garner enter her driveway and immediately walked outside, descended the steps, and motioned to a spot alongside the garage where he was to park his truck. As Garner stepped down from his vehicle, Rhea acknowledged, "I have our dinner."

Garner smiled. "I's hoping you were serious about the invitation because if you weren't, I's gonna have to go back out and find something."

Rhea replied in a serious tone. "If I tell you something, it's on the level." Rhea paused then said, "Unless I have to play a role to survive a situation, that is."

"I see." Garner looked at the second floor of the garage. "Is that to be my habitat?"

"Yes." Rhea handed Garner the keys.

"Just give me a few minutes to set my baggage inside the door."

"Sure, I'll get everything ready." As Rhea prepared hers and Garner's meal, she plotted her strategy to glean information from the latest addition to Eaton County High School.

*****

After Patty left with their orders, Hastings said, "The last time Rhea was here, she brought additional revelations. They described two people in the bell tower and around this office, the bank, and the newspaper office."

"Were they in verse form?" Hall looked at the candy jars sitting atop a wooden bookcase behind Hastings's desk.

"No," Hastings confirmed. "This time, they were written in prose." He paused. "But Michaels did leave an envelope for you and directed me, 'Don't open this envelope until Shepherd and Hall return.' So what's in here—your guess is as good as mine."

Shepherd also stared at the candy jars atop the bookcase. "Really?"

Hastings's response was direct. "Yes." Hastings then realized what Hall and Shepherd were thinking and confessed, "I'm trying to stop smoking with not much luck. I guess it's a mind-over-matter thing, and I need to set my mind in gear. But there's something all the time, and cigarettes calm me down." He turned around and focused toward the candy jars. "And they don't. So I'm smoking again, and keeping the candy jars handy just in case."

Shepherd voiced his concern. "What has happened besides the cartel and your encounters with Rhea Michaels?"

Hastings inhaled deeply then exhaled forcefully. "It's something all the time—one conflict after another. I'm tired of having to watch my back every time I walk out the door—even have to wonder what will enter the front office's door."

"Okay, Max." Shepherd attempted appeasement. "We understand."

Hastings shook his head and answered in a flat tone. "I doubt that, William. I doubt that very much."

*****

As Rhea set a choice of pizza or cheese sticks on the countertop, she asked, "What would you like to drink? I have soda or beer. I also have coffee or tea."

"Beer would be good." Garner eyed the choices that lay before him. "Thank you for your trouble."

Rhea smiled. "No trouble at all. It's the weekend, and I had no intention of cooking. I usually get carryout from somewhere in town. But if not here, then Will's Store or Villa."

"Where can I get meat and vegetables?"

"There's Ariel's in town. She and her husband, Stanley, are excellent cooks. It's on the corner across from the courthouse. They're always busy. In Will's Store, there's also a diner known as Henry's. He moved here from somewhere in the south. His breakfast specials are the best. So people congregate in droves. Both establishments are good places for you to become acquainted with the locals."

"The sooner I become acquainted with everyone, the better off I'm gonna be."

"I need to warn you about a couple of people. Actually, it's more like five."

After taking a bite of a cheese stick, Garner nodded. "I'm listening." He twisted the cap on his beer bottle then took a drink.

"You need to avoid Dee Burke and Jules Herman as much as possible."

"If you don't mind my asking, what was that exchange between Etta and Herman earlier?"

"They've been after Etta and me since they arrived. I say Etta and me, but they're really out to get me." Rhea paused momentarily to observe Garner's visage and body language. "I know how that sounds, but you can't imagine what they've done to us—again, more to me than Etta."

"Maybe they sense your energy, and the experience is daunting for them."

"My energy?" Rhea was shocked. "I guess my attitude about them is obvious."

"I wasn't talking about your attitude."

How am I going to wiggle out of this one? "I can't hide how I feel about both of them. Something doesn't click. I know eventually we'll have a confrontation, but when and where is the question. I just hope it occurs when I can be in control of the situation."

After taking another drink of beer and placing a couple of cheese sticks on his plate, Garner warned, "Just watch yourself."

Rhea laughed. "Wow! I wanted to warn you about those two, and you end up warning me." Rhea offered Garner a couple of napkins. "But I have to say, there's one good thing that's occurred since their arrival."

Garner accepted the napkins. "What's that?"

"Etta Smiley is an entirely different character. Before, Etta was meek. She never said anything untoward to anyone. Now, it's like she just waits for an opportunity to attack, but this afternoon was one for the records."

Garner took a drink of beer then nodded. "I heard bits, but they were fireballs. Now what about the other people I need to be warned about? Who are they?"

"Turner and Megan Ashton live next door, and both are extremely nosy. Don't be surprised if he'll ask you a lot of personal questions."

"So I need to keep my guard up."

"Yes."

"Anyone else?"

"Tobias Harding. He lives across the street. Tobias and Turner are buddies. I don't know if this could be a problem for you or not, but before you arrived, Benjamin Stillwater entered Tobias's driveway. There's nothing to Stillwater, and if Ashton, Harding, and Stillwater are plotting something, it can't be good for anybody."

"Thanks for the heads-up."

"You're welcome, but now, I need to ask you a question."

Garner laughed. "So you invited me to dinner to discover why I'm here."

Rhea giggled. "I don't understand why you would come to Eaton County. Of all the places on this planet, why here?"

"I was tired of sitting in a cubicle and staring at a computer screen."

Rhea laughed. "So you've swap one computer screen for another computer screen plus thirty to thirty-three sets of eyes staring at you every period all day."

Zeb Garner eyed Rhea intently. Then, with an almost flirtatious smiled, replied, "Yes, I guess you could say something like that."

Rhea liked Zeb Garner. He seemed amiable, intelligent, and fearless—unique.

Rhea's doorbell buzzed. "I wonder who that could be." *Probably Etta. She'll be here constantly to flirt with Zeb.*

When Rhea opened the door, Turner Ashton stood with a broad smile spreading across his face. "What is it, Turner?"

"I just wanted to see if you's all right. Never know—strange truck in your driveway."

When Garner walked to the door, Ashton pushed himself inside. "Hey, buddy, thought I'd introduce myself. I'm Turner Ashton. I live next door." Ashton extended his hand, but when Garner did not extend his own, Ashton rubbed his hand against his jeans.

Garner remained quiet, staring directly at Ashton.

"Turner," Rhea interrupted, "now's not a good time. We're having dinner, and"—realizing Garner did not want his name revealed to Ashton—"he needs to unpack. This gentleman is renting the apartment over my garage. So he'll be around until school's out—at least until then."

It appeared Ashton had no intention of leaving but suddenly said, "Sure. Talk later. You all have a good evening, ya hear."

As he watched Ashton descend the deck's steps, Garner's question was a statement. "What in the hell was that?"

"That was my—and now yours—next-door neighbor. But something's wrong. You bother him. He's never acted or talked that way before. His nosiness has reached a new level. He'll try to trip you up to find out all he can about you. It's obvious he's worried about who you are."

"People have tried to trip me up many times but never succeeded. He won't either."

Drums thundered from Garner's cell phone. When he looked at the ID, he said, "I need to take this."

After Garner stepped outside to speak on his phone, Rhea cleared the countertop of boxes, plates, and bottles.

When he returned to the kitchen, Garner smiled and eyed Rhea intently then leaned over and kissed her cheek. "Thank you for dinner, but I need to unpack."

Shocked from the kiss but pleased, Rhea replied, "You're welcome, and I hope you like the apartment."

"I'm sure I will." Garner stopped before he walked out the door and said, "Oh, I'll be leaving and returning a lot. I hope that won't be a problem."

"Not at all. Actually, I'm glad you're here."

Garner frowned. "In fact, next week, there's a course at the university I need to take, so I'll be driving back and forth. It was just verified, and it starts tomorrow with an eight-hour session. The remaining course is four hours from Monday through Friday only to finish with another eight hours next Saturday."

Rhea shook her head. "That sounds grueling."

"Yeah, but I need it to be certified. So I'll be leaving early tomorrow morning."

Rhea's response revealed concern. "Have a safe trip."

After Garner left and Rhea was alone, she said to herself. "Zeb Garner, you are a mysterious man. But your mystery—I like a lot."

Gigi entered the kitchen.

"Gigi, what have you been up to? What do you think about Zeb Garner?"

Gigi purred.

"Yes, I agree. He's a very handsome and sexy man, but now, I need to call Max Hastings."

24

Hastings eyed Shepherd and Hall. "So what's happened for you to appear out of nowhere on this cold evening?"

Shepherd's and Hall's visages remained noncommittal then Hall asked, "So what about the latest descriptions?"

Hastings frowned because his simple question had been ignored. "They describe a man in the bell tower and a woman around my office. The man in the courthouse tower applies to me, and the woman with the dagger applies to Rhea."

Shepherd interjected, "Dagger!"

"Yes," Hastings acknowledged, "the hilt was inlaid with mother-of-pearl."

Shepherd and Hall remained silent momentarily then Hall asked, "Anything else?"

Hastings sighed. "Rhea saw a horse-drawn hearse with no wheels or driver circle the courthouse, but she analyzed that scene had nothing to do with us but the county proper. More chaos, mayhem, death—I believe." He frowned. "Basically, a continuation of what's already happened."

"So the two of you are on a first-name basis now," Shepherd teased.

Hastings huffed. "I believe that's what you wanted, William, was it not? First-name basis. But that doesn't mean she trusts me or the two of you." Hastings frowned as he warned, "Sometimes, I wonder if I need to trust you. You need to be more transparent with me."

Shepherd replied, "Max, in time. As we've said in the past, keeping you in the dark about certain things is for your own good. And that's all we can say about the subject right now."

Patty Parks tapped on Hastings's closed door, entered, and announced, "Dinner is served. Ariel's special today is chicken and dumplings. You also have dried apple pies for dessert."

Hastings observed Park's angst and transformed his demeanor to be more jovial as he replied, "Thanks, Patty."

"And, Max, Ariel sent you a butterscotch pie. I set it in the refrigerator."

"Patty, you have a good evening."

"See you tomorrow." Patty closed the door and paused momentarily. *I wonder what those two want from Max. They always appear at odd times.* She shrugged and shook her head. *But I guess it's a wait and see concerning those two.*

Shepherd suggested, "Patty and Ariel, and no telling how many others, have spoiled you, Max. It's nice to know you have so many people taking care of you."

Hastings's reply was direct. "Sounds like you're jealous, William."

"Max, I just wanted to make a point about how much people care about you."

Hastings sighed. "All right, William, I'll acknowledge I am lucky to have people who care about me. I don't know what I'd do without them. I really don't."

Patty smiled as she walked away from the door.

When Hastings realized Patty had time to return to the outer office, he said, "Now, back to Rhea Michaels."

Hastings's office phone interrupted. "Yes, Patty, you didn't make it out the door, did you?"

"Max, Ad Haslett is on the line."

Hastings squeezed the phone until the skin across his knuckles turned three shades lighter than the flesh covering the remaining portion of his fingers and hands. "Tell Ad I can't talk now. Whatever the problem is, I'll take care of it tomorrow."

Returning the receiver to its cradle, Hastings again focused his attention toward Shepherd and Hall. "Now, gentlemen, I need to return to Rhea Michaels's directive concerning the delta nine. Have either one of you thought she might be testing you? And if she's testing you, you've failed."

Neither Shepherd nor Hall responded to Hastings's accusations and continued eating their chicken and dumplings.

Hastings smirked. "So it's the silent treatment." Then he asked, "So what's your purpose in all this mess anyway?"

William Shepherd attempted to ease the tension and replied as he had during previous visits. "Gabriel and I are here to help you."

Hastings opened his dessert box, removed the fried apple pie, and replied sarcastically. "William, I doubt that. And you want to know why?"

"Why?" Shepherd took a drink of soda.

Hastings declared, "When Michaels delivered these descriptions to me, I thought I'd ask her a simple question."

Hall had just taken a bite of dumplings, so Shepherd asked, "What was the question?"

Without hesitation, Hastings replied, "I asked her where she had been when no one knew where she was."

Hall interjected and asked nonchalantly. "And what was Michaels's answer?"

Hastings paused, eyed both men, and then answered forthrightly. "Oh, she flew around the world and took dips in both the Pacific and Atlantic Oceans." Hastings paused for his answer to register with Shepherd and Hall then set himself for their response and continued. "Oh, Antarctica is beautiful. She intends another flyover. And something else, there're more pyramids there than anyone could possibly imagine. But the ones in Alaska, they're really interesting."

"Max," Shepherd attempted to placate Hastings's attitude toward him and Hall, "I bet she's just teasing you."

Hastings huffed. "Really? That's your answer to me, William?"

Both Shepherd and Hall were surprised at Hastings's tone but even more so when he continued his revelation and warned, "Oh, she, the entity, also informed me that nothing had better happen to the Great Pyramid on the Giza plateau or any of the other future discoveries from ancient civilizations regardless of incumbent or revolutionary religious or secular leadership. That is if the—and this is how she said it profoundly—genus Homo sapiens sapiens continue to exist to make those discoveries. So I'm asking both of you again, who is this group she calls the delta nine? I want an answer."

Shepherd looked at Hall who responded, "We're working on it, Max. But now, we need to continue with those descriptions."

"Hell!" Hastings exclaimed, "You're not going to tell me a damn thing, are you?"

Shepherd attempted to placate Hastings's reaction to his repetitive excuse and replied calmly. "In time, Max, and that's all we can say right now."

Hastings hit his desk. "So you show up for a meal, see how my blood pressure is, try to glean information from me about Rhea Michaels—whom you're afraid to meet, I might add—give me the runaround, then leave with my having more questions after you leave than before you appeared from nowhere."

Horns from Hastings's cell phone blared. When he looked at the ID, Hastings warned, "It's Michaels." When he answered, Hastings changed his tone to amiability. "Rhea, how are you this evening?"

"I'm all right. But I need for you to tell William Shepherd and Gabriel Hall—"

Hastings pressed the speaker on his phone as he eyed the two men. "You want me to tell Shepherd and Hall what?"

"There was an incident today as Etta Smiley and I were leaving the school grounds."

"What happened?"

"We had an encounter with Jules Herman."

As Shepherd and Hall listened, Hastings asked, "What happened?"

"I'm not going into detail about what happened. It's obvious we survived the attack. The reason I'm calling you is I have a message for Shepherd and Hall."

"And what is—"

Rhea's responded forthrightly. "As I told you earlier in one of our conversations, Etta Smiley has become an entirely different character. Her persona is the exact opposite of what she used to be. And today she said something, which made me think covert operators have encouraged her to go after Herman and Burke. If that be the case, I am telling you and them—because I know they're in your office listening to this conversation—to back off."

Hastings shook his head as he observed Shepherd's and Hall's countenances. "How do you know Etta Smiley is in contact with a covert agency?"

Rhea replied pointedly, "Etta bragged to Herman she knew people in high places. She even accused him and Burke of killing Shirley Bass, and when I asked her whom she knew in high places, Etta replied, 'Rhea, you know I can't say anything.'"

After a moment of silence, Hastings asked, "Do you think Etta was just playing with Herman to cause him angst?"

"It didn't appear that way to me. And, gentlemen, you know you're not speaking to Rhea Michaels right now, so I want you to listen very carefully. If you have contacted Etta Smiley and encouraged her to taunt Burke and Herman, then you are now to tell her to stop. Herman and Burke are one of my tests, which I intend to pass. I know you understand the scenario."

Hall responded, "Yes, we understand."

There was an extended period of silence then the entity said, "Mr. Shepherd and Mr. Hall, since I have left Rhea Michaels's form, I now need for you to call Ira Abbott on your phone or phones then press speaker. I want all of you to hear my reading of the verses you have in the envelope, which you need to open now. I will wait until you do so."

Silence blanketed Hastings's office as the three men eyed one another while Hall opened the envelope.

The entity then spoke, "I'm waiting."

"We have the verses."

"Now, call Ira Abbott, and remember press speaker."

The entity waited until she knew contact had been made. "So, Ira Abbott, I need for you to listen to what I read to you."

"To whom am I speaking?"

"I believe you are aware of my existential character and host—even all of my existential hosts through the centuries, especially the crucifixion, the decapitations, and the burnings—are you not?"

Ira Abbott's response was flat. "Yes, I'm aware." His next statement was almost a whisper. "But what is your true name—your cosmic name—I never knew what it was."

The entity replied, "My true name remains and shall remain hidden. But you can refer to me as Zakira. The *Z* represents omega, the *a* represents alpha, *ki* represents the Sumerian Earth Goddess, *ra* is an alternate spelling for Re." Zakira paused for effect then said, "But enough of the chitchat. You need to listen to what I have to say both in verse and dialogue."

Ira Abbott sighed. "I'm listening."

"I know you've read *The Man,* and since you have, you understand the reference to tyrants, dictators, and dissidents—both politically and theologically. I know you understand the comparisons even to you and your comrades."

Ira Abbott acknowledged, "The verses have been discussed."

"Now I need for you to listen to this verse entitled *Notandum Nudis Verbis.*"

Ira Abbott translated, "Something noted in plain words."

"Close enough" was the entity's response.

Ira Abbott sighed before he said, "Please begin."

>
> Notandum Nudis Verbis
> I warn about man and woman too
>
> For thee need watch and listen
> To how they act and speak untruths.
> Even their rudeness reveals
> Their de classe attitudes.
>
> For all speech and acts
> Make asses
> Of sycophants.
> And when they speak in room—
> Know they mock all
> Who worship their suits.
> And when their tantrums

LIFTING THE VEIL

Start ruckus anew—
They keep turmoil
Boiling in cauldron stew.

So if thou ask,
"What be seen?'
Answer be clear—
I tell all
Keep the fiends away from seats.
And when the scene
Is clear of stool—
The world is better
And air be too.

Now, I say
Stop the man and woman too,
For they not care an ounce
About others—it's true.
And when they plot schemes—
It's to fill their pockets
And keep populace lean.

I do need
To say a hymn—
It's not good
When man and woman be dim.
For their mouths
Be flowing through,
And what be said
Is a tale of stool.

I say it more than once—
Man and woman not be
Way they seem,
For faces say one,
But mouths say two.

And when two forked—
Lie believed—
When bigots speak at meets.

For all they do
When in room
Is eat cakes and drink booze—
While they lie
And say—it's true.
But truth not be
Their creed,
For they never be
Righteous deans.

And yes I say
Stool it be
When speak words
Not good for seed.

So I end
With one more scene—
The man and woman no longer
Hold their seams,
And when they come to say their piece,
All will see their asses
For what they be.

But warning be true—
Don't let the man and woman
Continue their stew.
For you see
They harm the earth and its peoples
To maintain their selfish schemes.

Silence permeated all rooms, but when Zakira realized the men were waiting for her to speak, she continued her narrative. "My experience during this incarnation—as many others—has been a crucible. Over many millennia, I have resided in all countries, I have existed in all races, I have experienced all theological ideologies. So I'm well aware of the hardships endured by all peoples because of tyranny—economically, politically, socially, and theologically."

Ira Abbott attempted to respond.

"I'm not finished. The chains are heavy for those less fortunate. But the travesty is ignorance. It is not bliss to be subjected to the whims of those who worship leaders and wannabe dictators who subjugate their citizens and continue to harm the planet because of their narcissistic need for position, fame, and wealth. Homo sapiens sapiens need to pay attention to scientists in more ways than one." The entity paused then said, "I know now why I was directed to this location in this country. Every day it becomes more apparent."

Ira Abbott interrupted and asked, "So, Zakira, the entity who encouraged you to arrive at your present location is now Max Hastings?"

Hastings looked at Shepherd and Hall and exclaimed, "What!"

Both Shepherd and Hall waved their hands in negation.

Zakira ignored Hastings's outburst and replied, "No. I've checked. However, as you are aware, he is in the same boat as I with terrestrials attempting his demise. As for the one who encouraged me to enter this location, I'm still searching for him. But I'm sure his existential experience has been much better than mine."

Ira Abbott continued his interrogation, hoping to gain time to contact his comrades. "And the interdimensional traveler who is your enemy—"

"I have to play that game a little longer. It'll give me the edge I need." Zakira paused then warned, "Ira Abbott, you need to stop attempting to contact your comrades because your connector is blocked. You and they need to meet with me. I'm tired of being ignored because the at-present civilization is plagued with reincarnations from the Roman Empire and Dark Ages. Too many Homo sapiens sapiens—as I've just said—want to listen to political tyrants and religious leaders who subjugate and enslave their peoples."

Ira Abbott started to speak but was interrupted.

"I'm not finished," Zakira hissed. "The real travesty is ill-informed females are joining forces with a percentage of males—in authoritative and lucrative positions—to ensure the female gender is trapped. Evidently, the garden myth reigns, and females are still paying for the narrative. I've been betrayed more times than you can count, and I don't like betrayals. The imbalance has to be balanced. The female has to be equal to the male. Regardless of what is being preached and believed, the mother is equal to the father within the triangle."

Ira Abbott coughed and started to speak.

"I said I'm not finished, Ira Abbott, so listen. You mentioned Max Hastings, so I will refer to his name to make an analogy. The first letters of Maxwell Aaron Christian Hastings forms the acronym MACH, which pertains to sound. Sound destroys, sound builds. Likewise, the elements of fire, water, and wind destroy, yet in doing so, they continue the cycle of renewal. Earth is an entity unto herself, and pollution of the air, water, and land is destroying her. Earth Mother is angry, and she is revealing her anger in most profound ways. Homo sapiens sapiens are attacking Earth Mother with overpopulation, garbage, and emissions. If there is not a change in action and thought, Ira Abbott, Earth Mother will return with a force the at-present civilization has not yet experienced."

Again, Ira Abbott attempted to speak.

"Our extended dialogue is for you to listen while I speak. So I end with this warning. There must be peace on every continent even the seas, for there is turmoil and strife in all countries among all peoples politically, socially, and theologically."

"We understand—"

Zakira ignored Ira Abbott's attempt to interrupt her and chanted, "And if not stop what at present do, no more chances shall be granted free, and fall of breed shall be decreed. It come to be if not listen to Me. The fall of the killing breed come to pass. It be seen."

There was a moment of silence then Zakira warned, "Ira Abbott, you will be hearing from me in a more provocative way. In the meantime, do not send anyone to harm my host—whoever it be. If something happens to her—or any mask or cloak I wear—the chain reaction begins immediately. My interdimensional enemy is plotting schemes as I speak. The drug cartel is plotting schemes as I speak. Do not jump into their cauldrons. I assure you it would not be wise. My meeting with you and your comrades needs to be amiable, not contentious. And now our conversation ends."

Hall turned his phone off, which was connected to Ira Abbott.

Then, Hastings, Shepherd, and Hall realized the entity had remained on the phone, so Shepherd spoke, "Zakira?"

"I've been explicit concerning what I expect to occur, yet I know additional samples of the Earth Mother's retribution will happen." The entity paused then warned, "Mr. Shepherd and Mr. Hall, you can remind Ira Abbott what was revealed when one of those incidents presents itself."

The entity returned to Rhea's form and addressed Hastings. "Max, I'll be in touch, and remember what I said about a response and a visit."

Hastings eyed Shepherd and Hall as he said, "Yes, I remember."

Once their conversation ended, Shepherd asked, "What visit, Max?"

Hastings smiled as he replied, "All in good time, all in good time. After all, I'm here to help you two, right?" Hastings was silent momentarily then warned, "It would be wise for those individuals to whom the entity referred to think about—even do as directed. It's obvious she is here to ensure there is a paradigm shift to a better environment for all genera—even the planet itself."

*****

Rhea placed her phone on the counter, walked outside, gazed at Nut's navy cloak decorated with stars from horizon to horizon, and began her chant. "I am the Kali Ma, the Blue One. I am Wadjet Uraeus, the Green One. I am the Eye of Re. I am Sekhmet. I am Ki. I am Shekinah. I am the Truth of All Myths. Please protect and keep me safe. For I need thou presence due."

Epilogue

The young girl sat at the corner of the picnic table. Her family had been invited to dinner because the hosts needed her father to fry the fish for the picnic.

Sitting and eyeing those around the table, the young girl waited for the side dishes to be passed to her and her siblings. She knew the subject of the veil would be mentioned, so she made sure her prep for an answer had been practiced since that morning. She had even told her mother about the incident.

The woman, Carolyn, whose veil had been used for the symbolic act sat down opposite the young girl, looked toward the young girl's mother and said, "The silliest thing happened today. Your daughter asked to see then try my wedding veil on."

The young girl's mother looked at Carolyn then at her daughter. "She did?"

"Yes," Carolyn verified, "in fact, now that I think about it, it was ritualistic. First, she asked to see it. She then pleaded—almost demanded—to try it on. Frankly, I didn't understand why she wanted to see it in the first place, but to try it on and place it over her face the way she did was very upsetting. But what was really bizarre was the way she lifted the veil over her head and gave it back to me."

"Why?" The young girl's mother inquired, "Why was it bizarre?"

"It wasn't so much what she did, but what she said." Carolyn paused thoughtfully then continued. "When I asked her why she wanted to try the veil on, she said adamantly, 'It had to be done.'"

The young girl smiled as her father placed a piece of fish onto her plate. She then said with determination, "It is time the veil be lifted. I am here to do what I've been sent here to do."

NICHOLAS MOON

Prayer to the Sacred Feminine

Sacred Mother
I speak this plea—
Thou art one
Who be what need.

And I beseech thou presence due
For summer, winter, spring, fall,
Ensuring flora and fauna
Remain secure—be the call.

The earth and cosmos too
Travel through thee,
And forever be endeared,
To thou watchful see.

So I speak with words so true—
Keep the balance
For all to remain
Where due.

Sacred Mother
I say to thee—
Blend with father
To continue—

For thou seat
Awaits thou presence due
To keep earth and cosmos
Existent in stream of hues.

Bradford Wainwright's Review 3

While Wainwright returned his recliner to its standard position, his cell phone vibrated.

After checking the ID, Wainwright whispered, "Bertie, what's wrong?"

"Just wanted to check on you," Bertie replied. "You've lost your voice, Bradford."

"I told you, Bertie, my allergies have attacked me ferociously. So I can't talk much longer."

"Okay, I'll let you go, Bradford."

"Bertie?"

"Yes, Bradford."

"I really need to rest. I'm all right. Just hoarse from my latest battle with allergies. So—"

"You want me to leave you alone?"

"Yes. I'll talk to you later."

Tears welled in Bertie Schmidt's eyes as she whimpered, "Okay, Bradford. I'll leave you alone for now, but if I get the feeling I need to call you, I will."

"Bertie, I have to go to the bathroom."

After his conversation ended with Bertie Schmidt, Wainwright heated another couple slices of pizza in his countertop oven while he prepared himself a soda. "I don't know how much longer I can keep this charade up with Bertie, but I'm definitely going to plan, even plot, some kind of strategy. It might be better for both of us if I just level with her and tell her I want a break from our writing partnership."

Thinking about Bertie's response, Wainwright asked himself, "But do I want to put myself through that interrogation?"

Setting his food and drink on the table beside his recliner, Wainwright answered himself, "Hell no! I just need to play the game, make excuses, be ill. I know, I'll tell Bertie I have writer's block. She won't be able to argue with me about that. Yeah, writer's block it is. That'll solve my problem with Bertie. But now, I need to review what I've just read. I know a third book will be arriving because *Lifting the Veil* ended with a lead into exactly that—a third book.

"Whoever Mina Sille or Nicholas Moon are, both are introducing new characters whose roles connect to Rhea Michaels and Max Hastings and the overall plot development. And like the *When the Goddess Returns to Eden*, this work follows the pattern of multiple shifts within each chapter."

Collecting the manuscript from the table, Wainwright acknowledged, "And the last eight chapters of this work definitely have multiple shifts. Chapter 17 begins with Irma Wheels recuperating at home and her questioning Oscar about her attacker. There's a shift to Max Hastings's office where he and Ad Haslett, judge executive, are enjoying a break with tobacco chew and discussing county maintenance and political problems. Another shift occurs to Irma Wheels and her receiving a call from Edna Norton who tells Irma how angry Oscar was about their encounter with Ross Jackson. Another shift occurs to Hastings's office, and Daniel Rafter demands to speak to Hastings who is unavailable, so Rafter informs Patty Parks he'll return that afternoon. Another shift occurs to Rhea Michaels and her encounter with Zachary Milestone. Chapter 17 ends with a return to Hastings's office and his warning to Daniel Rafter about the murders of Race Webb, Eldon Nolan, and Emery Rafter and what could happen in the future.

"Chapter 18 opens with Rhea Michaels waiting to speak to Max Hastings and encounters Daniel Rafter as he is leaving the office. Rhea has brought descriptions of assassins in the area of the courthouse, bank, and Hastings's office. A shift occurs to Oscar Wheels's business where Daniel Rafter tells the cartel members he has met with Hastings. Samuel Meadows appears to inform the members he has established bank accounts in archipelagos. The chapter ends with Rhea still in Hastings's office where she shifts her form and communicates with him by telepathy. The form not only reveals about her trek, but she also warns Hastings both terrestrials and extraterrestrials need to acknowledge her. When Rhea leaves Hastings's office, she thinks she sees Samuel Meadows in Bell City.

"Except for one section, which occurs in Max Hastings's office and his dialogue with Patty Parks about the following day's appointments, chapter 19 is completely about Rhea Michaels and her encounters and dialogue with various characters. Initially, Rhea is sitting at a stoplight listening to music while she reflects on a past incident where a man verbally attacked her while sitting at that stoplight. Once Rhea arrives home, she receives a phone call from her sister, Charlotte. Their conversation is somewhat contentious, but they end it amicably.

"Megan Ashton rings Rhea's doorbell, and Etta Smiley calls simultaneously. Rhea speaks to Megan first, and again their conversation is contentious with Rhea being somewhat rude to Megan. After Megan leaves, Rhea speaks to Etta Smiley who wants to talk about the new male hire, Zebadiah Garner, at the high school. Etta convinces Rhea to go to a ball game in hopes of seeing Garner. The chapter ends with Rhea and Etta encountering Richard Calendar's mother, and Etta informing Rhea she has told Garner about Rhea's empty apartment.

"Chapter 20 returns to Irma Wheels's home where Edna Norton arrives with containers of food. The women discuss Irma's attack and how Oscar is acting toward Irma. There's a shift to Max Hastings's office where he is discussing Otis Borden's and Rudd Dewey's conflict with Alma Whirs. Another shift returns to Irma Wheels listening to Oscar entering their home. Irma suggests she and Edna meet with new members' wives, but Oscar's response is negative. After Oscar leaves, Irma calls Edna, and they plan to discover exactly what their husbands' business interests are.

"Chapter 21 opens with Rhea at the high school during her lunch break. Etta Smiley enters Rhea's room, and they begin their revelations about their morning's experiences. Etta's verbal encounter with Dee Burke and her inquiry about Zebadiah Garner still has Etta upset. But Rhea's revelation about Richard Calendar's striptease and 'mooning' of her outweighs Etta's verbal war with Burke. The fire alarm disrupts their conversation and lunch. The chapter shifts to Hastings's office where he is eating lunch while he's talking to Alma Whirs about her ongoing conflict with Otis Borden and Rudd Dewey. At the end of their conversation, Hastings realizes Whirs has no intention of listening to him and intends to do as she pleases. There's a return shift to the high school with Rhea, Etta, Burke, and Zebadiah Garner, a new character standing outside the building. Etta's and Burke's dialogue is contentious, but Etta ensures Rhea's apartment over her garage is mentioned to Garner. The chapter ends with the four characters returning to the high school at the end of the fire drill.

"Chapter 22 begins in Hastings's office. Ross Jackson appears to discover why Hastings needs to speak to him, but their initial dialogue reveals how disgruntled Jackson is concerning the murders and their not being solved. The chapter shifts to Rhea and Etta leaving the high school when Jules Herman thwarts their exit. Etta and Herman engage a contentious verbal exchange, which surprises Rhea. This section ends with Rhea discovering Etta knows covert individuals who will come to her aid, but Etta refuses to tell Rhea who they are. Another shift occurs to Ross Jackson and his visiting Alma Whirs. Their exchange is comedic yet contentious. The chapter ends with Jackson and Hastings eating their dinners in Ariel's with both concerned about what the next conflict could be.

"In chapter 23, there are shifts between Rhea's house and Max Hastings's office. It opens with Rhea waiting for Zebadiah Garner to arrive. During her wait, she reflects on a dream about a man in an aerodynamic craft. As she analyzes the dream, Rhea realizes the man was an extraterrestrial. While talking to herself, Turner Ashton appears, and the dialogue between the two is anything but amiable. Turner leaves and walks toward Tobias Harding's. The chapter shifts to Hastings's office with the appearance of William Shepherd and Gabriel Hall as Patty Parks is locking the door. Another shift occurs to Rhea and the arrival of Zebadiah Garner.

"There's a return shift to Hastings's office. While Patty has gone for carryout from Ariel's, the three men discuss Rhea Michaels. Hastings mentions Rhea's demands and the incidents that have occurred since Shepherd's and Hall's last visit. The chapter ends with Rhea and Zebadiah Garner eating dinner and becoming acquainted. When Garner leaves, Rhea comments to Gigi how sexy Zeb Garner is."

Wainwright flipped through the final pages and said, "So this work has twenty-four chapters, and chapter 24 opens in Hastings's inner office. The three men are discussing future events when Hastings mentions a dagger." Wainwright paused then said thoughtfully, "So another prop introduction, but back to the story—Patty delivers the men's dinners. After Patty leaves, their discussion returns to Rhea Michaels and her demands of Shepherd and Hall. Hastings's cell phone rings. It's Rhea Michaels, and she directs the men to warn Etta Smiley to withdraw from her attacks on Herman and Burke. She then directs the men to utilize their cell phones to contact Ira Abbott. The dialogue is contentious between the entity and Abbott, and a lot of what is said about the Earth Mother is redundant."

Wainwright analyzed, "But concerning this theme—and there are many—redundancy is important when it comes to climate change, subjugation and genocide of peoples because of religion and politics, the plague of distribution and ingestion of illegal drugs, the ongoing threat of nuclear annihilation from political and theological terrorism—both domestic and international."

Wainwright paused thoughtfully then said to himself, "What if these fictional works really are written by someone who is more than he or she appears to be and is warning Homo sapiens sapiens to make changes before it's too late?"

Wainwright shook his head. "But I digress—back to the chapter. When the conversation between Abbott and the entity ends and the entity reenters Rhea's body, she reminds Hastings about an upcoming visit. This stirs Shepherd's and Hall's curiosity, but Hastings ignores the men's inquiries. The chapter ends with a shift to Rhea where she walks outside, gazes at the cosmos, and chants her acknowledgment to different goddesses, seeking their protection.

"The epilogue returns to the young girl and her repeating the necessity for lifting the veil ritual. *Lifting the Veil* also has a prayer to the sacred feminine, but unlike *When the Goddess Returns to Eden* and utilizing Poe's poem, Nicholas Moon has written a prayer of his own, or is Mina Sille the author of the prayer? I guess in time all will be revealed. At least, I hope so."

Wainwright placed the manuscript on the table, collected his phone, and pressed numbers to contact his agent. After waiting momentarily, Wainwright heard a response and said, "Virgil, Emmaline Singer is to be placed on hold for now. The author plans a different format for it."

Virgil replied, "Okay, we'll wait about Emmaline Singer. I've started to read the initial work you emailed to me." He paused then asked, "What about the second one you've just read?"

"Yes, *Lifting the Veil* is definitely a sequel to *When the Goddess Returns to Eden*. But *Lifting the Veil* also leads to a third manuscript. And yes, I'm expecting it anytime. Whoever is sending these manuscripts to me knows when I've finished my review of the one I'm reading. It's kinda bizarre."

Wainwright's doorbell buzzed.

"Virgil, I believe the third manuscript has just arrived. Give me a second."

"Of course, Bradford. I'm in no hurry."

When Wainwright answered his door, "Ah, I've been expecting you."

The letter carrier nodded. "I need your signature, Dr. Wainwright."

Wainwright signed and accepted the package. "Take it easy out there. It's still treacherous."

"You too, Professor!"

"Virgil, I'm back. Give me a minute, and I'll see what this title is."

Wainwright opened the package, removed the manuscript, and said, "Virgil, the title of this manuscript is *Aila's Mission*. At the ending of *Lifting the Veil*, the main character, Rhea Michaels, decides a cousin needs to come and visit. That cousin's name is Aila. But listen to this, Aila is also a character's name in the one-act play in *When the Goddess Returns to Eden*. The author ensures there's continuity in the simplest of references."

Virgil then directed, "So, Bradford, email me *Lifting the Veil*, and I'll start reading it when I finish *When the Goddess Returns to Eden*."

"Will do."

"How long do you think it'll take to read the third manuscript in the series?"

Wainwright flipped through the pages. "*Aila's Mission* appears to have the same format as *Lifting the Veil*."

"Okay, Bradford, start reading, and I'll be in touch." Virgil paused then said, "Bradford, are you sure Bertie isn't involved in these works?"

"No, Virgil. It's not her style."

About the Author

Nicholas Moon, a former educator and attorney, upon the death of his wife and child, decided to move to a small town in south-central Kentucky where he is at present writing novels and poetry. Since becoming acquainted with local community leaders, Moon volunteers and participates in various charities and organizations, especially the food bank. His hobbies include hiking on designated trails and painting abstract works of art. *Lifting the Veil* is the sequel to *When the Goddess Returns to Eden* and the second book in a series that utilizes the genres of drama, mystery, science fiction, and horror—both existential and paranormal.

Printed in the USA
CPSIA information can be obtained
at www.ICGtesting.com
LVHW051052090924
790324LV00001B/54